Volume
1

NEW TJHSST

MATH WORKBOOK

By Brian Rhee

D1709191

As Close as the Quant-Q Math Test

14 Lessons with Key Summaries

10 Full-Length Practice Tests

Detailed Solutions for All Questions

Legal Notice

The Thomas Jefferson High School for Science and Technology (TJHSST) Admissions Test was not involved in the production of this publication nor endorses this book.

Acknowledgements

I wish to acknowledge my deepest appreciation to my wife, Sookyung, who has continuously given me wholehearted support, encouragement, and love. Without you, I could not have completed this book.

Thank you to my sons, Joshua and Jason, who have given me big smiles and inspiration. I love you all.

About Author

Brian(Yeon) Rhee obtained a Masters of Arts Degree in Statistics at Columbia University, NY. He served as the Mathematical Statistician at the Bureau of Labor Statistics, DC. He is the Head Academic Director at Solomon Academy due to his devotion to the community coupled with his passion for teaching. His mission is to help students of all confidence level excel in academia to build a strong foundation in character, knowledge, and wisdom. Now, Solomon academy is known as the best academy specialized in Math in Northern Virginia.

Brian Rhee has published more than seventeen books. The titles of his books are 7 full-length practice tests for the AP Calculus AB/BC Multiple choice sections, AP Calculus, SAT 1 Math, SAT 2 Math level 2, 12 full-length practice tests for the SAT 2 Math Level 2, SHSAT/TJHSST Math workbook, and IAAT (Iowa Algebra Aptitude Test) Volume 1 and 2, NNAT 2 Level B Grade 1, CogAT form 7 Level 8, CogAT form 7 Level 9, and five arithmetic workbooks for grade 1 through grade 6. He's currently working on other math books which will be introduced in the near future.

Brian Rhee has more than twenty years of teaching experience in math. He has been one of the most popular tutors among TJHSST (Thomas Jefferson High School For Science and Technology) students. Currently, he is developing many online math courses with www.masterprep.net for AP Calculus AB and BC, SAT 2 Math level 2 test, and other various math subjects.

SOLOMON ACADEMY

Solomon Academy is a prestigious institution of learning with numerous qualified teachers of various fields of education. Our mission is to thoroughly teach students of all ages and confidence levels, elevate skills to the highest standard of education, and provide them with all the tools and materials to succeed.

5723 Centre Square Drive
Centreville, VA 20120
Tel: 703-988-0019

Email: solomonacademyva@gmail.com
info@solomonacademy.net

CLASSES OFFERED

MATHEMATICS	TESTING	ENGLISH
1st-6th grade math	CogAt	1st-6th Reading
Algebra 1, 2	IAAT and SOL 7	1st-6th Writing
Geometry	TJHSST Prep	Essay Writing
Pre-Calculus	SAT/ACT Prep	SAT Writing
AP Calculus AB/BC	SAT 2 Subject Tests	
AP Statistics	MathCounts	
Multivariate Calculus	AMC 10/12	

LEARN FROM THE AUTHOR

Private sessions with Brian Rhee is also available on the following subjects: TJ Math, SAT Math, SAT 2 Subject Math Level 2, Pre-Calculus, AP Calculus AB/BC, AP Statistics, IB SL/HL, Multivariate Calculus, Linear Algebra, AMC 8/10/12, and AIME.

Feel free to contact me at solomonacademyva@gmail.com

About This Book

The Thomas Jefferson High School for Science and Technology (TJHSST) Admissions Test consists of three tests: Quant-Q Math test, Aspire Reading test, and Aspire Science test. The Quant-Q Math test measures pattern recognition, probability, combinatorics, out-of-the box algebra, geometry, and optimization.

This book is designed to help you master the Quant-Q Math test. The book contains 13 topic-specific summaries and 10 problems relevant to each section, and a summary of advanced topics for Quant-Q Math Test. Along with the topic-specific lessons, there are 10 full-length practice tests with detailed solutions and explanations. It is recommended that you take Test 1 as a diagnostic test to understand your current level of expertise and in which area you need improvement. Afterwards, review the key lessons and essential theorems of the Quant-Q Math test. After completing the lessons, use the nine remaining practice tests to help improve your score and exhibit real test-taking conditions. There is no greater substitute than to study and practice.

Be sure to time yourself during the mathematic test with the appropriate time limit of 50 minutes. After completing any lessons or tests, immediately use the answer key and detailed solution to check your answers. Review all answers. Take the time to carefully read the explanations of problems you got incorrect. If you find yourself continually missing the same type of questions, look back at the topic summaries and review the theorems and examples in the lesson. Set a goal of improvement for each practice test.

Contents

LESSON 1

Number Theory

Number theory is a branch of ~~mathematics devoted to~~ ... involves analyzing
relationships between integers ... ion, remainders, etc.

Factors

Factors are the numbers that ... , $10 = 1 \times 10$ and $10 = 2 \times 5$.
Thus, the factors of 10 are 1, ...

[handwritten note: •2 is the smallest and first, only even prime number •0 and 1 are neither prime nor composite]

Prime numbers

A prime number is a whole number that has only two factors: 1 and itself. The prime numbers less than
60 are 2, 3, 5, 7, 11, 13, 17, 19, 23, 29, 31, 37, 41, 43, 47, 53, and 59. It is worth noting that 2 is the first,
smallest, and only even prime number among the prime numbers. A composite number is a number that
has more than two factors. 0 and 1 are neither prime nor composite. For instance, 4 has three factors: 1, 2,
and 4. Thus, 4 is a composite number.

Prime factorization

A prime factorization of a number is a process of writing the number as the product of all its prime factors.
Since 12 can be written as $12 = 2 \times 2 \times 3$, the prime factorization of 12 is $2^2 \times 3$.

The prime factorization is useful when you count the total number of factors of a number. If a prime
factorization of a number, n, is $n = 2^a \times 3^b \times 5^c$, the total number of factors of n is $(a+1) \times (b+1) \times (c+1)$.
For instance, a prime factorization of 72 is $72 = 2^3 \times 3^2$. Thus, the total number of factors of 72 is
$(3+1) \times (2+1) = 12$.

The total number of factors of a perfect square is always odd. For instance, the prime factorization of 9 is
$9 = 3^2$. Thus, the total number of factors is $(2+1) = 3$.

Remainder

A remainder, r, is amount left over when a number, n, is divided by a divisor, p. When a number, n, is
divided by p, the quotient is q and the remainder is r. Then, the number, n, can be expressed in terms of p,
q, and r: $n = pq + r$. For instance, when 7 is divided by 2, the quotient is 3 and the remainder is 1. Thus,
7 can be expressed as $7 = 2 \times 3 + 1$.

When a number is divided by p, the possible values of the remainder are either $0, 1, 2, \cdots, p-2$, or $p-1$.
For instance, if a number, n, is divided by 5, the possible values of the remainder are either 0, 1, 2, 3, or, 4.

Example :   How many factors does 42 have?

The prime factorization of 42 is $42 = 2^1 \times 3^1 \times 7^1$. Thus, the total number of factors of 42 is $(1+1) \times (1+1) \times (1+1) = 8$. Or, you can find the total number factors of 42 by listing them out. Since $42 = 1 \times 42$, $42 = 2 \times 21$, $42 = 3 \times 14$, and $42 = 6 \times 7$, the total number of factors is 8: 1, 2, 3, 6, 7, 14, 21 and 42.

EXERCISES 100%

1. Which of the following number has 6 factors?

   (A) 25   (B) 24   (C) 22
   (D) 16   (E) 12

2. Which of the following number is a prime number?

   (A) 53   (B) 51   (C) 39
   (D) 21   (E) 1

3. Which of the following number has an odd number of factors?

   (A) 11   (B) 28   (C) 36
   (D) 45   (E) 60

4. If the prime factorization of 200 is $2^a \times 5^b$, what is the value of $a + b$?

   (A) 4   (B) 5   (C) 6
   (D) 7   (E) 8

5. How many factors does 60 have?

   (A) 10   (B) 12   (C) 13
   (D) 16   (E) 18

6. Which of the following number has only two factors?

   (A) 15   (B) 36   (C) 43
   (D) 49   (E) 51

7. If a positive integer, n, is divided by k, the quotient is 7 and the remainder is 2. What is n in terms of k ?

   (A) $2k + 7$ (B) $2k + 9$
   (C) $5k + 2$ (D) $5k + 7$
   (E) $7k + 2$

8. If the prime factorization of a number, k, is $2^3 \times 3^2$, what is the prime factorization of $3k$?

   (A) $2^4 \times 3^2$ (B) $2^3 \times 3^5$
   (C) $2^3 \times 3^4$ (D) $2^3 \times 3^3$
   (E) $2^2 \times 3^3$

9. Which of the following number is NOT a factor of 144?

   (A) 3   (B) 9   (C) 16
   (D) 24   (E) 27

10. If a positive integer, n, is divided by 4, the remainder is 3. What is the value of the remainder when $n + 3$ is divided by 4?

   (A) 2   (B) 3   (C) 4
   (D) 5   (E) 6

ANSWERS AND SOLUTIONS

1. (E)

   The prime factorization of 12 is $12 = 2^2 \times 3^1$. Thus, the total number of factors is $(2+1) \times (1+1) = 6$. Or, list the factors of 12: 1, 2, 3, 4, 6, and 12.

2. (A)

   Since 1 has only one factor, 1, it is not a prime number. 51, 39, and 21 are divisible by 3. Thus, they are not prime numbers. Only prime number in the answer choices is 53. Therefore, (A) is the correct answer.

3. (C)

   Any perfect squares have an odd number of factors. Since 36 is a perfect square, it has an odd number of factors. The prime factorization of 36 is $36 = 2^2 \times 3^2$. Thus, the total number of factors is $(2+1) \times (2+1) = 9$. Therefore, (C) is the correct answer.

4. (B)

   Since the prime factorization of 200 is $200 = 2^3 \times 5^2$, $a = 3$ and $b = 2$. Therefore, the value of $a + b = 3 + 2 = 5$.

5. (B)

   The prime factorization of 60 is $60 = 2^2 \times 3^1 \times 5^1$. Thus, the total number of factors is $(2+1) \times (1+1) \times (1+1) = 12$. Therefore, (B) is the correct answer.

6. (C)

   Any prime numbers have only two factors. Since 43 is a prime number, it has only two factors. Therefore, (C) is the correct answer.

7. (E)

   When a positive integer, n, is divided by k, the quotient is 7 and the remainder is 2. Thus, n can be expressed as $7k + 2$. Therefore, (E) is the correct answer.

8. (D)

   Since the prime factorization of k is $2^3 \times 3^2$, the prime factorization of $3k$ is $3k = 3 \times 2^3 \times 3^2 = 2^3 \times 3^3$. Therefore, (D) is the correct answer.

9. (E)

   144 is divisible by 3, 9, 16, and 24. However, it is not divisible by 27. Therefore, (E) is the correct answer.

10. (A)

    For simplicity, let n be 7 so that the remainder is 3 when 7 is divided by 4. Since $n + 3 = 10$, the remainder is 2 when 10 is divided by 4. Therefore, (A) is the correct answer.

LESSON 2

Simplifying Numerical Expressions

To simplify numerical expressions, use the **order of operations** (PEMDAS)

- **P** : Parenthesis
- **E** : Exponent
- **M** : Multiplication
- **D** : Division
- **A** : Addition
- **S** : Subtraction

The order of operations suggests to first perform any calculations inside parentheses. Afterwards, evaluate any exponents. Next, perform all multiplications and divisions working from left to right. Finally, do additions and subtractions from left to right.

Example: Simplify $12(3-4)^2 \div 4 - 2$

$$
\begin{aligned}
12(3-4)^2 \div 4 - 2 &= 12(-1)^2 \div 4 - 2 \qquad &&\text{Simplify inside the parenthesis} \\
&= 12(-1)^2 \div 4 - 2 &&\text{Evaluate the exponent} \\
&= 12 \div 4 - 2 &&\text{Do multiplication and division from left to right} \\
&= 3 - 2 &&\text{Do Subtraction} \\
&= 1
\end{aligned}
$$

EXERCISES

1. $1 + 2 + 3 - 4 + 5 + 6 + 7 - 8 =$

   (A) 4   (B) 6   (C) 8
   (D) 10   (E) 12

2. $6 \times 3 - 12 \div 2 =$

   (A) 12   (B) 9   (C) 6   (D) 3   (E) 1

3. Which of the following value is equal to
   $\frac{1}{2} \times 4 \times \frac{1}{3} \times 2 \times \frac{1}{4} \times 3$?

   (A) 1   (B) 2   (C) 3   (D) 4   (E) 5

4. Which of the following value is equal to the expression below?

   $$2(1+2)^2 + (2-6)$$

   (A) 5   (B) 10   (C) 14
   (D) 24   (E) 32

5. Which of the following value is equal to the expression $(-1)^2 + (-1)^3 + (-1)^4$?

   (A) 1   (B) 2   (C) 3   (D) 4   (E) 5

6. $\dfrac{10(3)^2 - 5 \times 4}{5(3+4)} =$

   (A) 1 (B) 2 (C) 3 (D) 4 (E) 5

7. Which of the following value is equal to the expression below?

   $$4\left(\sqrt{16} + \sqrt{25}\right) - 10^2 \div 4$$

   (A) 5 (B) 7 (C) 9
   (D) 11 (E) 13

8. What is the value of $\dfrac{3}{5}(3^2 + 4^2 + 5^2)$?

   (A) 30 (B) 40 (C) 50
   (D) 60 (E) 70

9. $10(2 + 3 - 4)^2 - 9(2 + 3 - 4)^2 =$

   (A) 0 (B) 1 (C) 2 (D) 3 (E) 4

10. $5|-2| - |4 - 2 \times 6| =$

   (A) 0 (B) 2 (C) 4 (D) 6 (E) 8

ANSWERS AND SOLUTIONS

1. (E)

   Since the expression has only additions and subtractions, simplify the expression from the left to right.

   $$1 + 2 + 3 - 4 + 5 + 6 + 7 - 8 = 12$$

2. (A)

   Do multiplication and division first. Then, add and subtract.

   $$6 \times 3 - 12 \div 2 = 18 - 6$$
   $$= 12$$

3. (A)

   Since the expression has only multiplications, rearrange the integers and fractions to simplify the expression easily.

   $$\frac{1}{2} \times 4 \times \frac{1}{3} \times 2 \times \frac{1}{4} \times 3 = \left(2 \times \frac{1}{2}\right) \times \left(3 \times \frac{1}{3}\right) \times \left(4 \times \frac{1}{4}\right)$$
   $$= 1 \times 1 \times 1$$
   $$= 1$$

4. (C)

   Use the order of operations (PEMDAS).

   $$2(1 + 2)^2 + (2 - 6) = 2(3)^2 - 4$$
   $$= 2 \times 9 - 4$$
   $$= 14$$

5. (A)

   $(-1)^2 = 1$, $(-1)^3 = -1$, and $(-1)^4 = 1$. Therefore, $(-1)^2 + (-1)^3 + (-1)^4 = 1$

6. (B)

Use the order of operations (PEMDAS).

$$\frac{10(3)^2 - 5 \times 4}{5(3+4)} = \frac{10(9) - (5 \times 4)}{5(7)}$$
$$= \frac{90 - 20}{35}$$
$$= 2$$

7. (D)

Since $\sqrt{16} = 4$ and $\sqrt{25} = 5$,

$$4(\sqrt{16} + \sqrt{25}) - 10^2 \div 4 = 4(4+5) - (10^2 \div 4)$$
$$= 36 - 25$$
$$= 11$$

8. (A)

Simplify the expression inside the parenthesis: $(3^2 + 4^2 + 5^2) = 50$. Therefore,

$$\frac{3}{5}(3^2 + 4^2 + 5^2) = \frac{3}{5} \times 50$$
$$= 30$$

9. (B)

Since the expression inside the parenthesis is $(2 + 3 - 4)^2 = 1$,

$$10(2+3-4)^2 - 9(2+3-4)^2 = 10(1) - 9(1)$$
$$= 1$$

10. (B)

Since $|-2| = 2$ and $|4 - (2 \times 6)| = |-8| = 8$,

$$5|-2| - |4 - 2 \times 6| = 5(2) - 8$$
$$= 2$$

LESSON 3

Simplifying and Evaluating Algebraic Expressions

Like terms are terms that have same variables and same exponents; only the coefficients may be different but can be the same. Knowing like terms is essential when you simplify algebraic expressions. For instance,

- $2x$ and $3x$: (Like terms)

- $2x$ and $3x^2$: (Not like terms since the two expressions have different exponents)

- 2 and 3: (Like terms)

Use the **distributive property** to expand an algebraic expression that has a parenthesis.

$$x(y + z) = x \times y + x \times z$$

To simplify an algebraic expression, expand the expression using the distributive property. Then group the like terms and simplify them. For instance,

$$2(-x + 2) + 3x + 5 = -2x + 4 + 3x + 5 \qquad \text{Use distributive property to expand}$$
$$= (-2x + 3x) + (4 + 5) \qquad \text{Group the like terms and simplify}$$
$$= x + 9$$

To evaluate an algebraic expression, substitute the numerical value into the variable. When substituting a negative numerical value, make sure to use a **parenthesis** to avoid a mistake.

Example 1:   Simplify the expression $3(x^2 - 2x + 3) - 2(x^2 - x + 2)$

$$3(x^2 - 2x + 3) - 2(x^2 - x + 2) = 3x^2 - 6x + 9 - 2x^2 + 2x - 4$$
$$= (3x^2 - 2x^2) + (-6x + 2x) + (9 - 4)$$
$$= x^2 - 4x + 5$$

Example 2:   Evaluate the expression $-2x^2 + 3x$ when $x = -3$

$$-2x^2 + 3x = -2(-3)^2 + 3(-3)$$
$$= -2(9) - 9$$
$$= -27$$

15

EXERCISES

1. Which of the following expression equals $-(2-x)+2$?

   (A) x (B) $x-2$ (C) $x-4$
   (D) $2x$ (E) $3x$

2. Evaluate $(x-4)(x-1)$ when $x=3$

   (A) -2 (B) -1 (C) 0
   (D) 1 (E) 2

3. Simplify $3x-4y+5y-2x$

   (A) $5x+9$ (B) $-x-y$ (C) $-x+y$
   (D) $x+y$ (E) $x-y$

4. If the length of a square is $2x-3$, what is the perimeter of the square?

   (A) $4x-6$ (B) $8x-12$ (C) x^2-2x
   (D) x^2-9 (E) $4x^2+9$

5. Evaluate $x^2-yz+x+yz$ when $x=3$, $y=-2$, and $z=-3$.

   (A) 8 (B) 10 (C) 12
   (D) 14 (E) 16

6. Which of the following expression is equal to the sum of $4x+y$ and $2x+3y$ subtracted from $9x+5y$?

   (A) $x+3y$ (B) $3x+y$ (C) $3x-y$
   (D) $6x+4y$ (E) $5x+4y$

7. If $x=30$, evaluate the expression below.

   $$\frac{2x-10}{3}+\frac{3x-20}{3}+\frac{4x+30}{3}$$

   (A) 30 (B) 45 (C) 60
   (D) 75 (E) 90

8. What is the average of $9x+5$ and $5x+7$?

   (A) $6x+7$ (B) $7x+6$ (C) $7x+12$
   (D) $14x+6$ (E) $14x+12$

9. Evaluate $(\sqrt{x}-\sqrt{y})^2$ if $x=9$ and $y=25$

   (A) 256 (B) 64 (C) 16
   (D) 4 (E) 1

10. If Joshua is y years old now and his brother Jason is 7 years younger, what is Jason's age in 10 years from now?

    (A) $y-7$ (B) $y-3$ (C) $y+3$
    (D) $3y+3$ (E) $3y+7$

ANSWERS AND SOLUTIONS

1. (A)

   Use the distributive property to expand the expression inside the parenthesis.

   $$-(2-x)+2 = x-2+2$$
   $$= x$$

   Therefore, the expression $-(2-x)+2$ equals to x.

16

2. (A)

In order to evaluate the expression, it is not necessary to expand the expression $(x-4)(x-1)$. Just substitute 3 for x in the expression.

$$
\begin{aligned}
(x-4)(x-1) &= (3-4)(3-1) \qquad \text{Substitute 3 for } x \\
&= (-1)(2) \\
&= -2
\end{aligned}
$$

Therefore, the value of $(x-4)(x-1)$ when $x=3$ is -2.

3. (D)

Group the like terms and simplify them.

$$
\begin{aligned}
3x - 4y + 5y - 2x &= (3x - 2x) + (-4y + 5y) \\
&= x + y
\end{aligned}
$$

4. (B)

The length of the square is $2x - 3$. The perimeter of the square is four times the length of the square. Therefore,

$$
\text{Perimeter of square} = 4(2x-3) = 8x - 12
$$

5. (C)

Before substituting 3 for x, -2 for y, and -3 for z in the expression, look at the expression carefully. You will notice that $-yz$ and yz are like terms that cancel each other out. Thus, the expression simplifies to $x^2 + x$. So, substitute 3 for x in $x^2 + x$.

$$
\begin{aligned}
x^2 - yz + x + yz &= x^2 + x + (yz - yz) \\
&= x^2 + x \qquad \text{Substitute 3 for } x \\
&= (3)^2 + 3 \\
&= 12
\end{aligned}
$$

Therefore, the value of $x^2 - yz + x + yz$ when $x = 3$, $y = -2$, and $z = -3$ is 12.

6. (B)

The sum of $4x + y$ and $2x + 3y$ equals to $6x + 4y$, which is subtracted from $9x + 5y$.

$$
\begin{aligned}
9x + 5y - (4x + y + 2x + 3y) &= 9x + 5y - (4x + 2x + y + 3y) \\
&= 9x + 5y - (6x + 4y) \\
&= 9x + 5y - 6x - 4y \\
&= (9x - 6x) + (5y - 4y) \\
&= 3x + y
\end{aligned}
$$

Therefore, the expression equals to the sum of $4x + y$ and $2x + 3y$ which is subtracted from $9x + 5y$ is $3x + y$.

7. (E)

Before substituting 30 for x, simplify the expression by adding the three fractions with the same denominators.

$$\frac{2x-10}{3} + \frac{3x-20}{3} + \frac{4x+30}{3} = \frac{2x-10+3x-20+4x+30}{3}$$

$$= \frac{2x+3x+4x-10-20+30}{3}$$

$$= \frac{9x}{3}$$

$$= 3x$$

Thus, the expression simplifies to $3x$. Therefore, the value of the expression is $3x = 3(30) = 90$.

8. (B)

To evaluate an average of two expressions, divide the sum of the two expressions by two.

$$\text{Average} = \frac{\text{Sum of two expressions}}{2}$$

$$= \frac{9x+5+5x+7}{2}$$

$$= \frac{14x+12}{2}$$

$$= 7x+6$$

Therefore, the average of $9x+5$ and $5x+7$ is $7x+6$.

9. (D)

Since $\sqrt{9} = 3$ and $\sqrt{25} = 5$, $\sqrt{9} - \sqrt{25} = -2$. Therefore,

$$(\sqrt{x} - \sqrt{y})^2 = (\sqrt{9} - \sqrt{25})^2 \qquad \text{Substitute 9 for } x \text{ and 25 for } y$$

$$= (3-5)^2$$

$$= (-2)^2$$

$$= 4$$

10. (C)

Jason is 7 years younger than his brother, Joshua, who is y years old now. So, Jason's current age is $y - 7$ years old. Therefore, 10 years from now, Jason's age will be $y - 7 + 10 = y + 3$ years old.

LESSON 4

Properties of Exponents

In the expression 2^4, 2 is the base, 4 is the exponent, and 2^4 is the power. Exponents represent how many times the base is multiplied by. $2^4 = 2 \times 2 \times 2 \times 2$. The table below shows a summary of the properties of exponents .

Properties of Exponents	Example
1. $\quad a^m \cdot a^n = a^{m+n}$	1. $\quad 2^4 \cdot 2^6 = 2^{10}$
2. $\quad \frac{a^m}{a^n} = a^{m-n}$	2. $\quad \frac{2^{10}}{2^3} = 2^{10-3} = 2^7$
3. $\quad (a^m)^n = a^{mn} = (a^n)^m$	3. $\quad (2^3)^4 = 2^{12} = (2^4)^3$
4. $\quad a^0 = 1$	4. $\quad (-2)^0 = 1,\ (3)^0 = 1,\ (100)^0 = 1$
5. $\quad a^{-1} = \frac{1}{a}$	5. $\quad 2^{-1} = \frac{1}{2}$
6. $\quad a^{\frac{1}{n}} = \sqrt[n]{a}$	6. $\quad 2^{\frac{1}{2}} = \sqrt{2}, \qquad x^{\frac{1}{3}} = \sqrt[3]{x}$
7. $\quad (ab)^n = a^n b^n$	7. $\quad (2 \cdot 3)^6 = 2^6 \cdot 3^6,\quad (2x)^2 = 2^2 x^2$
8. $\quad \left(\frac{a}{b}\right)^n = \frac{a^n}{b^n}$	8. $\quad \left(\frac{2}{x}\right)^3 = \frac{2^3}{x^3}$

To solve an exponential equation, make sure that expressions on both sides have the same base. If the expressions have the same base, then exponents on both sides are the same.

$$a^x = a^y \implies x = y \qquad\qquad \text{Example: } 2^x = 2^3 \implies x = 3$$

Example 1: Simplify $\left(\frac{1}{8}\right)^{\frac{2}{3}} \left(\frac{1}{8}\right)^{-\frac{2}{3}}$

Since the two expressions have the same base, $\frac{1}{8}$, you can combine both expressions using the first exponent property shown on the table above.

$$\left(\frac{1}{8}\right)^{\frac{2}{3}} \left(\frac{1}{8}\right)^{-\frac{2}{3}} = \left(\frac{1}{8}\right)^{\frac{2}{3}-\frac{2}{3}} = \left(\frac{1}{8}\right)^{0} = 1$$

Example 2: Solve $3^{x+1} = 27$

$$3^{x+1} = 3^3 \qquad \text{Since both expressions have the same base}$$
$$x + 1 = 3$$
$$x = 2$$

EXERCISES

1. Simplify $\dfrac{x^3 \cdot x^4}{x^2}$

   (A) x^6 (B) x^5 (C) x^4

   (D) x^3 (E) x^2

2. What is the value of $2 \cdot 2^0 \cdot 2^{-1}$?

   (A) 4   (B) 3   (C) 2   (D) 1   (E) 0

3. If $x = \frac{1}{2}$, what is the value of x^{-2} ?

   (A) 1   (B) 2   (C) 4   (D) 6   (E) 8

4. If $x^2 = 3$, what is the value of x^6 ?

   (A) 6   (B) 8   (C) 9

   (D) 15   (E) 27

5. If $2^x = 64$, what is the value of x^2 ?

   (A) 64   (B) 36   (C) 25

   (D) 12   (E) 8

6. If $10^x = a$, what is 100^x in terms of a ?

   (A) $2a$ (B) $5a$ (C) $10a$

   (D) a^2 (E) 2^a

7. If $\dfrac{x}{y} = 3$, what is the value of $\dfrac{y^3}{x^3}$?

   (A) $\dfrac{1}{27}$ (B) $\dfrac{1}{18}$ (C) $\dfrac{1}{9}$

   (D) 9   (E) 27

8. If $x^2 = 2$ and $y^3 = 3$, what is the value of $(xy)^6$?

   (A) 6   (B) 8   (C) 48

   (D) 54   (E) 72

9. If $4^{3x+1} = 256$, what is the value of x ?

   (A) 0   (B) 1   (C) 2   (D) 3   (E) 4

10. If two positive integers, x and y, satisfy the following equation $24 \times 18 = 2^x 3^y$, what is the sum of the values of x and y ?

   (A) 3   (B) 4   (C) 7   (D) 12   (E) 81

ANSWERS AND SOLUTIONS

1. (B)

Since the expressions have the same base, x, use the properties of exponents. Therefore,

$$\frac{x^3 \cdot x^4}{x^2} = x^{3+4-2} = x^5$$

2. (D)

Since $2^0 = 1$ and $2^{-1} = \frac{1}{2}$,

$$2 \cdot 2^0 \cdot 2^{-1} = 2 \cdot 1 \cdot \frac{1}{2} = 1$$

3. (C)

If $x = \frac{1}{2}$, $x^2 = \frac{1}{4}$. Since $x^{-2} = (x^2)^{-1} = \frac{1}{x^2}$,

$$x^{-2} = \frac{1}{x^2} = \frac{1}{\frac{1}{4}} = 4$$

Therefore, the value of x^{-2} is 4.

4. (E)

Since $x^2 = 3$, $x^6 = (x^2)^3 = 3^3 = 27$.

5. (B)

$2^6 = 64$. Thus, $x = 6$. Therefore, the value of x^2 is $6^2 = 36$.

6. (D)

Since $10^x = a$,

$$100^x = (10^2)^x = 10^{2x} = (10^x)^2 = a^2$$

Therefore, 100^x in terms of a is a^2.

7. (A)

Since $\frac{x}{y} = 3$, $\frac{y}{x} = \frac{1}{3}$. Thus,

$$\frac{y^3}{x^3} = \left(\frac{y}{x}\right)^3 = \left(\frac{1}{3}\right)^3 = \frac{1}{27}$$

Therefore, the value of $\frac{y^3}{x^3}$ is $\frac{1}{27}$.

8. (E)

First, expand $(xy)^6$ by using the properties of exponents. Afterwards, substitute 2 for x^2 and 3 for y^3 in the expression.

$$
\begin{aligned}
(xy)^6 &= x^6 y^6 \\
&= (x^2)^3 (y^3)^2 \qquad \text{Substitute 2 for } x^2 \text{ and 3 for } y^3 \\
&= 8(9) \\
&= 72
\end{aligned}
$$

Therefore, the value of $(xy)^6$ is 72.

9. (B)

To solve an exponential equation, both expressions must have the same base. Change 256 to 4^4 and then solve the equation.

$$4^{3x+1} = 256$$
$$4^{3x+1} = 4^4 \qquad \text{Since both sides have the same base}$$
$$3x + 1 = 4$$
$$x = 1$$

Therefore, the value of x is 1.

10. (C)

Find the prime factorization of 24 and 18 separately: $24 = 2^3 \times 3$, and $18 = 2 \times 3^2$.

$$24 \times 18 = 2^x 3^y$$
$$2^3 \times 3 \times 2 \times 3^2 = 2^x 3^y$$
$$2^4 \times 3^3 = 2^x 3^y$$

Thus, $x = 4$ and $y = 3$. Therefore, the sum of the values of $x + y$ is $4 + 3 = 7$.

LESSON 5

Solving Equations and Word Problems

Solving an equation is finding the value of the variable that makes the equation true. In order to solve an equation, use the rule called SADMEP with inverse operations (SADMEP is the reverse order of the order of operations, PEMDAS). Inverse operations are the operations that cancel each other. Addition and subtraction, and multiplication and division are good examples.

SADMEP suggests to first cancel subtraction or addition. Then, cancel division or multiplication next by applying corresponding inverse operation. Below is an example that shows you how to solve $2x - 1 = 5$, which involves subtraction and multiplication.

$$
\begin{array}{ll}
& \checkmark \qquad \checkmark \\
2x - 1 = 5 & S\ A\ D\ M\ E\ P \\
+1 = +1 & \text{Addition to cancel substraction} \\
2x = 6 & \text{Division to cancel multiplication} \\
x = 3 &
\end{array}
$$

Solving word problems involve translating verbal phrases into mathematical equations. The table below summarizes the guidelines.

Verbal Phrase	Expression
A number	x
Is	$=$
Of	$\times$
Percent	0.01 or $\frac{1}{100}$
The sum of x and y	$x + y$
Three more than twice a number	$2x + 3$
The difference of x and y	$x - y$
3 is subtracted from a number	$x - 3$
4 less than a number	$x - 4$
A number decreased by 5	$x - 5$
6 less a number	$6 - x$
The product of x and y	xy
6 times a number	$6x$
The quotient of x and y	$\frac{x}{y}$
A number divided by 9	$\frac{x}{9}$

Example: 5 more than the quotient of x and 3 is 14. What is the number?

$\checkmark \checkmark$

$$\frac{x}{3} + 5 = 14$$

$S \ A \ D \ M \ E \ P$

$$-5 = -5$$

Subtraction to cancel addition

$$\frac{x}{3} = 9$$

Multiplication to cancel division

$$x = 27$$

EXERCISES

1. If $5x - 3 = 7$, what is the value of $2x$?

   (A) 0   (B) 1   (C) 2   (D) 3   (E) 4

2. If $3(x-2) = 2(x-2)$, then $x =$

   (A) 2   (B) 3   (C) 4   (D) 6   (E) 8

3. If $5x - (x + 6) = 18$, what is the value of $x + 6$?

   (A) 4   (B) 8   (C) 12
   (D) 16   (E) 20

4. If $x^2 - x - 2 = x^2 - 2x - 3$, then $x =$

   (A) -3 (B) -2 (C) -1
   (D) 1   (E) 3

5. If $2x$ subtracted from 6 equals 9 less than x, what is the value of x ?

   (A) 6   (B) 5   (C) 4   (D) 3   (E) 2

6. If $2(x+y) = 6$, what is the value of $3x+3y$?

   (A) 5   (B) 7   (C) 8   (D) 9   (E) 12

7. If $4xy - 6 = 2x + 3y$ and $y = 2$, then what is the value of x ?

   (A) 2   (B) 3   (C) 4   (D) 5   (E) 6

8. If two thirds of the sum of $6x$ and 9 equals $2x$ less 8, what is the value of x ?

   (A) -8 (B) -7 (C) -5
   (D) 3   (E) 7

9. If $x = \frac{2y}{a}$, which of the following expression equals $6a$?

   (A) $\frac{3x}{y}$ (B) $\frac{6x}{y}$ (C) $\frac{6y}{x}$
   (D) $\frac{12x}{y}$ (E) $\frac{12y}{x}$

10. Joshua has \$300 in his savings account. If he saves \$200 per week, in how many weeks will he have saved a total amount of \$2100 in his savings account?

    (A) 5   (B) 6   (C) 7   (D) 8   (E) 9

ANSWERS AND SOLUTIONS

1. (E)

$$5x - 3 = 7$$
$$+3 = +3$$
$$5x = 10$$
$$x = 2$$

✓ ✓

$S\ A\ D\ M\ E\ P$

Addition to cancel substraction

Division to cancel multiplication

Therefore, the value of $2x$ is $2(2) = 4$.

2. (A)

Expand the expressions inside the parenthesis on the left and right side by using the distributive property.

$$3(x - 2) = 2(x - 2)$$
$$3x - 6 = 2x - 4$$
$$3x - 2x = -4 + 6$$
$$x = 2$$

Use the distributive property

3. (C)

Simplify the expression on the left side and solve the equation.

$$5x - (x + 6) = 18$$
$$5x - x - 6 = 18$$
$$4x = 24$$
$$x = 6$$

Therefore, $x + 6 = 12$.

4. (C)

Cancel out x^2 on each side and solve for x.

$$x^2 - x - 2 = x^2 - 2x - 3$$
$$-x - 2 = -2x - 3$$
$$2x - x = -3 + 2$$
$$x = -1$$

Subtract x^2 from each side

5. (B)

$2x$ subtracted from 6 can be expressed as $6 - 2x$. 9 less than x can be expressed as $x - 9$.

$$6 - 2x = x - 9$$
$$-3x = -15$$
$$x = 5$$

6. (D)

You can not solve for the value of x and y separately since you only have one equation with two variables. Instead, multiply the equation by $\frac{3}{2}$ and find the value of $3x + 3y$.

$$\frac{3}{2} \times 2(x + y) = \frac{3}{2} \times 6 \qquad \text{Multiply both sides by } \frac{3}{2}$$
$$3(x + y) = 9$$
$$3x + 3y = 9$$

7. (A)

Substituting 2 for y simplifies the equation to $8x - 6 = 2x + 6$.

$$4xy - 6 = 2x + 3y \qquad \text{Substitute 2 for } y$$
$$8x - 6 = 2x + 6$$
$$6x = 12$$
$$x = 2$$

8. (B)

Two thirds of the sum of $6x$ and 9 can be expressed as $\frac{2}{3}(6x + 9)$ and $2x$ less 8 can be expressed as $2x - 8$.

$$\frac{2}{3}(6x + 9) = 2x - 8 \qquad \text{Use the distributive property}$$
$$4x + 6 = 2x - 8$$
$$2x = -14$$
$$x = -7$$

9. (E)

From the equation $x = \frac{2y}{a}$, write a in terms of y and x. Afterwards, evaluate $6a$.

$$x = \frac{2y}{a} \qquad \text{Multiply both sides by } a$$
$$ax = 2y \qquad \text{Divide both sides by } x$$
$$a = \frac{2y}{x} \qquad \text{Multiply both sides by } 6$$
$$6a = \frac{12y}{x}$$

10. (E)

Define x as the number of weeks Joshua needs to save the total amount of \$2100. Since Joshua will save \$200 per week, the amounts that Joshua will save in x weeks will be $200x$. Thus,

$$200x + 300 = 2100$$
$$200x = 1800$$
$$x = 9$$

Therefore, Joshua needs 9 weeks to save the total amount of \$2100.

LESSON 6

Solving Inequalities and Compound Inequalities

Solving Inequalities

Solving an inequality is exactly the same as solving an equation. To solve an inequality, use SADMEP (Reverse order of the PEMDAS). In most cases, the inequality symbol remains unchanged. However, there are only two cases in which the inequality symbol must be reversed. The first case is when you multiply or divide each side by a negative number. The second case is when you take a reciprocal of each side. For instance,

Case 1	Case 2
$2 < 3$	$2 < 3$
$-2 > -3$	$\dfrac{1}{2} > \dfrac{1}{3}$

Solving Compound Inequalities

There are two types of compound inequalities: **And** compound inequality and **Or** compound inequality.

And Compound Inequality: $\qquad -5 \leq 2x - 1 \leq 7$

Or Compound Inequality: $\qquad x - 4 < -3 \quad$ or $\quad 2x + 1 > 7$

Below shows how to solve each type of compound inequality.

$$-5 \leq 2x - 1 \leq 7 \qquad \text{And compound inequality}$$
$$+1 \leq \quad +1 \leq +1 \qquad \text{Add 1 to each side}$$
$$-4 \leq 2x \leq 8 \qquad \text{Divide each side by 2}$$
$$-2 \leq x \leq 4$$

Thus, x is greater than or equal to -2 <u>and</u> less than or equal to 4

$$x - 4 < -3 \quad \text{or} \quad 2x + 1 > 7 \qquad \text{Or compound inequality}$$
$$x < 1 \quad \text{or} \quad x > 3$$

Thus, x is less than 1 <u>or</u> greater than 3

Example: Solve $-3x + 2 > x + 10$

$-3x + 2 > x + 10$	Subtract x from each side
$-4x + 2 > 10$	Subtract 2 from each side
$-4x > 8$	Divide each side by -4
$x < -2$	Reverse the inequality symbol

EXERCISES

(handwritten: $2x < 4$ $x < 2$)

1. Solve the inequality $2x + 1 < 5$

   (A) $x < 2$ (B) $x < -2$ (C) $x > 2$
   (D) $x > -2$ (E) $x < -3$

2. Solve the inequality $-2 \leq 3x + 1 \leq 10$

   (A) $-3 \leq x \leq 3$ (B) $-1 \leq x \leq 1$
   (C) $0 \leq x \leq 2$ (D) $-3 \leq x \leq 1$
   (E) $-1 \leq x \leq 3$ *(handwritten: $-3 \leq 3x \leq 9$)*
   (handwritten: $-1 \leq x \leq 3$)

3. Solve the inequality $-4x - 8 > 12$

   (A) $x > -5$ (B) $x < -5$ (C) $x > 5$
   (D) $x < 5$ (E) $x < 1$ *(handwritten: $-4x > 20$)*
   (handwritten: $x \leq -5$)

4. What is the solution to the following inequality $3x + 1 < -5$ or $2x - 1 > 7$?

   (A) $x < -2$ or $x > 4$ *(handwritten: $3x < -6$)*
   (B) $x < -2$ or $x > -4$ *(handwritten: $x \leq -2$)*
   (C) $x < 2$ or $x > 4$
   (D) $-2 < x < 4$ *(handwritten: $2x > 6$)*
   (E) $2 < x < 4$ *(handwritten: $x > 3$)*

5. Solve $3(2x - 4) < 2(x + 4)$

   (A) $x < 3$ (B) $x > 4$ (C) $x < 5$
   (D) $x > 6$ (E) $x < 7$

(handwritten: $6x - 12 < 2x + 8$)
(handwritten: $4x < 20$ $x < 5$)

6. How many positive integer values of x satisfy $-2(x - 8) > x - 2$?

   (handwritten: $-2x + 16 > x - 2$)
   (handwritten: $18 > 3x$)   (A) 1   (B) 2   (C) 3
   (handwritten: $x < 6$)   (D) 4   (E) 5

7. If the solution to $4 - 2x > x + 16$ is $x < a$, what is the value of a ?

   (A) 6   (B) 4   (C) 2
   (D) -4 (E) -6

8. Solve $-10 \leq -3x - 4 < 5$

   (A) $-3 \leq x < 2$ (B) $-3 < x \leq 2$
   (C) $-2 \leq x < 3$ (D) $-2 < x \leq 3$
   (E) $2 \leq x < -3$

9. If 4 less than a number is less than 4 and greater than -3, find the number.

   (A) $0 < x < 7$ (B) $1 < x < 7$
   (C) $1 < x < 8$ (D) $0 < x < 8$
   (E) $2 < x < 9$

10. If 3 more than twice a number is at most 11 and at least 5, find the number.

   (A) $2 < x < 8$ (B) $2 \leq x \leq 8$
   (C) $1 \leq x < 4$ (D) $1 < x \leq 4$
   (E) $1 \leq x \leq 4$

ANSWERS AND SOLUTIONS

1. (A)

$$2x + 1 < 5 \quad \text{Subtract 1 from each side}$$
$$2x < 4 \quad \text{Divide each side by 2}$$
$$x < 2$$

2. (E)

$$-2 \leq 3x + 1 \leq 10$$ Subtract 1 from each side

$$-3 \leq 3x \leq 9$$ Divide each side by 3

$$-1 \leq x \leq 3$$

3. (B)

$$-4x - 8 > 12$$ Add 8 to each side

$$-4x > 20$$ Divide each side by -4

$$x < -5$$ Reverse the inequality symbol

4. (A)

$$3x + 1 < -5 \qquad \text{or} \qquad 2x - 1 > 7$$
$$3x < -6 \qquad \text{or} \qquad 2x > 8$$
$$x < -2 \qquad \text{or} \qquad x > 4$$

5. (C)

$$3(2x - 4) < 2(x + 4)$$ Expand each side using the distributive property

$$6x - 12 < 2x + 8$$ Subtract $2x$ from each side

$$4x - 12 < 8$$ Add 12 to each side

$$4x < 20$$ Divide each side by 4

$$x < 5$$

6. (E)

$$-2(x - 8) > x - 2$$ Expand left side using the distributive property

$$-2x + 16 > x - 2$$ Subtract x from each side

$$-3x + 16 > -2$$ Subtract 16 from each side

$$-3x > -18$$ Divide each side by -3 and reverse the inequality symbol

$$x < 6$$

The positive integer values of x for which $x < 6$ are 1, 2, 3, 4, and 5. Therefore, there are 5 positive integer values of x that satisfy the original inequality.

7. (D)

$$4 - 2x > x + 16$$ Subtract x from each side

$$4 - 3x > 16$$ Subtract 4 from each side

$$-3x > 12$$ Divide each side by -3 and reverse the inequality symbol

$$x < -4$$

Therefore, the value of a is -4.

8. (B)

$$-10 \leq -3x - 4 < 5 \qquad \text{Add 4 to each side}$$
$$-6 \leq -3x < 9 \qquad \text{Divide each side by } -3 \text{ and reverse the inequality symbols}$$
$$2 \geq x > -3 \qquad \text{Rearrange the inequality}$$
$$-3 < x \leq 2$$

9. (C)

Translate the verbal phrases into an **And compound** inequality. Let x be the number. Then, 4 less than a number can be expressed as $x - 4$.

$$-3 < x - 4 < 4 \qquad \text{Add 4 to each side}$$
$$1 < x < 8$$

10. (E)

At most means $\leq$ and **at least** means $\geq$. Let x be the number. Then, 3 more than a twice a number can be expressed as $2x + 3$.

$$5 \leq 2x + 3 \leq 11 \qquad \text{Subtract 3 from each side}$$
$$2 \leq 2x \leq 8 \qquad \text{Divide each side by 2}$$
$$1 \leq x \leq 4$$

LESSON 7

Fractions, Ratios, Rates, and Proportions

A **fraction** represents a part of a whole. In the fraction $\frac{4}{5}$, the numerator 4 means that the fraction represents 4 equal parts, and the denominator 5 means that 5 parts make up a whole.

A **ratio** is a fraction that compares two quantities measured in the same units. The ratio of a to b can be written as $a : b$ or $\frac{a}{b}$. If the ratio of a number of apples to that of oranges in a store is $3 : 4$ or $\frac{3}{4}$, it means that there are 3 apples to every 4 oranges in the store.

A **rate** is a ratio that compares two quantities measured in different units. A rate is usually expressed as a unit rate. A unit rate is a rate per one unit of a given quantity. The rate of a per b can be written as $\frac{a}{b}$. If a car travels 100 miles in 2 hours, the car travels at a rate of 50 miles per hour.

A **proportion** is an equation that states that two ratios are equal. A proportion can be written as

$$a : b = c : d \qquad \text{or} \qquad \frac{a}{b} = \frac{c}{d}$$

The proportion above reads a is to b as c is to d. To solve the value of a variable in a proportion, use the cross product property and then solve for the variable. For instance,

$$\frac{x}{2} = \frac{6}{3} \qquad \text{Cross product property}$$
$$3x = 2 \times 6$$
$$x = 4$$

Example: Simplify $\frac{x}{2} + \frac{x}{3}$

$$\frac{x}{2} + \frac{x}{3} = \frac{3x}{6} + \frac{2x}{6} \qquad \text{Common denominator is 6}$$
$$= \frac{5x}{6}$$

EXERCISES

1. Simplify $\frac{2x-3y}{y}$

   (A) $\frac{2x}{y} - 3$ (B) $\frac{2x}{y} + 2$ (C) $\frac{2}{xy} - 3$

   (D) $\frac{2}{xy} + 2$ (E) $2x - 2y$

   $$\frac{2x}{y} - \frac{3y}{y}$$

2. Two-thirds of students in a class are girls. If one-half of the girls wear glasses, what fractional part of students are girls who wear glasses?

   (A) $\frac{1}{8}$ (B) $\frac{1}{6}$ (C) $\frac{1}{5}$

   (D) $\frac{1}{4}$ (E) $\frac{1}{3}$

3. If the ratio of a to b is $2:3$ and the ratio of c to b is $3:4$, which of the following is equal to the ratio of a to c ?

(A) $\dfrac{1}{2}$ (B) $\dfrac{2}{3}$ (C) $\dfrac{3}{4}$

(D) $\dfrac{8}{9}$ (E) $\dfrac{9}{10}$

4. If a student can type 120 words in 3 minutes, at this rate, how many words can she type in 5 minutes?

(A) 240   (B) 200   (C) 180

(D) 160   (E) 120

5. A 45-inch string is cut into two pieces. If the ratio of the longer piece to the shorter piece is $3:2$, what is the length of the shorter piece?

(A) 9   (B) 12   (C) 18

(D) 27   (E) 36

6. If $2x - 3y = 0$, what is $\dfrac{x}{y}$?

(A) $\dfrac{3}{2}$ (B) $\dfrac{2}{3}$ (C) $\dfrac{5}{3}$

(D) $\dfrac{3}{5}$ (E) $\dfrac{5}{2}$

7. $\dfrac{x}{2} + \dfrac{x}{3} + \dfrac{x}{4} = 26$, $x =$

(A) 12   (B) 16   (C) 18

(D) 20   (E) 24

8. If a car travels at a rate of 48 miles per hour, how many miles does it travel in 40 minutes?

(A) 28   (B) 32   (C) 36

(D) 40   (E) 42

9. 10 people who build at the same rate can frame a house in 6 days. What fractional part of a house can 4 people frame a house in 3 days?

(A) $\dfrac{1}{2}$ (B) $\dfrac{1}{3}$ (C) $\dfrac{1}{4}$

(D) $\dfrac{1}{5}$ (E) $\dfrac{1}{6}$

10. If Joshua can wash x cars in y hours, how many cars does he wash in z hours?

(A) $\dfrac{xy}{z}$ (B) $\dfrac{yz}{x}$ (C) $\dfrac{xz}{y}$

(D) $\dfrac{x}{yz}$ (E) $\dfrac{z}{xy}$

ANSWERS AND SOLUTIONS

1. (A)

$$\frac{2x - 3y}{y} = \frac{2x}{y} - \frac{3y}{y}$$
$$= \frac{2x}{y} - 3$$

2. (E)

Let x be the total number of students in the class. Two-thirds of the students are girls. Thus, the number of girls can be expressed as $\frac{2}{3}x$. Since one-half of the girls wear glasses, the number of girls who wear glasses can be expressed as $\frac{1}{2}(\frac{2}{3}x)$ or $\frac{1}{3}x$. Therefore, one-third of the students are girls who wear glasses.

3. (D)

Since $\frac{a}{b} = \frac{2}{3}$ and $\frac{c}{b} = \frac{3}{4}$, the ratio $\frac{a}{c}$ can be calculated using the two given ratios.

$$\begin{aligned} \frac{a}{c} &= \frac{a}{b} \times \frac{b}{c} \\ &= \frac{2}{3} \times \frac{4}{3} \\ &= \frac{8}{9} \end{aligned} \qquad \left(\text{Since } \frac{c}{b} = \frac{3}{4} \implies \frac{b}{c} = \frac{4}{3} \right)$$

4. (B)

If a student can type 120 words in 3 minutes, she can type $120 \div 3 = 40$ words in 1 minute. Therefore, she can type $40 \times 5 = 200$ words in 5 minutes.

5. (C)

The ratio of the longer piece to the shorter piece is $3 : 2$. Instead of using 3 for the longer piece and 2 for the shorter piece directly, multiply the ratio $3 : 2$ by x so that a new ratio is $3x : 2x$. Now, $3x$ represents the length of the longer piece and $2x$ represents the length of the shorter piece. If you add the longer and shorter pieces together, the sum of these lengths is equal to the length of the original string, 45 inches. Thus,

$$\begin{aligned} 3x + 2x &= 45 \\ 5x &= 45 \\ x &= 9 \end{aligned}$$

Therefore, the length of the shorter piece is $2x = 2(9) = 18$ inches.

6. (A)

$$\begin{aligned} 2x - 3y &= 0 && \text{Add } 3y \text{ to each side} \\ 2x &= 3y && \text{Divide each side by 2} \\ x &= \frac{3}{2}y && \text{Divide each side by } y \\ \frac{x}{y} &= \frac{3}{2} \end{aligned}$$

7. (E)

The least common multiple of 2, 3, and 4 is 12. Multiply each side by 12 to eliminate fractions.

$$\begin{aligned} 12 \times \left(\frac{x}{2} + \frac{x}{3} + \frac{x}{4} \right) &= 26 \times 12 && \text{Use the distributive property} \\ 6x + 4x + 3x &= 26(12) \\ 13x &= 26(12) \\ x &= \frac{26(12)}{13} \\ x &= 24 \end{aligned}$$

Therefore, the value of x is 24.

8. (B)

48 miles per hour means that the car travels 48 miles in one hour. There are 60 minutes in one hour. Set up a proportion in terms of miles and minutes.

$$48_{\text{miles}} : 60_{\text{minutes}} = x_{\text{miles}} : 40_{\text{minutes}}$$
$$\frac{48}{60} = \frac{x}{40} \qquad \text{Use cross product property}$$
$$60x = 48 \times 40$$
$$x = 32$$

Therefore, the car travels 32 miles in 40 minutes.

9. (D)

Let's define work as the number of people times the number of days. The work required to frame a house is $10_{\text{people}} \times 6_{\text{days}} = 60_{\text{people}\times\text{days}}$. If 4 people frame in 3 days, the work they finish is $4_{\text{people}} \times 3_{\text{days}} = 12_{\text{people}\times\text{days}}$. Thus,

$$\text{A fractional part of a house} = \frac{12_{\text{people}\times\text{days}}}{60_{\text{people}\times\text{days}}}$$
$$= \frac{1}{5}$$

Therefore, 4 people can frame $\frac{1}{5}$ of the house in 3 days.

10. (C)

Let's set up a proportion and solve for w.

$$x_{\text{cars}} : y_{\text{hours}} = w_{\text{cars}} : z_{\text{hours}}$$
$$\frac{x}{y} = \frac{w}{z} \qquad \text{Use cross product property}$$
$$yw = xz$$
$$w = \frac{xz}{y}$$

Therefore, Joshua can wash $\frac{xz}{y}$ cars in z hours.

LESSON 8

Linear Equations

The **slope**, m, of a line is a number that describes the steepness of the line. The larger the absolute value of the slope, $|m|$, the steeper the line is (closer to y-axis). If a line passes through the points (x_1, y_1) and (x_2, y_2), the slope m is defined as

$$m = \frac{\text{Rise}}{\text{Run}} = \frac{y_2 - y_1}{x_2 - x_1}$$

If the points (x_1, y_1) and (x_2, y_2) are given, the following formulas are useful in solving TJHSST and SHSAT math problems.

Midpoint Formula: $\left(\dfrac{x_1 + x_2}{2}, \dfrac{y_1 + y_2}{2} \right)$

Distance Formula: $D = \sqrt{(x_2 - x_1)^2 + (y_2 - y_1)^2}$

An equation of a line can be written in three different forms.

1. **Slope-intercept form:** $y = mx + b$, where m is slope and b is y-intercept.

2. **Point-slope form:** If the slope of a line is m and the line passes through the point (x_1, y_1),

$$y - y_1 = m(x - x_1)$$

3. **Standard form:** $Ax + By = C$, where A, B, and C are integers.

Below classifies the lines by slope.

- Lines that rise from left to right have positive slope.
- Lines that fall from left to right have negative slope.
- Horizontal lines have zero slope (example: $y = 2$).
- Vertical lines have undefined slope (example: $x = 2$).
- Parallel lines have the same slope.
- Perpendicular lines have negative reciprocal slopes (product of the slopes equals -1).

The x-intercept of a line is a point where the line crosses x-axis. **The y-intercept** of a line is a point where the line crosses y-axis.

To find the x-intercept of a line $\implies$ Substitute 0 for y and solve for x
To find the y-intercept of a line $\implies$ Substitute 0 for x and solve for y

Example: If the slope of a line is 3 and the y-intercept is -4, write an equation of the line.

In slope-intercept form, $y = mx + b$, m represents the slope and b represents the y-intercept. Thus, $m = 2$ and $b = -4$. Therefore, the equation of the line is $y = 2x - 4$.

EXERCISES

1. If a line passes through the points $(-2, 3)$ and $(1, 9)$, what is the slope of the line?

   (A) -3 (B) -2 (C) -1
   (D) $\frac{1}{3}$ (E) 2

2. What are the x and y coordinates of the midpoint between $(6, 5)$ and $(-2, 1)$?

   (A) $(4, 3)$ (B) $(2, 4)$ (C) $(4, 2)$
   (D) $(3, 2)$ (E) $(2, 3)$

3. What is the distance between $(-1, -3)$ and $(4, 9)$?

   (A) 13 (B) 12 (C) 10
   (D) 8 (E) 5

4. Which of the following line has a slope of zero?

   (A) $y = 2x - 3$ (B) $y = -2x + 3$
   (C) $y = -2$ (D) $x = -2$
   (E) $x + y = 0$

5. If a point $(1, a)$ lies on the line $y = -3x + 4$, what is the value of a ?

   (A) -1 (B) 0 (C) 1
   (D) 2 (E) 3

6. If the equation of the line is $2x + 3y = 6$, what is the x-intercept of the line?

   (A) -6 (B) -3 (C) 2
   (D) 3 (E) 6

7. Which of the following line is parallel to $y = 4x + 1$?

   (A) $y = 4x + 2$ (B) $y = -4x + 2$
   (C) $y = \frac{1}{4}x + 2$ (D) $y = -\frac{1}{4}x + 2$
   (E) $y = -\frac{1}{4}x - 2$

8. What is the equation of the line that is parallel to $y = \frac{1}{2}x + 3$ and passes $(4, 7)$?

   (A) $y = \frac{1}{2}x - 5$ (B) $y = \frac{1}{2}x + 5$
   (C) $y = -\frac{1}{2}x + 5$ (D) $y = -\frac{1}{2}x - 3$
   (E) $y = -2x + 5$

9. Which of the following line is perpendicular to $y = \frac{1}{3}x - 2$?

   (A) $-x + 3y = 6$ (B) $-x - 3y = 6$
   (C) $-2x + y = 4$ (D) $3x - y = 4$
   (E) $3x + y = 4$

10. What is the equation of the perpendicular bisector of a line segment connected by $(1, 5)$ and $(5, 3)$?

   (A) $y = 2x + 2$ (B) $y = 2x - 2$
   (C) $y = \frac{1}{2}x + 2$ (D) $y = \frac{1}{2}x - 2$
   (E) $y = -\frac{1}{2}x + 2$

ANSWERS AND SOLUTIONS

1. (E)

$$\text{Slope} = \frac{y_2 - y_1}{x_2 - x_1} = \frac{9 - 3}{1 - (-2)} = \frac{6}{3} = 2$$

2. (E)

$$\text{Midpoint} = \left(\frac{x_1 + x_2}{2}, \frac{y_1 + y_2}{2} \right) = \left(\frac{6 + (-2)}{2}, \frac{5 + 1}{2} \right) = (2, 3)$$

3. (A)

$$\begin{aligned}
\text{Distance} &= \sqrt{(x_2 - x_1)^2 + (y_2 - y_1)^2} \\
&= \sqrt{(4 - (-1))^2 + (9 - (-3))^2} \\
&= \sqrt{5^2 + 12^2} \\
&= 13
\end{aligned}$$

Therefore, the distance between $(-1, -3)$ and $(4, 9)$ is 13.

4. (C)

Horizontal lines have a slope of zero. Any horizontal lines can be written as $y = k$, where k=constant. Therefore, $y = -2$ is the answer.

5. (C)

Since point, $(1, a)$, is on the line, $(1, a)$ is the solution to the equation $y = -3x + 4$. Substitute 1 for x and a for y in the equation and solve for a.

$$\begin{aligned}
y &= -3x + 4 \qquad & \text{Substitute 1 for } x \text{ and } a \text{ for } y \\
a &= -3(1) + 4 \\
a &= 1
\end{aligned}$$

Therefore, the value of a is 1.

6. (D)

To find the x-intercept of the line $2x + 3y = 6$, substitute 0 for y in the equation and solve for x.

$$\begin{aligned}
2x + 3y &= 6 \qquad & \text{Substitute 0 for } y \\
2x + 3(0) &= 6 \\
x &= 3
\end{aligned}$$

Therefore, the x-intercept of the line is 3.

7. (A)

Two lines are parallel if they have the same slope. Thus, the slope of the parallel line must be 4. Since the only equation of the line that has the slope of 4 is $y = 4x + 2$ in the answer choices, (A) is the correct answer.

8. (B)

Two parallel lines have the same slope. Thus, the slope of the parallel line is $\frac{1}{2}$. Start with the slope-intercept form, $y = mx + b = \frac{1}{2}x + b$. Since the point $(4, 7)$ is on the line, $(4, 7)$ is a solution to the equation $y = \frac{1}{2}x + b$. Substitute 4 for x and 7 for y in the equation and then solve for b.

$$y = \frac{1}{2}x + b \qquad\qquad \text{Substitute 4 for } x \text{ and 7 for } y$$

$$7 = \frac{1}{2}(4) + b \qquad\qquad \text{Solve for } b$$

$$b = 5$$

Therefore, the equation of the parallel line that passes through $(4, 7)$ is $y = \frac{1}{2}x + 5$.

9. (E)

The slope of the perpendicular line to $y = \frac{1}{3}x - 2$ is -3. Each equation in the answer choices is written in standard form. Rewrite each equation of the line in slope-intercept form and choose the equation of the line that has the slope of -3.

$$\text{(A)} \quad -x + 3y = 6 \quad\Longrightarrow\quad y = \frac{1}{3}x + 2$$

$$\text{(B)} \quad -x - 3y = 6 \quad\Longrightarrow\quad y = -\frac{1}{3}x - 2$$

$$\text{(C)} \quad -2x + y = 4 \quad\Longrightarrow\quad y = 2x + 4$$

$$\text{(D)} \quad 3x - y = 4 \quad\Longrightarrow\quad y = 3x - 4$$

$$\text{(E)} \quad 3x + y = 4 \quad\Longrightarrow\quad y = -3x + 4$$

Therefore, (E) is the correct answer.

10. (B)

The slope of the line segment connected by $(1, 5)$ and $(5, 3)$ is

$$\text{Slope} = \frac{3 - 5}{5 - 1} = -\frac{1}{2}$$

The midpoint between $(1, 5)$ and $(5, 3)$ is

$$\text{Midpoint} = \left(\frac{1 + 5}{2}, \frac{5 + 3}{2} \right) = (3, 4)$$

The slope of the perpendicular bisector is the negative reciprocal of $-\frac{1}{2}$, or 2. The equation of the perpendicular bisector in slope-intercept form is $y = 2x + b$. Since the perpendicular bisector passes through the midpoint of the line segment, $(3, 4)$ is the solution to the equation $y = 2x + b$.

$$y = 2x + b \qquad\qquad \text{Substitute 3 for } x \text{ and 4 for } y$$

$$4 = 2(3) + b$$

$$b = -2$$

Therefore, the equation of the perpendicular bisector is $y = 2x - 2$.

LESSON 9

Solving Systems of Linear Equations

A system means more than one. A linear equation represents a line. Thus, a **system of linear equations** represent more than one line. Below is an example of a system of linear equations.

$$2x - y = 5$$
$$3x + y = 10$$

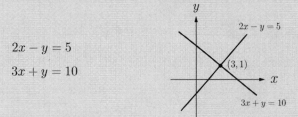

A solution to a system of linear equations is an ordered pair (x, y) that satisfies each equation in the system. In other words, a solution to a system of linear equation is an intersection point that lies on both lines. In the figure above, $(3, 1)$ is an ordered pair that satisfies each equation,

$$2x - y = 5 \implies 2(3) - 1 = 5$$
$$3x + y = 10 \implies 3(3) + 1 = 10$$

and is the intersection point of both lines.

Solving a system of linear equations means finding the x and y coordinates of the intersection point of the lines. There are two methods to solve a system of linear equations: **substitution** and **linear combinations**.

1. Substitution method
In the example above, write y in terms of x in the first equation. $2x - y = 5 \implies y = 2x - 5$. Substitute $2x - 5$ for y in the second equation.

$$3x + y = 10 \implies 3x + (2x - 5) = 10$$
$$5x - 5 = 10$$
$$x = 3 \implies y = 2x - 5 = 2(3) - 5 = 1$$

The solution to the system using the substitute method is $(3, 1)$.

2. Linear combinations method
In the example above, the coefficient of the y variable in each equation is opposite. Thus, adding the two equations eliminates the y variables. Then, solve for x.

$$
\begin{array}{ll}
2x - y = 15 & \\
\underline{3x + y = 10} & \text{Add two equations} \\
5x \quad = 15 & \\
x = 3 &
\end{array}
$$

39

Substitute 3 for x in the first equation and solve for y.

$$2x - y = 5 \quad \Longrightarrow \quad 2(3) - y = 5 \quad \Longrightarrow \quad y = 1$$

The solution to the system using the linear combinations method is $(3, 1)$.

Example: Solve the system of linear equations below.

$$y = x - 4$$
$$2x + y = 2$$

Solve the system of equations using the substitution method.

$$2x + y = 2 \qquad \text{Substitute } y = x - 4 \text{ for } y$$
$$2x + (x - 4) = 2$$
$$3x - 4 = 2$$
$$x = 2 \quad \Longrightarrow \quad y = x - 4 = (2) - 4 = -2$$

Therefore, the solution to the system is $(2, -2)$.

EXERCISES 100%

1. If $3x + 2y = 5$ and $5x - 2y = 3$, what is the value of $x + 3$?

   (A) 1 (B) 2 (C) 3
   (D) 4 (E) 5

2. If $-x + 3y = 16$ and $y = 2x - 3$, what is the value of y ?

   (A) 3 (B) 4 (C) 5
   (D) 6 (E) 7

3. If $x - y = 6$ and $2x + 4y = 9$, what is the value of $2x + 2y$?

   (A) 8 (B) 10 (C) 12
   (D) 15 (E) 18

4. If $-2x + 2y = 12$ and $\frac{x}{2} = \frac{y}{6}$, what is the value of x ?

   (A) 2 (B) 3 (C) 4
   (D) 5 (E) 6

$$3x - y = m$$
$$-2x + 5y = n$$

5. If $x = 3$ and $y = 2$ are solutions to the system of equations above, what is the value of $m + n$?

   (A) 11 (B) 9 (C) 7
   (D) 5 (E) 3

6. If the two lines, $y = 2x$ and $y = 6 - x$ intersect, what are the x and y coordinates of the intersection point?

   (A) $(4, 8)$ (B) $(4, 2)$ (C) $(3, 6)$
   (D) $(3, 2)$ (E) $(2, 4)$

7. If $x - y = 1$ and $x + y = 7$, what is the value of $3x - 2y$?

   (A) 6 (B) 5 (C) 4
   (D) 3 (E) 2

8. If $3x - 4y = -1$ and $-4x + 3y = 6$, what is the solution to the system of equations?

   (A) $(-3, -2)$ (B) $(-2, -3)$
   (C) $(3, -2)$ (D) $(3, 2)$
   (E) $(2, 3)$

9. Joshua and Jason saved $1000 together. Joshua saved $100 more than twice the amount that Jason saved. How much did Jason save?

   (A) $400   (B) $350   (C) $300
   (D) $250   (E) $200

10. A store sells desks and chairs. A store makes a profit of $15 per desk and $8 per chair. If the store sold a total of 23 desks and chairs and made the total profit of $240, how many chairs did the store sell?

    (A) 5   (B) 8   (C) 10
    (D) 12   (E) 15

ANSWERS AND SOLUTIONS

1. (D)

   Use the linear combinations method.

   $$3x + 2y = 5$$
   $$5x - 2y = 3$$
   $$8x = 8$$
   $$x = 1$$

   Add two equations

   Therefore, $x + 3 = 4$.

2. (E)

   Use the substitution method.

   $$-x + 3y = 16$$
   $$-x + 3(2x - 3) = 16$$
   $$5x - 9 = 16 \implies x = 5$$

   Substitute $2x - 3$ for y

   Therefore, $y = 2x - 3 = 2(5) - 3 = 7$.

3. (B)

   Add the two equations and divide the result by $\frac{2}{3}$ to find the value of $2x + 2y$.

   $$x - y = 6$$
   $$2x + 4y = 9$$
   $$3x + 3y = 15$$
   $$2x + 2y = 10$$

   Add two equations

   Multiply each side by $\frac{2}{3}$

   Therefore, the value of $2x + 2y = 10$.

4. (B)

Multiply each side of the equation $\frac{x}{2} = \frac{y}{6}$ by 6 to obtain $y = 3x$. Then, use the substitution method.

$$-2x + 2y = 12 \qquad \text{Substitute } 3x \text{ for } y$$
$$-2x + 2(3x) = 12$$
$$4x = 12$$
$$x = 3$$

Therefore, the value of x is 3.

5. (A)

Substitute 3 for x and 2 for y in the first equation to solve for m.

$$3x - y = m \qquad \text{Substitute 3 for } x \text{ and 2 for } y$$
$$3(3) - 2 = m \qquad \text{Solve for } m$$
$$m = 7$$

Then, substitute 3 for x and 2 for y in the second equation to solve for n.

$$-2x + 5y = n \qquad \text{Substitute 3 for } x \text{ and 2 for } y$$
$$-2(3) + 5(2) = n \qquad \text{Solve for } n$$
$$n = 4$$

Thus, $n = 4$. Therefore, the value of $m + n = 11$.

6. (E)

In order to find the intersection point that lies on both lines $y = 2x$ and $y = 6 - x$, use the substitution method.

$$y = 6 - x \qquad \text{Substitute } 2x \text{ for } y$$
$$2x = 6 - x$$
$$3x = 6$$
$$x = 2$$

Thus, $x = 2$ and $y = 2x = 2(2) = 4$. Therefore, the x and y coordinates of the intersection point is $(2, 4)$.

7. (A)

Use the linear combinations method.

$$x - y = 1$$
$$\underline{x + y = 7} \qquad \text{Add two equations}$$
$$2x \quad = 8$$
$$x = 4$$

Since $x = 4$, substitute 4 for x in the first equation to solve for y.

$$x - y = 1 \qquad \text{Substitute 4 for } x$$
$$4 - y = 1 \qquad \text{Solve for } y$$
$$y = 3$$

Thus, $x = 4$ and $y = 3$. Therefore, the value of $3x - 2y = 3(4) - 2(3) = 6$.

8. (A)

Use the linear combinations method. Since the coefficients of x in the first and second equation are 3 and -4, find the least common multiple (LCM) of 3 and 4, which is 12. Thus, multiply the first equation by 4, and multiply the second equation by 3 to obtain the same coefficient of x, 12.

$$3x - 4y = -1 \quad \xrightarrow{\text{Multiply by 4}} \quad 12x - 16y = -4$$
$$-4x + 3y = 6 \quad \xrightarrow{\text{Multiply by 3}} \quad -12x + 9y = 18$$

Add two equations to eliminate x variables.

$$\begin{array}{r} 12x - 16y = -4 \\ \underline{-12x + 9y = 18} \\ -7y = 14 \\ y = -2 \end{array} \qquad \text{Add two equations}$$

Substitute -2 for y in the first equation and solve for x.

$$3x - 4y = -1 \qquad \text{Substitute } -2 \text{ for } y$$
$$3x - 4(-2) = -1$$
$$3x = -9$$
$$x = -3$$

Thus, $x = -3$ and $y = -2$. Therefore, the solution to the system of equations is $(-3, -2)$.

9. (C)

Let x be the amount that Jason saved. Since Joshua saved $100 more than twice the amount that Jason saved, $2x + 100$ represents the amount that Joshua saved. Joshua and Jason saved $1000 together. Thus, the sum of x and $2x + 100$ equals 1000.

$$x + 2x + 100 = 1000$$
$$3x + 100 = 1000$$
$$3x = 900$$
$$x = 300$$

Therefore, the amount that Jason saved, x, is $300.

10. (E)

Let's define x as the number of desks that the store sold and y as the number of chairs that the store sold. Set a system of equations using the x and y variables. First, set up the first equation in terms of a total number of desks and chairs that the store sold. The store sold a total of 23 desks and chairs: $x + y = 23$. Then, set up the second equation in terms of $240 profit that the store made after selling x numbers of desks and y numbers of chairs: $15x + 8y = 240$. Next, multiply each side of the first equation by -15.

$$x + y = 23 \xrightarrow{\text{Multiply by } -15} -15x - 15y = -345$$
$$15x + 8y = 240$$

Use the linear combinations method.

$$
\begin{aligned}
-15x - 15y &= -345 \\
\underline{15x + 8y} &= \underline{240} \qquad \text{Add two equations} \\
-7y &= -105 \\
y &= 15
\end{aligned}
$$

Therefore, the number of chairs that the store sold, y, is 15.

LESSON 10

Classifying Angles

An angle is formed by two rays and is measured in degrees (°). The angle A is expressed as $\angle A$ and the measure of the angle A is expressed as $m\angle A$.

Two angles, A and B, that have the same measure are called **congruent angles**. They are expressed as $\angle A \cong \angle B$.

Angles are classified by their measures.

- Acute angle is less than 90°.

- Right angle is 90°.

- Obtuse angle is greater than 90°.

- Straight angle is 180°.

- Vertical angles are formed by intersecting two lines. Vertical angles are congruent. In the figure below, $\angle 1$ and $\angle 3$, and $\angle 2$ and $\angle 4$ are vertical angles.

- Complementary angles are two angles whose sum of their measures is 90°. In the figure below, $\angle 5$ and $\angle 6$ are complementary angles.

- Supplementary angles are two angles whose sum of their measures is 180°. In the figure below, $\angle 7$ and $\angle 8$ are supplementary angles.

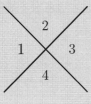

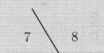

Vertical angles	Complementary angles	Supplementary angles

Example: Two angles are complementary. If one angle measures $x + 10$ and the other angle measures $2x + 5$, what is the value of x ?

Two angles are complementary angles if the sum of their measures is 90°.

$$x + 10 + 2x + 5 = 90$$
$$3x + 15 = 90$$
$$3x = 75$$
$$x = 25$$

45

When two parallel lines are cut by a third line called the transversal, the following angles are formed.

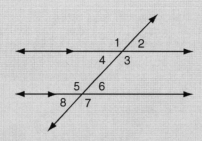

- Corresponding angles are congruent: $\angle 1 \cong \angle 5$, $\angle 4 \cong \angle 8$, $\angle 2 \cong \angle 6$, and $\angle 3 \cong \angle 7$.

- Alternate interior angles are congruent: $\angle 4 \cong \angle 6$, and $\angle 3 \cong \angle 5$.

- Alternate exterior angles are congruent: $\angle 1 \cong \angle 7$, and $\angle 2 \cong \angle 8$.

- Consecutive angles are supplementary: $\angle 4$ and $\angle 5$, and $\angle 3$ and $\angle 6$ are supplementary. In other words, $m\angle 4 + m\angle 5 = 180°$, and $m\angle 3 + m\angle 6 = 180°$.

EXERCISES

1. In the figure below, two lines intersect to form two pairs of vertical angles. What is the value of x ?

$3x + 10$

$2x + 40$

(A) 30   (B) 50   (C) 70

(D) 90   (E) 110

2. Two angles are supplementary. If one angle measures x and the other angle measures $x + 30$, what is the value of x ?

(A) 60   (B) 65   (C) 70

(D) 75   (E) 80

3. Two angles are complementary. If the measure of one angle is twice the measure of the other angle, what is the measure of the larger angle?

(A) 20   (B) 30   (C) 40

(D) 50   (E) 60

4. Two angles are supplementary. If the ratio of the measure of the smaller angle to that of the larger angle is 5 : 7, what is the measure of the smaller angle?

(A) 60   (B) 65   (C) 70

(D) 75   (E) 80

5. Two angles are complementary angles. What is the mean of the complementary angles?

(A) 30   (B) 45   (C) 60

(D) 75   (E) 90

6. If the two lines are parallel in the figure below, what is the value of $x + y$?

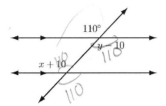

(A) 220   (B) 200   (C) 180
(D) 160   (E) 140

7. $\angle A$ and $\angle B$ are complementary angles. $\angle B$ and $\angle C$ are complementary angles. If $m\angle A = 40$, what is the $m\angle C$?

(A) 30   (B) 35   (C) 40
(D) 45   (E) 50

8. A straight angle is divided into three smaller angles. If the measures of three smaller angles are consecutive even integers, what is the measure of the largest angle?

(A) 58   (B) 59   (C) 60
(D) 61   (E) 62

9. If the two lines are parallel in the figure below, what is the value of x ?

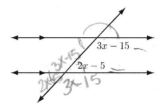

(A) 40   (B) 45   (C) 50
(D) 55   (E) 60

10. Angles A and B are supplementary angles. Angles B and C are complementary angles. If the measure of angle B is 10 less than three times the measure of angle C, what is the sum of the measures of angle A and C ?

(A) 150   (B) 140   (C) 130
(D) 120   (E) 110

ANSWERS AND SOLUTIONS

1. (A)

Vertical angles are congruent. Thus, set $3x + 10$ and $2x + 40$ equal to each other and solve for x.

$$3x + 10 = 2x + 40$$
$$x = 30$$

Therefore, the value of x is 30.

2. (D)

Since the two angles are supplementary, the sum of their measures is $180°$.

$$x + x + 30 = 180$$
$$2x + 30 = 180$$
$$x = 75$$

Therefore, the value of x is 75.

3. (E)

Define x as the measure of the smaller angle. Then, $2x$ is the measure of the larger angle. Since the two angles are complementary, the sum of their measures is $90°$.

$$x + 2x = 90$$
$$3x = 90$$
$$x = 30$$

Therefore, the measure of the larger angle is $2x = 2(30) = 60°$.

4. (D)

The ratio of the measures of the two angles is $5 : 7$. So, let $5x$ be the measure of the smaller angle and $7x$ be the measure of the larger angle. Since the two angles are supplementary, the sum of their measures is $180°$.

$$5x + 7x = 180$$
$$12x = 180$$
$$x = 15$$

Therefore, the measure of the smaller angle is $5x = 5(15) = 75°$.

5. (B)

The definition of the mean is the sum of the two numbers divided by 2. Since the two angles are complementary, the sum of their measures is $90°$. Therefore, the mean of two complementary angles is $\frac{90}{2} = 45°$.

6. (A)

The angles $110°$ and $y - 10$ are vertical angles and congruent. Thus,

$$y - 10 = 110$$
$$y = 120$$

Additionally, angles $110°$ and $x + 10$ are corresponding angles and congruent. Thus,

$$x + 10 = 110$$
$$x = 100$$

Thus, $x = 100$ and $y = 120$. Therefore, the value of $x + y = 220$.

7. (C)

The angles A and B are complementary. Thus, the sum of their measures is $90°$. Since the measure of angle A is $40°$, the measure of angle B is $50°$. Additionally, since angles B and C are complementary and the measure of angle B is $50°$, the measure of angle C is $40°$. Furthermore, the measure of angle C can be obtained according to the congruent complements theorem.

$$m\angle A + m\angle B = 90°$$
$$m\angle C + m\angle B = 90°$$
$$\therefore \ \ m\angle A = m\angle C = 40°$$

8. (E)

Let x be the measure of the middle angle. Since the measures of the three angles are consecutive even integer, $x + 2$ is the measure of the largest angle and $x - 2$ is the measure of the smallest angle. Because the three angles are formed from the straight angle, the sum of their measures is 180°.

$$x - 2 + x + x + 2 = 180$$
$$3x = 180$$
$$x = 60$$

Therefore, the measure of the largest angle is $x + 2 = 60 + 2 = 62°$.

9. (A)

Since angles $3x - 15$ and $2x - 5$ are consecutive angles, they are supplementary angles whose sum of their measures is 180°.

$$3x - 15 + 2x - 5 = 180$$
$$5x - 20 = 180$$
$$x = 40$$

Therefore, the value of x is 40.

10. (B)

Angles B and C are complementary angles whose sum of their measures is 90°. Let x be the measure of angle C. Then, $3x - 10$ is the measure of angle B.

$$3x - 10 + x = 90$$
$$4x - 10 = 90$$
$$x = 25$$

Thus, the measure of angle C is 25° and the measure of angle B is $3x - 10 = 3(25) - 10 = 65°$. Since angle A and B are supplementary, the measure of angle A is $180 - 65 = 115°$. Therefore, the sum of the measures of angle A and C is $115 + 25 = 140°$.

LESSON 11

Properties and Theorems of Triangles

A triangle is a figure formed by three segments joining three points called **vertices**. A triangle ABC is expressed as $\triangle ABC$. A triangle can be classified according to its sides or its angles.

Classification by Sides

- Equilateral triangle: All sides are equal in length. The measure of each angle is 60°.

- Isosceles triangle: Two sides are equal in length. If two sides of a triangle are congruent, then the angles (**base angles**) opposite them are congruent as shown in the figure below.

- Scalene triangle: All sides are unequal in length.

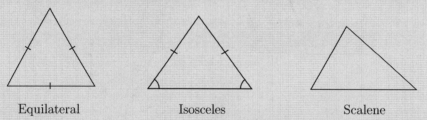

| Equilateral | Isosceles | Scalene |

Classification by Angles

- Acute triangle: All interior angles measure less than 90°.

- Right triangle: One of the interior angles measures 90°.

- Obtuse triangle: One of the interior angles measures more than 90°.

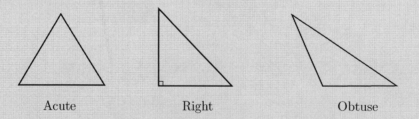

| Acute | Right | Obtuse |

Area of a Triangle

- The area of a triangle is $A = \frac{1}{2}bh$, where b is base and h is height.

- The area of an equilateral triangle with side length of s is $A = \frac{\sqrt{3}}{4}s^2$.

- The areas of two triangles are equal if the bases and heights of the two triangles are the same.

Theorems of triangles

Triangle sum theorem

The sum of the measures of interior angles of a triangle is 180°.

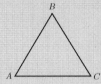

$$m\angle A + m\angle B + m\angle C = 180°$$

Right triangles

In the right triangle, shown at the right, the longest side opposite the right angle is called the **hypotenuse** and the other two sides are called **legs** of the triangle. There is a special relationship between the length of the hypotenuse and the lengths of the legs. It is known as the Pythagorean theorem.

Pythagorean theorem

In the right triangle above, the square of the length of the hypotenuse is equal to the sum of the squares of the lengths of the legs.

$$c^2 = a^2 + b^2$$

The Pythagorean theorem is very useful because it helps you find the length of the third side of a right triangle when the lengths of two sides of the right triangle are known.

45°-45°-90° special right triangles

In a 45°-45°-90° right triangle, the sides of the triangle are in the ratio $1 : 1 : \sqrt{2}$, respectively. In other words, the length of the hypotenuse is $\sqrt{2}$ times the length of each leg.

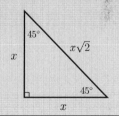

$$\text{Hypotenuse} = \text{Leg} \times \sqrt{2} \iff \text{Leg} = \frac{\text{Hypotenuse}}{\sqrt{2}}$$

Example: If the measures of the angles of a triangle are $x + 5$, $2x + 10$, and $3x + 15$, what is the measure of the largest angle?

The sum of the measures of interior angles of a triangle is 180°. Thus,

$$x + 5 + 2x + 10 + 3x + 15 = 180$$
$$6x + 30 = 180$$
$$x = 25$$

Therefore, the measure of the largest angle is $3x + 15 = 3(25) + 15 = 90°$.

EXERCISES

1. What is the area of the equilateral triangle with side length of 6 ?

    (A) $6\sqrt{3}$ (B) $9\sqrt{3}$ (C) $12\sqrt{3}$

    (D) $15\sqrt{3}$ (E) $18\sqrt{3}$

2. In a right triangle, the length of the hypotenuse is 13 and the length of one leg is 5. What is the length of the other leg?

    (A) 4   (B) 6   (C) 8

    (D) 10   (E) 12

3. If the equal sides of an isosceles triangle are $3x+3$ and $2x+7$, what is the length of the equal sides of the isosceles triangle?

    (A) 18   (B) 15   (C) 12

    (D) 10   (E) 8

4. If the area of a square is 100, what is the length of the diagonal?

    (A) $5\sqrt{2}$ (B) $10\sqrt{2}$ (C) $10\sqrt{3}$

    (D) 20   (E) $20\sqrt{2}$

5. In an isosceles triangle, the ratio of the measure of the base angle to that of the vertex angle is 2 : 1, what is the measure of the vertex angle?

    (A) 18   (B) 24   (C) 36

    (D) 48   (E) 72

6. Two trains leave a station at the same time. One train is traveling North at a rate of 30 mph and the other train is traveling East at a rate of 40 mph. After 5 hours, how far apart are they in miles?

    (A) 200   (B) 225   (C) 250

    (D) 300   (E) 350

7. If the x and y coordinates of three vertices of a triangle are $(4,0)$, $(9,0)$ and $(2,4)$, what is the area of the triangle?

    (A) 30   (B) 20   (C) 15

    (D) 10   (E) 5

8. In the triangle below, $AC = BC$. What is $m\angle BCD$?

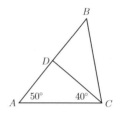

    (A) 40   (B) 45   (C) 50

    (D) 55   (E) 60

9. In an isosceles right triangle ABC, B is the right angle. If $AC = 20$, what is the perimeter of the triangle?

    (A) 20   (B) 40

    (C) $20 + 20\sqrt{2}$ (D) $20 + 30\sqrt{2}$

    (E) $40 + 20\sqrt{2}$

10. In the figure below, $AB = 1$, $BC = 2$, and $CD = 2$. What is AD ?

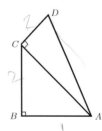

    (A) $\sqrt{29}$ (B) 4   (C) $\sqrt{13}$

    (D) 3   (E) 2

1. (B)

The area of the equilateral triangle with side length of s is $\frac{\sqrt{3}}{4}s^2$.

$$\text{Area of equilateral triangle} = \frac{\sqrt{3}}{4}(6)^2 = 9\sqrt{3}$$

Therefore, the area of the equilateral triangle with side length of 6 is $9\sqrt{3}$.

2. (E)

Since the triangle is a right triangle, use the Pythagorean theorem: $c^2 = a^2 + b^2$, where c is the hypotenuse, and a and b are the legs of the triangle. The length of the hypotenuse is 13 and the length of one leg is 5. Thus, $c = 13$ and $a = 5$.

$$
\begin{aligned}
c^2 &= a^2 + b^2 && \text{Substitute 13 for } c \text{ and 5 for } a \\
13^2 &= 5^2 + b^2 && \text{Subtract 25 from each side} \\
b^2 &= 144 && \text{Solve for } b \\
b &= 12 && \text{Since } b > 0
\end{aligned}
$$

Therefore, the length of the other leg is $b = 12$.

3. (B)

Since $3x + 3$ and $2x + 7$ are the equal sides of the isosceles triangle, set $3x + 3$ and $2x + 7$ equal to each other and solve for x.

$$
\begin{aligned}
3x + 3 &= 2x + 7 \\
3x - 2x &= 7 - 3 \\
x &= 4
\end{aligned}
$$

Therefore, the length of the equal sides of the isosceles triangle is $3x + 3 = 3(4) + 3 = 15$.

4. (B)

In the figure below, the area of the square is 100 which means that the length of the side of the square is 10. The square consists of two $45°$-$45°$-$90°$ triangles whose sides are in the ratio $1 : 1 : \sqrt{2}$.

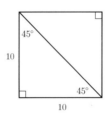

The diagonal of the square is the hypotenuse of the two triangles. The length of the hypotenuse is $\sqrt{2}$ times the length of each leg. Therefore, the length of the diagonal of the square is $10\sqrt{2}$.

53

5. (C)

Since the ratio of the measure of the base angle to that of the vertex angle is $2 : 1$, let x be the measure of the vertex angle and $2x$ be the measure of the each base angle in the isosceles triangle. Since the sum of the measures of interior angles of triangle BDC is $180°$,

$$x + 2x + 2x = 180$$
$$5x = 180$$
$$x = 36$$

Therefore, the measure of the vertex angle is $36°$.

6. (C)

After 5 hours, the train heading North travels $5 \times 30 = 150$ miles and the other train heading East travels $5 \times 40 = 200$ miles. In order to find out how far they are apart in 5 hours, Use the Pythagorean theorem: $c^2 = 150^2 + 200^2$. Thus, $c = 250$. Therefore, the two trains are 250 miles apart in 5 hours.

7. (D)

In the figure below, the two points $(4, 0)$ and $(9, 0)$ are on the x axis.

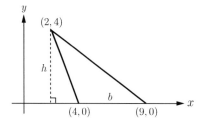

Thus, the base of the triangle is $b = 9 - 4 = 5$. Since the point $(2, 4)$ is 4 units above the x axis, the height of the triangle is $h = 4$. Therefore, the area of the triangle is $A = \frac{1}{2}bh = \frac{1}{2}(5)(4) = 10$.

8. (A)

Since $AC = BC$, triangle ACB is an isosceles triangle. $\angle B$ and $\angle A$ are base angles of the isosceles triangle and are congruent. Thus, $m\angle B = m\angle A = 50°$. Additionally, $\angle BDC$ is an exterior angle of the triangle ADC. Thus, $m\angle BDC = m\angle DAC + m\angle DCA = 90°$. Since the sum of the measures of interior angles of triangle BDC is $180°$,

$$m\angle BCD + m\angle BDC + m\angle B = 180° \qquad \text{Substitute } m\angle BDC = 90° \text{ and } m\angle B = 50°$$
$$m\angle BCD + 90° + 50° = 180°$$
$$m\angle BCD = 40°$$

9. (C)

An isosceles right triangle is a $45°$-$45°$-$90°$ right triangle whose sides are in the ratio $1 : 1 : \sqrt{2}$. AC is the length of the hypotenuse of the isosceles right triangle and $AC = 20$. The length of each leg is $\frac{\text{hypotenuse}}{\sqrt{2}} = \frac{20}{\sqrt{2}} = 10\sqrt{2}$. Therefore, the perimeter of the isosceles right triangle is

$$\text{Perimeter of isosceles right triangle} = 20 + 10\sqrt{2} + 10\sqrt{2} = 20 + 20\sqrt{2}$$

10. (D)

In the figure below, find AC using the Pythagorean theorem.

$$AC^2 = AB^2 + BC^2 = 1^2 + 2^2$$
$$AC^2 = 5 \quad \implies \quad AC = \sqrt{5}$$

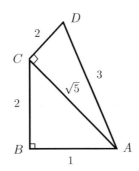

Since AC and CD are known, use the Pythagorean theorem again to find AD.

$$AD^2 = AC^2 + CD^2 = (\sqrt{5})^2 + 2^2$$
$$AD^2 = 9 \quad \implies \quad AD = 3$$

LESSON 12

Patterns and Data Analysis

Patterns

A **pattern** is a set of numbers or objects that are closely related by a specific rule. Understanding a pattern is very important because it helps you predict what will happen next in the set of numbers or objects.

For instance, the figure above shows a pattern which consists of a circle, a triangle, and a square in that order. If the pattern is repeated continuously, how do you predict which one of the three figures is the 36th figure? Since 36 is a multiple of 3 and every third figure is a square, the 36th figure is a square.

Arithmetic sequence and Geometric sequence

There are two most common number patterns: arithmetic sequence and geometric sequence.
A **sequence or progression** is an ordered list of numbers.

- In an arithmetic sequence, add or subtract the same number (common difference) to one term to get the next term.

- In geometric sequence, multiply or divide one term by the same number (common ratio) to get the next term.

- In both sequences, the first term, the second term, and n^{th} term are expressed as a_1, a_2, and a_n respectively.

Type	Definition	Example	n^{th} term
Arithmetic sequence	The common difference between any consecutive terms is constant.	$1, 3, 5, 7, \ldots$	$a_n = a_1 + (n-1)d$ where d is the common difference.
Geometric sequence	The common ratio between any consecutive terms is constant	$2, 4, 8, 16, \ldots$	$a_n = a_1 \times r^{n-1}$ where r is the common ratio.

Data Analysis

Mean, or **Average**, is the sum of all elements in a set divided by the number of elements in the set. For instance, if there are 3, 7, and 11 in a set, the mean $= \frac{3+7+11}{3} = 7$.

Median is the middle number when a set of numbers is arranged from least to greatest.

- If there is a n (odd number) number of numbers in a set, the median is the middle number which is $(\frac{n+1}{2})^{\text{th}}$ number in the set. For instance, if there are 3, 2, 5, 7, and 10 in a set, arrange the numbers in the set from least to greatest: 2, 3, 5, 7, and 10. Since there are 5 numbers in the set, the median is the $\frac{5+1}{2} = 3^{\text{rd}}$ number in the set. Thus, the median is 5.

- If there is a n (even number) number of numbers in a set, the median is the average of the two middle numbers which are the $(\frac{n}{2})^{\text{th}}$ and $(\frac{n}{2}+1)^{\text{th}}$ numbers. For instance, if there are 1, 4, 6, 8, 9, and 11 in a set, the median is the average of 3rd number and 4th number in the set. Thus, the median is $\frac{6+8}{2} = 7$.

Mode is a number that appears most frequently in a set. It is possible to have more than one mode or no mode in a set.

Range is the difference between the greatest number and the least number in a set.

Example: There are 2, 4, 8, 10, and x in a set. If the range of the set is 13, what is the value of x ?

The range is the difference between the greatest number and the least number. The least number in the set is 2. If 10 is the greatest number in the set, the range would be 8. Thus, x must be the greatest number. Therefore, the value of x is 15.

EXERCISES

1. If the pattern below is repeated continuously, what is the 48th letter in the pattern?

$$B, \quad C, \quad D, \quad E, \quad A, \quad B, \quad C, \ldots$$

(A) A (B) B (C) C

(D) D (E) E

2. In the sequence below, the nth term is defined as $a_n = n^2 + 1$. What is the 7th term in the sequence?

$$2, 5, 10, 17, \ldots$$

(A) 50   (B) 42   (C) 35

(D) 26   (E) 20

3. In a set of 5, 1, 10, x, and 16, where $10 < x < 16$, which of the following is the median of the set?

(A) 1   (B) 5   (C) 10

(D) x (E) 16

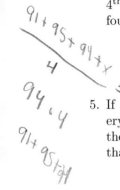

4. Jason scored 91, 95, and 94 in the first three tests. What score does he get on the 4th test so that his overall average for the four tests is 94 ?

(A) 96   (B) 97   (C) 98

(D) 99   (E) 100

5. If the volume of a balloon is doubled every three minutes, in how many minutes is the volume of the balloon eight times larger than the initial volume of the balloon?

(A) 6   (B) 8   (C) 9

(D) 12   (E) 16

6. In the arithmetic sequence $3, 7, 11, 15, \ldots$ what is the value of the 17th term?

(A) 76   (B) 67   (C) 56

(D) 45   (E) 37

7. There are 1, 3, 4, 7, and 10 in a set. If 3 is added to each number in the set, what is the positive difference of the new mean and the new median of the set?

(A) 1   (B) 2   (C) 3

(D) 4   (E) 5

8. In a set of five positive integers, the mode is 4, the median is 5, and the mean is 6. What is the greatest of these integers?

(A) 7   (B) 8   (C) 9

(D) 10   (E) 11

9. A car travels at 60 miles per hour for 2 hours on a trip and travels at 40 miles per hour for three hours on the returning trip. What is the average speed of the entire trip?

(A) 55   (B) 50   (C) 48

(D) 45   (E) 42

10. In the arithmetic sequence, the 3rd term is 17 and the 10th term is 73. What is the 15th term?

(A) 95   (B) 97   (C) 103

(D) 108   (E) 113

ANSWERS AND SOLUTIONS

1. **(D)**

   The pattern consists of B, C, D, E and A. It is repeated continuously. Since every 5th letter is A, the 45th letter is also A. Thus, the 46th letter is B, the 47th letter is C, and the 48th letter is D.

2. **(A)**

   To find the 7th term in the sequence, substitute 7 for n in $a_n = n^2 + 1$.

   $$a_n = n^2 + 1 \qquad \text{Substitute 7 for } n$$
   $$a_7 = (7)^2 + 1 = 50$$

   Therefore, the 7th term in the sequence is 50.

3. (C)

Arrange the numbers in the set from least to greatest: 1, 5, 10, x, 16. The median is the middle number of the set. Therefore, the median is 10.

4. (A)

The average of four tests is 94. This means that Jason should get a total score of $94 \times 4 = 376$ for the four tests. The sum of scores of the first three tests is $91 + 95 + 94 = 280$. Therefore, the score of the fourth test is $376 - 280 = 96$.

5. (C)

Let's define V_0 as the initial volume of the balloon. The volume of the balloon is doubled every 3 minutes:

$$\text{In 3 minutes} = 2V_0$$
$$\text{In 6 minutes} = 2(2V_0) = 4V_0$$
$$\text{In 9 minutes} = 2(4V_0) = 8V_0$$

Therefore, in 9 minutes, the volume of the balloon is eight times larger than the initial volume of the balloon.

6. (B)

In an arithmetic sequence, the first term, $a_1 = 3$ and the common difference, $d = 7 - 3 = 4$. Use the nth term formula to find the 17th term.

$$a_n = a_1 + (n - 1)d \qquad \text{Substitute 17 for } n, \text{ 3 for } a_1, \text{ and 4 for } d$$
$$a_{17} = 3 + (17 - 1)4 = 67$$

Therefore, the value of the 17th term is 67.

7. (A)

The mean of the set is $\frac{1+3+4+7+10}{5} = 5$. The median of the set is the middle number, 4. If 3 is added to each number in the set, the new mean is $5 + 3 = 8$, and the new median is $4 + 3 = 7$. Therefore, the positive difference of the new mean the new median is $8 - 7 = 1$.

8. (E)

Since the mean of the five positive integers is 6, the sum of the five positive integers is $5 \times 6 = 30$. Define x as the second greatest integer and y as the greatest integer in the set. Let's consider three cases shown below. In case 1, the median is 4 because there are three 4's. This doesn't satisfy the given information such that the median is 5. Thus, case 1 is false.

Case 1:	$4 + 4 + 4 + x + y = 30$	mode=4, median=4: It doesn't work
Case 2:	$4 + 4 + 5 + 5 + y = 30$	mode=4 and 5, median=5: It doesn't work
Case 3:	$4 + 4 + 5 + x + y = 30$	mode=4, median=5: It works

In case 2, there are two 4's and two 5's in which the mode are both 4 and 5. This doesn't satisfy the given information such that the mode is 4. Thus, case 2 is false. Finally, in case 3, there are two 4's and one 5. If x is greater than 5, the mode is 4 and median is 5 which satisfy the given information. x must be smallest positive integer greater than 5 so that y will have the greatest possible value. Thus, $x = 6$ and $y = 11$. Therefore, the greatest of these integers is 11.

9. (C)

On the trip, the car travels $60 \times 2 = 120$ miles. On the returning trip, the car travels $40 \times 3 = 120$ miles. Thus,

$$\text{The average speed} = \frac{\text{Total distance}}{\text{Total number of hours}}$$

$$= \frac{120 \text{ miles} + 120 \text{ miles}}{2 \text{ hours} + 3 \text{ hours}}$$

$$= \frac{240 \text{ miles}}{5 \text{ hours}}$$

$$= 48 \text{ miles per hour}$$

Therefore, the average speed of the entire trip is 48 miles per hour.

10. (E)

Write the 10th term and 3rd term of the arithmetic sequence in terms of a_1 and d using the nth term formula: $a_n = a_1 + (n-1)d$.

$$a_{10} = a_1 + 9d = 73$$
$$a_3 = a_1 + 2d = 17$$

Use the linear combinations method to solve for d and a_1.

$$a_1 + 9d = 73$$
$$\underline{a_1 + 2d = 17} \qquad \text{Subtract two equations}$$
$$7d = 56 \qquad \text{Divide both sides by 7}$$
$$d = 8$$

Substitute $d = 8$ in $a_3 = a_1 + 2d = 17$ and solve for a_1. Thus, $a_1 = 1$. Therefore, the 15th term of the arithmetic sequence is $a_{15} = a_1 + 14d = 1 + 14(8) = 113$.

LESSON 13

Counting and Probability

Counting

Counting integers

How many positive integers are there between 42 and 97 inclusive? Are there 54, 55, or 56 integers? Even in this simple counting problem, many students are not sure what the right answer is. A rule for counting integers is as follows:

$$\text{The number of integers} = \text{Greatest integer} - \text{Least integer} + 1$$

According to this rule, the number of integers between 42 and 97 inclusive is $97 - 42 + 1 = 56$ integers.

Counting points on a line

There is a line whose length is 200 feet. If points are placed every 2 feet starting from one end, how many points are on the line?

The pattern above suggests that a rule for counting the number of points on a line is as follows:

$$\text{Total number of points on a line} = \frac{\text{Length of a line}}{\text{Distance between each point}} + 1$$

For instance, if a line is 6 feet long, there are $\frac{6}{2} + 1 = 4$ points on the line as shown above. Therefore, if a line is 200 feet long, there are $\frac{200}{2} + 1 = 101$ points on the line.

Counting points on a circle

There is a circle whose circumference is 200 feet. If points are placed every 2 feet on the circumference of the circle, how many points are on the circle?

$$C = 2 \text{ ft} \qquad C = 4 \text{ ft} \qquad C = 6 \text{ ft}$$

The pattern above suggests that a rule for counting the total number of points on a circle is as follows:

$$\text{Total number of points on a circle} = \frac{\text{Circumference of a circle}}{\text{Distance between each point}}$$

According to this rule, if the circumference of a circle is 200 feet, there are $\frac{200}{2} = 100$ points on the circle.

The fundamental counting principle

If one event can occur in m ways and another event can occur in n ways, then the number of ways both events can occur is $m \times n$. For instance, Jason has three shirts and four pairs of jeans. He can dress up in $3 \times 4 = 12$ different ways.

Venn Diagram

A venn diagram is very useful in counting. It helps you count numbers correctly.

$A \qquad B$

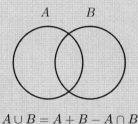

$$A \cup B = A + B - A \cap B$$

In the figure above, $A \cup B$ represents the combined area of two circles A and B. $A \cap B$ represents the common area where the two circles overlap. The venn diagram suggests that the combined area $(A \cup B)$ equals the sum of areas of circles $(A + B)$ minus the common area $(A \cap B)$.

In counting, each circle A and B represents a set of numbers. $n(A)$ and $n(B)$ represent the number of elements in set A and B, respectively. For instance, $A = \{2, 4, 6, 8, 10\}$ and $n(A) = 5$. Thus, the total number of elements that belong to either set A or set B, $n(A \cup B)$, can be counted as follows:

$$n(A \cup B) = n(A) + n(B) - n(A \cap B)$$

Let's find out how many positive integers less than or equal to 20 are divisible by 2 or 3. Define A as the set of numbers divisible by 2 and B as the set of numbers divisible by 3.

$$A = \{2, 4, 6, \cdots, 18, 20\}, \qquad n(A) = 10$$
$$B = \{3, 6, 9, 12, 15, 18\}, \qquad n(B) = 6$$
$$A \cap B = \{6, 12, 18\}, \qquad n(A \cap B) = 3$$

Notice that $A \cap B = \{6, 12, 18\}$ are multiples of 2 and multiples of 3. They are counted twice so they must be excluded in counting. Thus,

$$n(A \cup B) = n(A) + n(B) - n(A \cap B)$$
$$= 10 + 6 - 3$$
$$= 13$$

Therefore, the total number of positive integers less than or equal to 20 that are divisible by 2 or 3 is 13.

Probability

The definition of probability of an event, E, is as follows:

$$\text{Probability(E)} = \frac{\text{The number of outcomes event } E \text{ can happen}}{\text{The total number of possible outcomes}}$$

Probability is a measure of how likely an event will happen. Probability can be expressed as a fraction, a decimal, and a percent, and is measured on scale from 0 to 1. Probability can not be less than 0 nor greater than 1.

- Probability equals 0 means an event will never happen.

- Probability equals 1 means an event will always happen.

- Higher the probability, higher chance an event will happen.

For instance, what is the probability of selecting a prime number at random from 1 to 5? In this problem, the event E is selecting a prime number from three possible prime numbers: 2, 3, and 5. The total possible outcomes are numbers from 1 to 5. Thus, the probability of selecting a prime number is $P(E) = \frac{\{2,3,5\}}{\{1,2,3,4,5\}} = \frac{3}{5}$.

Geometric probability

Geometric probability involves the length or area of the geometric figures. The definition of the geometric probability is as follows:

$$\text{Geometric probability} = \frac{\text{Area of desired region}}{\text{Total area}}$$

In the figure below, a circle is inscribed in the square with side length of 10. Assuming that a dart always lands inside the square, what is the probability that a dart lands on a region that lies outside the circle and inside the square?

The area of the square is $10^2 = 100$, and the area of the circle is $\pi(5)^2 = 25\pi$. Thus, the area of desired region is $100 - 25\pi$.

$$\begin{aligned}
\text{Geometric probability} &= \frac{\text{Area of desired region}}{\text{Total area}} \\
&= \frac{100 - 25\pi}{100} \\
&= \frac{25(4 - \pi)}{100} \\
&= \frac{4 - \pi}{4}
\end{aligned}$$

Example: You toss a coin four times. How many different outcomes are possible?

Event 1, event 2, event 3, and event 4 are tossing a first coin, second coin, third coin, and fourth coin, respectively. For each event, there are two possible outcomes: head or tail. According to the fundamental counting principle, there are $2 \times 2 \times 2 \times 2 = 16$ possible outcomes for the four events.

EXERCISES

1. There are three red, two yellow, and five blue cards. What is the probability that a blue card is selected at random?

   (A) $\dfrac{3}{5}$ (B) $\dfrac{1}{2}$ (C) $\dfrac{2}{5}$

   (D) $\dfrac{3}{10}$ (E) $\dfrac{1}{5}$

2. How many positive integers are there between 19 and 101 exclusive?

   (A) 78   (B) 79   (C) 80
   (D) 81   (E) 82

3. There are four types of breads, five types of meats, and three types of cheese. Assuming you have to select one of each category, how many different sandwiches can you make?

   (A) 60   (B) 50   (C) 40
   (D) 30   (E) 12

4. Toss a coin twice. What is the probability that you have one head and one tail?

   (A) $\dfrac{1}{4}$ (B) $\dfrac{1}{2}$ (C) $\dfrac{3}{4}$

   (D) $\dfrac{4}{5}$ (E) 1

5. On a road that is 200 feet long, trees are placed every 4 feet starting from one end. How many tree are on the road?

   (A) 49   (B) 50   (C) 51
   (D) 52   (E) 53

6. There are two concentric circles whose radii are 2 and 3, respectively. Assuming a dart never land outside the larger circle, what is the probability that a dart lands on the shaded region?

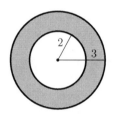

   (A) $\dfrac{1}{3}$ (B) $\dfrac{1}{2}$ (C) $\dfrac{2}{3}$

   (D) $\dfrac{3}{4}$ (E) $\dfrac{5}{9}$

7. There is a square-shaped plot of land whose side length is 50 feet. If posts are placed every 5 feet on the perimeter of the land, how many posts are on the land?

   (A) 39   (B) 40   (C) 41
   (D) 42   (E) 43

8. How many three digit numbers are there whose digits in the hundreds place and ones place are the same? (Assume that a nonzero digit is in the hundreds place.)

   (A) 80   (B) 81   (C) 90
   (D) 100   (E) 121

9. There are 36 marbles in a bag. They are either blue, red, or green marbles. The number of green marbles is twice the number of blue marbles. The number of the red marbles is 8 more than the number of blue marbles. What is the probability that a red marble is selected at random in a bag?

(A) $\frac{1}{3}$ (B) $\frac{13}{36}$ (C) $\frac{7}{18}$

(D) $\frac{5}{12}$ (E) $\frac{4}{9}$

10. If a number is selected at random from 1 to 30 inclusive, what is the probability that the selected integer is divisible by 2 or 3 ?

(A) $\frac{8}{15}$ (B) $\frac{9}{15}$ (C) $\frac{2}{3}$
(D) $\frac{11}{15}$ (E) $\frac{4}{5}$

ANSWERS AND SOLUTIONS

1. (B)

There are 10 cards. Out of these cards, there are 5 blue cards. Therefore, the probability of selecting a blue card is $\frac{5}{10} = \frac{1}{2}$.

2. (D)

The two numbers, 19 and 101, are excluded. Therefore, the number of integers from 20 and 100 is $100 - 20 + 1 = 81$.

3. (A)

Event 1, event 2, and event 3 are selecting one out of 4 types of breads, one out of 5 types of meats, and one out of 3 types of cheese, respectively. According to the fundamental counting principle, you can make $4 \times 5 \times 3 = 60$ different sandwiches.

4. (B)

Event 1 is tossing a first coin and event 2 is tossing a second coin. According to the fundamental counting principle, there are $2 \times 2 = 4$ outcomes. The four outcomes are HH, HT, TH, and TT. Out of these outcomes, there are two outcomes that have one head and one tail: HT and TH. Therefore, the probability that you have one head and one tail is $\frac{2}{4} = \frac{1}{2}$.

5. (C)

This problem is exactly the same as counting points on the line. The road is 200 feet long and trees are placed every 4 feet.

$$\text{Total number of trees on the road} = \frac{\text{Length of the road}}{\text{Distance between each tree}} + 1$$
$$= \frac{200}{4} + 1$$
$$= 51$$

Therefore, there are 51 trees on the road.

6. (E)

The area of the larger circle is $\pi(3)^2 = 9\pi$. The area of the shaded region is $\pi(3)^2 - \pi(2)^2 = 5\pi$.

$$\text{Geometric probability} = \frac{\text{Area of the shaded region}}{\text{Area of larger circle}} = \frac{5\pi}{9\pi} = \frac{5}{9}$$

Therefore, the probability that a dart lands on the shaded region is $\frac{5}{9}$.

7. (B)

This problem is exactly the same as counting points on the circle. The perimeter of the square-shaped plot of land is $50 \times 4 = 200$ feet. The posts are placed every 5 feet.

$$\text{Total number of posts on the land} = \frac{\text{Perimeter of the land}}{\text{Distance between each post}}$$

$$= \frac{200}{5}$$

$$= 40$$

Therefore, there are 40 posts on the land.

8. (C)

Event 1 is selecting a digit in the hundreds place and ones place. There are 9 possible outcomes: 1 through 9. Event 2 is a selecting a digit in the tens place. There are 10 possible outcomes: 0 through 9. Therefore, according to the fundamental counting principle, there are $9 \times 10 = 90$ three digit numbers whose digits in hundreds place and the ones place are the same.

9. (D)

Let x be the number of blue marbles. Then, the number of green marbles is $2x$, and the number of red marble is $x + 8$. Since there are 36 marbles, set up an equation and solve for x.

$$x + x + 8 + 2x = 36$$
$$4x + 8 = 36$$
$$4x = 28$$
$$x = 7$$

Thus, the number of the red marble is $x + 8 = 15$. Therefore, the probability that a red marble is selected at random is $\frac{15}{36} = \frac{5}{12}$.

10. (C)

Let's define A as the set of integers that are divisible by 2, B as the set of integers that are divisible by 3, and $A \cap B$ as the set of integers that are divisible by 2 and 3, respectively.

$$A = \{2, 4, 6, \cdots, 28, 30\}, \qquad n(A) = 15$$
$$B = \{3, 6, 9, \cdots, 27, 30\}, \qquad n(B) = 10$$
$$A \cap B = \{6, 12, 18, 24, 30\}, \qquad n(A \cap B) = 5$$

Thus, the number of integers less than or equal to 30 that are divisible by 2 or 3, $n(A \cup B)$, is

$$n(A \cup B) = n(A) + n(B) - n(A \cap B)$$
$$= 15 + 10 - 5$$
$$= 20$$

Out of the integers from 1 to 30 inclusive, there are 20 integers that are divisible by 2 or 3. Therefore, the probability that a selected integer is divisible by 2 or 3 is $\frac{20}{30} = \frac{2}{3}$.

LESSON 14

ADVANCED MATH TOPICS

Divisibility Rule for 3

A number is divisible by 3 if the sum of the digits is divisible by 3. For instance, the number 2241 is divisible by 3 since the sum of digits, $2 + 2 + 4 + 1 = 9$, is divisible by 3.

Divisibility Rule for 11

Take the alternating sum of the digits in the number, read from left to right. If it is 0 or divisible by 11, so is the original number. For instance, 8173 has alternating sum of digits 8-1+7-3 = 11. Since 11 is divisible by 11, so is 8173.

GCF and LCM

The product of two numbers ab equals the product of $GCF(a, b)$ and $LCM(a, b)$.

$$ab = GCF \times LCM$$

For instance, the product of 4 and 6 is 24. The GCF(4, 6)=2, and LCM(4, 6)=12. Thus,

$$4 \times 6 = GCF(4,6) \times LCM(4,6)$$
$$4 \times 6 = 2 \times 12$$

The Product of Factors

When the prime factorization of a number n is $2^a \cdot 3^b$,

$$\text{Number of factors} = (a+1) \times (b+1)$$

$$\text{Product of factors} = n^{\frac{\text{Number of factors}}{2}}$$

How to Determine a Prime Number

How to determine whether a number n is a prime number:

- Step 1: Check whether the number n is divisible by 2, 3, 5, 7.

- Step 2: Find the prime numbers less than or equal to $\sqrt{n}$.

- Step 3: Check whether n is divisible by the prime numbers that you found in step 2.

For instance, the number 127 is not divisible by 2, 3, 5, and 7. $\sqrt{144} = 12$ and $\sqrt{127} < \sqrt{144}$. Thus, the prime numbers less than $\sqrt{127}$ are 2, 3, 5, 7, and 11. Since 127 is not divisible by 11, 127 is a prime number.

Proportions

If $\frac{a}{b} = \frac{c}{d} = \frac{e}{f}$, the following equalities are true.

$$\frac{a}{b} = \frac{c}{d} = \frac{e}{f} = \frac{a+c+e}{b+d+f}$$

Special Product Patterns

- **Sum and Difference**

$$(a + b)(a - b) = a^2 - b^2$$

- **Square of a binomial**

$$(a + b)^2 = a^2 + 2ab + b^2$$
$$(a - b)^2 = a^2 - 2ab + b^2$$
$$(a - b)^2 = (a + b)^2 - 4ab$$

- **Sum of squares**

$$a^2 + b^2 = (a + b)^2 - 2ab$$

- **Sum and difference of two cubes**

$$a^3 + b^3 = (a + b)(a^2 - ab + b^2)$$
$$a^3 - b^3 = (a - b)(a^2 + ab + b^2)$$

- **Cube of a binomial**

$$(a + b)^3 = a^3 + 3a^2b + 3ab^2 + b^3$$
$$(a - b)^3 = a^3 - 3a^2b + 3ab^2 - b^3$$

- **Square of a trinomial**

$$(a + b + c)^2 = a^2 + b^2 + c^2 + 2ab + 2ac + 2bc$$

AM-GM Inequality

For non-negative real numbers a and b, the arithmetic mean $\left(\dfrac{a + b}{2}\right)$ is greater than or equal to the geometric mean($\sqrt{ab}$).

$$\frac{a + b}{2} \geq \sqrt{ab}$$

Vieta's Formulas

Vieta's formulas relate the coefficients of a polynomial to the sum and product of its zeros. Let s and t be the solutions to $ax^2 + bx + c = 0$.

$$s + t = -\frac{b}{a}$$
$$st = \frac{c}{a}$$

The Remainder Theorem

If a polynomial function $f(x)$ is divided by $x - k$, the remainder is $r = f(k)$, where k is the value of x for which the divisor $x - k$ equals to zero. For instance, if $f(x) = x^2 + 2$ is divided by $x - 1$, the remainder is $r = f(1) = 3$.

Arithmetic Sequences and Geometric Sequences

There are two most common sequences: Arithmetic sequences and geometric sequences.

- In an **arithmetic sequence**, add or subtract the same number (common difference) to one term to get the next term.

- In a **geometric sequence**, multiply or divide one term by the same number (common ratio) to get the next term.

Type	Definition	Example	nth term
Arithmetic sequence	The common difference between any consecutive terms is constant.	$1, 3, 5, 7, \ldots$	$a_n = a_1 + (n-1)d$ where d is the common difference.
Geometric sequence	The common ratio between any consecutive terms is constant	$2, 4, 8, 16, \ldots$	$a_n = a_1 \times r^{n-1}$ where r is the common ratio.

Series

A **series** is the sum of a sequence. A series can be either a finite series, S_n or infinite series, S. The finite series S_n is the sum of a finite number of terms. Whereas, the infinite series is the sum of an infinite number of terms. Often, the finite series S_n is called the **nth partial sum** and the infinite series is called an **infinite sum**.

A series can be represented in a compact form, called summation notation or sigma notation $\sum$. Using the summation notation, the nth partial sum S_n and infinite sum S can be expressed as follows:

$$S_n = a_1 + a_2 + \cdots + a_n = \sum_{k=1}^{n} a_k,$$

$$S = a_1 + a_2 + a_3 \cdots = \sum_{k=1}^{\infty} a_k$$

where k is called the **index** of the sum. $k = 1$ indicates where to start the sum and $k = n$ indicates where to end the sum. For instance,

$$\sum_{k=1}^{5} k^2 = 1^2 + 2^2 + 3^2 + 4^2 + 5^2$$

Arithmetic Series and Geometric Series

An arithmetic series is the sum of an arithmetic sequence. A geometric series is the sum of a geometric sequence. For instance, $1 + 3 + 5 + 7 + \cdots$ is an arithmetic series and $\frac{1}{2} + \frac{1}{4} + \frac{1}{8} + \frac{1}{16} + \cdots$ is a geometric series.

Below summarizes the nth partial sum and infinite sum for an arithmetic series and a geometric series.

Type	Arithmetic Series	Geometric Series
nth Partial Sum	$S_n = \frac{n}{2}(a_1 + a_n)$	$S_n = \frac{a_1(1-r^n)}{1-r}$
Infinite Sum	$S = \infty$	$S = \begin{cases} \dfrac{a_1}{1-r}, & \|r\| < 1 \\ \infty, & \|r\| \geq 1 \end{cases}$

Tips

1. Note that the infinite sum S of a geometric series converges to $\frac{a_1}{1-r}$ if $|r| < 1$, where r is the common ratio of a geometric sequence.

2. $1 + 2 + 2^2 + 2^3 + \cdots + 2^n = 2^{n+1} - 1$

Properties of Sigma Notation

1. $\displaystyle\sum_{k=1}^{n}(a_k \pm b_k) = \sum_{k=1}^{n} a_k \pm \sum_{k=1}^{n} b_k$

2. $\displaystyle\sum_{k=1}^{n} c \cdot a_k = c \cdot \sum_{k=1}^{n} a_k$, where c is a constant.

3. $\displaystyle\sum_{k=1}^{n} c = cn$, where c is a constant.

4. $\displaystyle\sum_{k=1}^{n} k = 1 + 2 + \cdots + n = \frac{n(n+1)}{2}$

5. $\displaystyle\sum_{k=1}^{n} k^2 = 1^2 + 2^2 + \cdots + n^2 = \frac{n(n+1)(2n+1)}{6}$

6. $\displaystyle\sum_{k=1}^{n} k^3 = 1^3 + 2^3 + \cdots + k^3 = \left(\frac{n(n+1)}{2}\right)^2$

Tips $\displaystyle\sum_{k=1}^{n}(a_k \cdot b_k) \neq \sum_{k=1}^{n} a_k \cdot \sum_{k=1}^{n} b_k$

Tag-recapture Method

The assumption behind tag-recapture method is that the proportion of tagged individuals recaptured in the second sample represent the proportion of tagged individuals in the population as a whole. In other words,

$$\frac{R}{S} = \frac{T}{N}$$

where

- R is the number of fish recaptured on the second day

- S is the number of sample on the second day

- T is the number of fish captured and tagged on the first day

- N is the fish population

Perpendicular Bisector Theorem

If a point is on the perpendicular bisector of a segment, it is equidistant from the segment's endpoints.

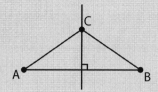

For instance, point C is on the perpendicular bisector of a segment $\overline{AB}$ as shown above. Thus, $CA = CB$.

Partial Fraction Decomposition

$$\frac{1}{n(n+1)} = \frac{1}{n} - \frac{1}{n+1}$$

For instance, $\dfrac{1}{2 \cdot 3} = \dfrac{1}{2} - \dfrac{1}{3}$.

An inscribed Triangle Inside a Semi-Circle

A triangle that is inscribed inside a semi-circle is a right triangle.

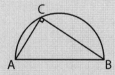

For instance, if point C is chosen on the semi-circle, $\triangle ABC$ that is inscribed inside the semi-circle is a right triangle.

Permutation and Combination

Factorial notation

n factorial, denoted by $n!$, is defined as $n! = n(n-1)(n-2)\cdots 3\cdot 2\cdot 1$. In other words, n factorial is the product of all positive integers less than or equal to n. For instance, $3! = 3\cdot 2\cdot 1 = 6$. Please notice that $0! = 1$ and $n! = n\times(n-1)!$.

Permutations without repetition

A permutation, denoted by $_nP_r$, represents a number of ways to select r objects from the total number of objects n where the order is important. The permutation $_nP_r$ is given by

$$_nP_r = \frac{n!}{(n-r)!}, \qquad \text{where } r \le n$$

For instance, how many words can be formed using all the letters in the word ABCDE?

Since all the letters A, B, C, D, and E are distinguishable, the order is important. Thus, this is a permutation problem. The number of different words can be formed using the letters in word ABCDE is $_5P_5 = \frac{5!}{0!} = 120$.

Permutations with repetition

The number of permutations of n objects, where there are n_1 indistinguishable objects of one kind, and n_2 indistinguishable objects of a second kind, is given by

$$\text{Permutations with repetition} = \frac{n!}{n_1!\cdot n_2!}$$

For instance, how many words can be formed using all the letters in the word AABBB?

Since letters A and B are distinguishable, the order is important. However, there are 2 A's and 3 B's out of 5 letters. Therefore, the number of different words can be formed using the letters in word AABBB is $\frac{5!}{2!\cdot 3!} = 10$.

Combinations

A combination, denoted by $_nC_r$ or $\binom{n}{r}$, represents a number of ways to select r objects from the total number of objects n where the order is NOT important. The combination $\binom{n}{r}$ is given by

$$\binom{n}{r} = \frac{n!}{(n-r)!\cdot r!}, \qquad \text{where } r \le n$$

For instance, how many 2 different books can be selected from a list of 10 books?

Since 2 books are indistinguishable, the order is not important. Thus, this is a combination problem. Therefore, the number of selecting 2 different books from a list of 10 books is $\binom{10}{2} = \frac{10!}{8!\cdot 2!} = 45$.

The sum of the entries in the nth row of Pascal's triangle

The sum of the entries in the nth row of Pascal's triangle is 2^n.

$$\binom{n}{0} + \binom{n}{1} + \binom{n}{2} + \cdots + \binom{n}{n} = 2^n$$

The Sum of the Coefficients of a Binomial Expansion

In the binomial expansion shown below,

$$(x+y)^n = \sum_{k=0}^{n} \binom{n}{k} x^{n-k} y^k$$

the sum of the coefficients of a binomial expansion is obtained by substituting $x = 1$ and $y = 1$. For instance, the sum of the coefficients of a binomial expansion $(x+y)^2 = x^2 + 2xy + y^2$ is $(1+1)^2 = 4$.

The number of ways n people can sit around a circular table

In a circular arrangement, you have to fix the position for the first person, which can be performed in only one way since every position is considered same if no one is already sitting on any of the seats. Once you have fixed the position for the first person, you can arrange the remaining $n-1$ people in $(n-1)!$ ways. Therefore, the number of ways n people can sit around a circular table is $(n-1)!$.

The Volume and Surface Area of a Sphere

Volume of a sphere: $= \dfrac{4}{3}\pi r^3$

Surface area of a sphere: $= 4\pi r^2$

The Area of a triangle with three vertices

If three vertices of a triangle are $(0,0)$, (a,b), and (c,d), the area A of the triangle is as follows:

$$A = \pm\frac{1}{2}(ad - bc)$$

TJHSST MATH PRACTICE TEST 1
Time — 50 minutes
Number of questions — 28

Directions: Solve each of the following problems using the available space for scratch work. Choose the best answer among the answer choices given and fill in the corresponding circle on the answer sheet.

1. On a road that is 200 feet long, trees are placed every 4 feet starting from one end. How many trees are on the road?

   (A) 49

   (B) 50

   (C) 51

   (D) 52

   (E) 53

$$B, \quad C, \quad D, \quad E, \quad A, \quad B, \quad C, \cdots$$

2. If the pattern above is repeated continuously, what is the 48th letter in the pattern?

   (A) A

   (B) B

   (C) C

   (D) D

   (E) E

3. A bus leaves Fairfax city at 9:10 AM traveling at a speed of 45 mph. 25 minutes later, a car leaves Fairfax city in the same direction as the bus at 60 mph. At what time would the car catch up with the bus?

   (A) 10:40 AM

   (B) 10:50 AM

   (C) 11:00 AM

   (D) 11:10 AM

   (E) 11:20 AM

4. The 3-digit number 98A is divisible by 6. What is the remainder when this number is divisible by 5?

   (A) 0

   (B) 1

   (C) 2

   (D) 3

   (E) 4

5. The numbers 1 through 10 inclusive are in a hat. If a number is selected at random, what is the probability that the number is neither divisible by 3 nor 4?

(A) $\frac{1}{4}$

(B) $\frac{1}{3}$

(C) $\frac{1}{2}$

(D) $\frac{2}{3}$

(E) $\frac{3}{10}$

7. A store sells desks and chairs. A store makes a profit of $15 per desk and $8 per chair. If the store sold a total of 23 desks and chairs and made the total profit of $240, how many chairs did the store sell?

(A) 5

(B) 8

(C) 10

(D) 12

(E) 15

6. A drawer contains 10 red socks, 9 white socks, 8 green socks, and 7 black socks. Without looking at the color, how many socks do you need to pull out to be sure of having a matching color?

(A) 4

(B) 5

(C) 6

(D) 7

(E) 8

8. If you toss a coin three times, what is the probability that one head will be shown?

(A) $\frac{3}{4}$

(B) $\frac{2}{3}$

(C) $\frac{5}{8}$

(D) $\frac{1}{2}$

(E) $\frac{3}{8}$

9. A palindrome is a number that reads the same backward as forward. For instance, the number 2552 is a 4-digit palindrome. How many 4-digit palindromes are there?

(A)   70

(B)   80

(C)   90

(D)   100

(E)   110

$T = \{\, L2, \quad F3, \quad W4 \,\}$

11. Set T has three elements. Which of the following is the most similar to the elements in set T ?

(A)   A4

(B)   T3

(C)   E5

(D)   H4

(E)   K3

10. Joshua has 100 mL of a 25% acid solution. How much of a 60% solution should he add so that the final solution is 40% solution?

(A)   75 mL

(B)   80 mL

(C)   85 mL

(D)   90 mL

(E)   95 mL

12. ABC represents a three-digit number greater than 200, where $A < B < C$. If B and C are multiples of A, and C is three more than B, which of the following number can be the three-digit number ABC ?

(A)   136

(B)   248

(C)   269

(D)   369

(E)   447

79

$$3, 7, 11, 15, \cdots$$

13. In the sequence above, what is the value of the 34th term?

    (A) 134

    (B) 135

    (C) 136

    (D) 137

    (E) 138

15. Joshua rolls two dice to form a two-digit integer. If the number on the first die represents the tens digit and the number on the second die represents the units digit, what is the probability that the integer formed is divisible by 8?

    (A) $\dfrac{2}{9}$

    (B) $\dfrac{7}{36}$

    (C) $\dfrac{1}{6}$

    (D) $\dfrac{5}{36}$

    (E) $\dfrac{1}{9}$

14. Jason has a total of 11 coins worth $1.23. 11 coins consist of pennies, nickels, dimes, and quarters. If Jason has at least one coin of each type, how many dimes does he have?

    (A) 1

    (B) 2

    (C) 3

    (D) 4

    (E) 5

$$2, 3, 5, 6, 7, 10, \cdots$$

16. The sequence above consists of all positive integers that are neither squares nor cubes. Which of the following is the value of the 100th term of the sequence?

    (A) 111

    (B) 112

    (C) 113

    (D) 114

    (E) 115

80

$S = \{ F6, \quad B2, \quad I9 \}$

17. Set S has three elements. Which of the following is the most similar to the elements in set S ?

    (A)   A0

    (B)   C3

    (C)   G5

    (D)   D6

    (E)   H7

    B 2nd

    F 6th

    19th

19. What is the sum of the first 100 positive even integers?

    (A)   5050

    (B)   10100

    (C)   15500

    (D)   20200

    (E)   22500

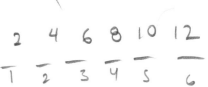

18. A larger cube with side length 3 is painted with the color red. Then each side of the larger cube is divided by 3 to form 27 smaller cubes. As a result, there are m unpainted smaller cube(s) and n smaller cube(s) with only 2 painted sides. What is the value of $m + n$?

    (A)   11

    (B)   12

    (C)   13

    (D)   14

    (E)   15

20. If a number, n, is divided by k, the remainder is 5. What is the remainder if $n - k$ is divided by k ?

    (A)   1

    (B)   2

    (C)   3

    (D)   4

    (E)   5

21. The prime factorization of $3,000,000$ is $2^a \cdot 3^b \cdot 5^c$. What is the value of $a + b + c$?

    (A) 11

    (B) 12

    (C) 13

    (D) 14

    (E) 15

22. The sum of two numbers is 6, and the sum of the reciprocals of the two numbers is $\frac{3}{4}$. What is the sum of the squares of the two numbers?

    (A) 12

    (B) 14

    (C) 16

    (D) 18

    (E) 20

23. There are 4 boys and 5 girls in Mr. Rhee's class. Mr. Rhee wants to select a team of 2 boys and 2 girls from his class. How many different teams can Mr. Rhee can select?

    (A) 80

    (B) 60

    (C) 50

    (D) 40

    (E) 30

24. Two numbers are selected without replacement from the set $\{3, 5, 7, 11\}$ to form a fraction. What is the probability that the fraction formed is an improper fraction?

    (A) $\frac{4}{5}$

    (B) $\frac{3}{4}$

    (C) $\frac{2}{3}$

    (D) $\frac{1}{2}$

    (E) $\frac{1}{3}$

25. What is the units digit of the product of the first 55 odd integers?

    (A)   5

    (B)   6

    (C)   7

    (D)   8

    (E)   9

26. Jason has many marbles in his bag. If he removes marbles 2 at a time from his bag, 1 marble is remaining. If he removes marbles 3, 4, 5, 6, or 7 at a time from his bag, 1 marble is still remaining. What is the least number of marbles he could have in his bag?

    (A)   421

    (B)   543

    (C)   681

    (D)   751

    (E)   841

$$a \oplus b = 2a + 3b$$
$$a \otimes b = ab$$

27. Two operators $\oplus$ and $\otimes$ are defined above. Let x and y be both positive integers. What is the largest possible value of x that satisfies $x \oplus y = x \otimes y$?

    (A)   6

    (B)   7

    (C)   8

    (D)   9

    (E)   10

$$\frac{x}{4y} + \frac{9y}{x}$$

28. What is the minimum possible value of the expression above? (Assume x and y are real numbers)

    (A)   1

    (B)   2

    (C)   3

    (D)   4

    (E)   5

$$\frac{1}{4(2)} + \frac{9(2)}{1}$$

$$\frac{18}{8} = 2\frac{1}{4}$$

Answers and Solutions
TJHSST Math Practice Test 1

Answers

1. C	11. E	21. C
2. D	12. D	22. E
3. B	13. B	23. B
4. E	14. D	24. D
5. C	15. D	25. A
6. B	16. B	26. A
7. E	17. B	27. D
8. E	18. C	28. C
9. C	19. B	
10. A	20. E	

Solutions

1. (C)

    This problem is exactly the same as counting points on the line. The road is 200 feet long and trees are placed every 4 feet.

$$\text{Total number of trees on the road} = \frac{\text{Length of the road}}{\text{Distance between each tree}} + 1$$
$$= \frac{200}{4} + 1$$
$$= 51$$

    Therefore, there are 51 trees on the road.

2. (D)

    The pattern consists of B, C, D, E and A. It is repeated continuously. Since every 5th letter is A, the 45th letter is also A. Thus, the 46th letter is B, the 47th letter is C, and the 48th letter is D.

3. (B)

Let x be the number of hours that the bus traveled until the car catches up with the bus.

$$\text{Distance that the bus traveled: } 45x$$
$$\text{Distance that the car traveled: } 60\left(x - \frac{25}{60}\right)$$

The car catches up with bus means that the distances that the bus and car traveled are the same.

$$45x = 60\left(x - \frac{25}{60}\right)$$
$$45x = 60x - 25$$
$$15x = 25$$
$$x = \frac{5}{3}$$

The bus traveled $\frac{5}{3}$ hours or 1 hour and 40 minutes. Therefore, the car catches up with the bus at 10:50 AM.

4. (E)

Only 984 is divisible by 6. Therefore, the remainder is 4 when 984 is divided by 5.

5. (C)

There are three numbers that are divisible by 3: 3, 6, and 9. Also, there are two numbers that are divisible by 4: 4, and 8. Thus, there are five numbers that are divisible by three or four. Since there are 10 numbers in the hat, five numbers are neither divisibly by 3 nor 4. Therefore, the probability that the number is neither divisible by 3 nor 4 is $\frac{5}{10}$ or $\frac{1}{2}$.

6. (B)

There are four different colors: red, white, green, and black. Let's assume that you pulled out 4 socks with 4 different colors. So you haven't found a matching pair yet. The fifth sock will match one of 4 socks that you pulled out. Therefore, 5 socks will guarantee a matching pair.

7. (E)

Let's define x as the number of desks that the store sold and y as the number of chairs that the store sold. Set a system of equations using the x and y variables. First, set up the first equation in terms of a total number of desks and chairs that the store sold. The store sold a total of 23 desks and chairs: $x + y = 23$. Second, set up the second equation in terms of $240 profit that the store made after selling x numbers of desks and y numbers of chairs: $15x + 8y = 240$. Next, multiply each side of the first equation by -15.

$$x + y = 23 \xrightarrow{\text{Multiply by } -15} -15x - 15y = -345$$
$$15x + 8y = 240$$

Use the linear combinations method.

$$
\begin{aligned}
-15x - 15y &= -345 \\
15x + 8y &= 240 \qquad \text{Add two equations} \\
\hline
-7y &= -105 \\
y &= 15
\end{aligned}
$$

Therefore, the number of chairs that the store sold, y, is 15.

8. (E)

When a coin is tossed, there are two possible outcomes: heads or tails. If you toss a coin three times, according to the fundamental counting principle, the total number of the possible outcomes is $2 \times 2 \times 2 = 8$. The table below shows the 8 possible outcomes.

H	H	H
H	H	T
H	T	H
H	T	T ✓
T	H	H
T	H	T ✓
T	T	H ✓
T	T	T

Out of 8 possible outcomes, there are 3 outcomes that have one head: $H\,T\,T$, $T\,H\,T$, and $T\,T\,H$. Therefore, the probability that one head will be shown is $\dfrac{3}{8}$.

9. (C)

> **Tips** The fundamental counting principle: If one event can occur in m ways and another event can occur in n ways, then the number of ways both events can occur is $m \times n$.

Event 1 is selecting a digit for thousands and units digit, and event 2 is selecting a digit for hundreds and tens digit. Event 1 has 9 ways$(1, 2, \cdots, 9)$ and event 2 has 10 ways$(0, 1, \cdots, 9)$. According to the fundamental counting principle, there are $9 \times 10 = 90$ 4-digit palindromes.

10. (A)

Let x be the amount of 60% solution. Then total amount of 40% solution is $100 + x$. Set up an equation in term of amount of acid and solve for x.

$$0.25 \times 100 + 0.6x = 0.4(100 + x)$$
$$0.6x + 25 = 40 + 0.4x$$
$$0.2x = 15$$
$$x = 75$$

Therefore, the amount of 60% solution that Joshua should add is 75 mL.

11. (E)

The letter L has 2 line segments, the letter F has 3 line segments, and the letter W has 4 line segments.

Letter	L	F	W	A	T	E	H	K
Number of segments	2	3	4	3	2	4	3	3

Since the letter K has 3 segments, $K3$ is the most similar to the elements in set T.

12. (D)

Use the answer choices to determine which number satisfies the given conditions. ABC represents a three-digit number greater than 200. Eliminate answer choice (A) because 136 is less than 200. Digits B and C are multiples of digit A. Thus, eliminate both answer choices (C) and (E) because they do not satisfy it. The remaining answer choices are (B) and (D) Since digit C is three more than digit B, eliminate answer choice (B) because 8 is not three more than 4. Therefore, (D) is the correct answer.

13. (B)

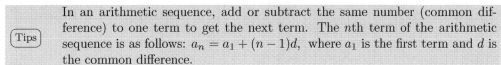

Tips — In an arithmetic sequence, add or subtract the same number (common difference) to one term to get the next term. The nth term of the arithmetic sequence is as follows: $a_n = a_1 + (n-1)d$, where a_1 is the first term and d is the common difference.

The sequence $3, 7, 11, 15, \cdots$ is an arithmetic sequence, where the first term, $a_1 = 3$ and the common difference, $d = 7 - 3 = 4$. Use the nth term formula to find the 34th term.

$$a_n = a_1 + (n-1)d \qquad \text{Substitute 34 for } n$$
$$a_{34} = 3 + (34 - 1)4 = 135$$

Therefore, the value of the 34th term is 135.

14. (D)

Jason has at least 1 penny, 1 nickel, 1 dime, and 1 quarter which is worth 40 cents. Since the total value of 11 coins is 123 cents, Jason must have 3 pennies. Now, Jason has 6 coins worth 43 cents: 3 pennies, 1 nickel, 1 dime, and 1 quarter. He has 5 coins remaining to make 80 cents. It is easy to see that 5 coins (2 quarters and 3 dimes) worth 80 cents. Therefore, the number of dimes that Jason has is 4.

15. (D)

Joshua rolls two dice to form a two-digit integer. Since the number on the first die represents the tens digit and the number on the second die represents the units digit, there are a total number of $6 \times 6 = 36$ possible two-digit integers. Out of these 36 integers, there are only 5 integers that are divisible by 8: 16, 24, 32, 56, 64. Note that 40 and 48 cannot be formed because a die has numbers 1 through 6. Therefore, the probability that the integer formed is divisible by 8 is $\dfrac{5}{36}$.

16. (B)

There are 10 squares $(1^2, 2^2, \cdots, 9^2, 10^2)$ and 4 cubes $(1^3, 2^3, 3^3, 4^3)$ from 1 to 100, inclusive. However, $1 = 1^2 = 1^3$ and $64 = 8^2 = 4^3$ are counted twice, the total number of squares and cubes from 1 to 100, inclusive is 12. Thus, $100 - 12$ or 88th term of the sequence is 99 as shown below.

Term	a_{88}	a_{89}	a_{90}	$\cdots$	a_{98}	a_{99}	a_{100}
Value	99	101	102	$\cdots$	110	111	112

Therefore, the value of the 100th term of the sequence is 112.

17. (B)

B is the second letter, F is the 6th, and I is the 9th letter in an alphabet as shown below.

Alphabet	A	B	C	D	E	F	G	H	I
Order	1	2	3	4	5	6	7	8	9

Therefore, C3 is the most similar to the elements in set S.

18. (C)

A larger cube with side length 3 is painted with the color red. Then each side of the larger cube is divided by 3 to form 27 smaller cubes. The table below shows the result.

Painted	0 side	1 side	2 sides	3 sides
Number of cubes	1	6	12	8

Thus, there are 1 unpainted smaller cube and 12 smaller cube(s) with only 2 painted sides. Therefore, the value of $m + n = 13$.

19. (B)

$$\sum_{k=1}^{n} k = 1 + 2 + 3 \cdots + n = \frac{n(n+1)}{2}$$

The sum of the first 100 positive integers is 5050 as shown below.

$$\sum_{k=1}^{100} k = 1 + 2 + 3 \cdots + 100 = \frac{100(101)}{2} = 5050$$

Thus,

$$2 + 4 + 6 \cdots + 200 = 2(1 + 2 + 3 \cdots + 100)$$
$$= 2(5050)$$
$$= 10100$$

the sum of the first 100 positive even integers is 10100.

20. (E)

When n is divided by k, the quotient is q and the remainder is r. Then, n can be written as $n = kq + r$

When 100 is divided by 3, the quotient is 33 and the remainder is 1. Thus, 100 can be expressed as $100 = 3 \times 33 + 1$. Likewise, when n is divided by k, the quotient is q and the remainder is 5. Thus, n can be expressed as $n = kq + 5$. To find the remainder when $n - k$ is divided by k,

$$n = kq + 5 \qquad \text{Subtract } k \text{ from each side}$$
$$n - k = kq - k + 5 \qquad \text{Factor } kq - k$$
$$n - k = k(q - 1) + 5$$

$n - k = k(q - 1) + 5$ implies that the remainder is 5 when $n - k$ is divided by k.

21. (C)

$$(a \cdot b)^n = a^n \cdot b^n$$

The prime factorization of $3,000,000$ is as follows.

$$3,000,000 = 3 \cdot 10^6$$
$$= 3 \cdot (2 \cdot 5)^6$$
$$= 3 \cdot 2^6 \cdot 5^6$$
$$= 2^6 \cdot 3^1 \cdot 5^6$$

Since $3,000,000 = 2^6 \cdot 3^1 \cdot 5^6$, $a = 6$, $b = 1$, and $c = 6$. Therefore, the value of $a + b + c = 13$.

22. (E)

> **Tips** $\qquad x^2 + y^2 = (x+y)^2 - 2xy$

Let x and y be the two numbers. The sum of two numbers is 6 can be written as $x + y = 6$. The sum of the reciprocals of the two numbers is $\dfrac{3}{4}$ can be written as $\dfrac{1}{x} + \dfrac{1}{y} = \dfrac{3}{4}$, which gives $xy = 8$ as shown below.

$$\frac{1}{x} + \frac{1}{y} = \frac{3}{4}$$
$$\frac{y+x}{xy} = \frac{3}{4} \qquad \text{where } x + y = 6$$
$$\frac{6}{xy} = \frac{3}{4}$$
$$\frac{1}{xy} = \frac{1}{8}$$
$$xy = 8$$

Thus, the sum of the squares of the two numbers, $x^2 + y^2$, can be calculated using $x + y = 6$ and $xy = 8$.

$$x^2 + y^2 = (x+y)^2 - 2xy$$
$$= 6^2 - 2(8)$$
$$= 20$$

Therefore, the sum of the squares of the two numbers is 20.

23. (B)

Event 1 is selecting 2 boys out of 4 boys. Since 4 boys are indistinguishable, the number of ways to select 2 boys out of 4 boys is $\binom{4}{2} = 6$. Event 2 is selecting 2 girls out of 5 girls. Since 5 girls are indistinguishable, the number of ways to select 2 girls out of 5 girls is $\binom{5}{2} = 10$. Each team that Mr. Rhee selects consists of 2 boys and 2 girls. Therefore, according to the fundamental counting principle, the number of different teams that Mr. Rhee can select is $\binom{4}{2} \times \binom{5}{2} = 6 \times 10 = 60$.

24. (D)

Two numbers are selected at random without replacement from the set $\{3, 5, 7, 11\}$ to form a fraction: one number for the numerator and another number for the denominator. If the numerator of the fraction is 3, there are three possible numbers for the denominator: 5, 7, and 11. Thus, there are three fractions that can be formed using these numbers: $\frac{3}{5}, \frac{3}{7}, \frac{3}{11}$. All of the fractions are proper fractions. The table below shows a list of all possible fractions that can be formed when the numerator of fractions are 3, 5, 7, or 11.

Numerator	Denominator	Fraction	Improper fraction
3	5	$\frac{3}{5}$	
3	7	$\frac{3}{7}$	
3	11	$\frac{3}{11}$	
5	3	$\frac{5}{3}$	✓
5	7	$\frac{5}{7}$	
5	11	$\frac{5}{11}$	
7	3	$\frac{7}{3}$	✓
7	5	$\frac{7}{5}$	✓
7	11	$\frac{7}{11}$	
11	3	$\frac{11}{3}$	✓
11	5	$\frac{11}{5}$	✓
11	7	$\frac{11}{7}$	✓

Out of 12 fractions, there are 6 improper fractions. Therefore, the probability that the fraction formed is an improper fraction is $\frac{6}{12}$ or $\frac{1}{2}$.

25. (A)

The product of the first 55 odd integers is

$$1 \times 3 \times 5 \times \cdots \times 105 \times 107 \times 109$$

is very hard to calculate. Thus, finding the units digit after finding the product of the first 55 odd integers is not a good way to solve this problem. Instead, let's group 5 odd integers and then find the units digit of the product of the 5 odd integers.

The units digit of the product of the first 5 odd integers $1 \times 3 \times 5 \times 7 \times 9$ is 5. The units digit of the product of the next 5 odd integers $11 \times 13 \times 15 \times 17 \times 19$ is also 5 as shown below.

$$U_1 = \text{Units digit of } 1 \times 3 \times 5 \times 7 \times 9 = 5$$
$$U_2 = \text{Units digit of } 11 \times 13 \times 15 \times 17 \times 19 = 5$$
$$\vdots$$
$$U_{10} = \text{Units digit of } 91 \times 93 \times 95 \times 97 \times 99 = 5$$
$$U_{11} = \text{Units digit of } 101 \times 103 \times 105 \times 107 \times 109 = 5$$

Thus, the units digit of the product of first 55 odd integers is the same as the units digit of the product of $U_1 \times U_2 \times \cdots U_{10} \times U_{11}$.

$$\text{Units digit of } U_1 \times U_2 \times \cdots U_{10} \times U_{11} = 5$$

Therefore, the units digit of the product of first 55 odd integers is 5.

26. (A)

Let n be the number of marbles that Jason has in his bag. When n is divided by 2, 3, 4, 5, 6, or 7, the remainder is 1. This means that $n - 1$ is divisible by 2, 3, 4, 5, 6, or 7. In other words, $n - 1$ is a LCM(Least Common Multiple) of 2, 3, 4, 5, 6, and 7. Thus, $n - 1 = 420$ which gives $n = 421$. Therefore, the least number of marbles that Jason could have in his bag is 421.

27. (D)

Find x in terms of y using $x \otimes y = x \oplus y$.

$$x \otimes y = x \oplus y$$
$$xy = 2x + 3y$$
$$xy - 2x = 3y$$
$$x(y - 2) = 3y$$
$$x = \frac{3y}{y - 2}$$

Since $x = \dfrac{3y}{y - 2}$ is a positive integer, y must be an integer greater or equal to 3.

y	$x = \frac{3y}{y-2}$
3	9
4	6
5	5
$\vdots$	$\vdots$

The value of x decreases when the value of y increases. Therefore, the largest possible value of x that satisfies $x \oplus y = x \otimes y$ is 9.

28. (C)

Tips

The arithmetic mean $\left(\dfrac{a + b}{2}\right)$ is greater than or equal to the geometric mean($\sqrt{ab}$).

$$\frac{a + b}{2} \geq \sqrt{ab}$$
$$a + b \geq 2\sqrt{ab}$$

Since the Arithmetic mean is greater than or equal to the geometric mean,

$$\frac{x}{4y} + \frac{9y}{x} \geq 2\sqrt{\frac{x}{4y} \cdot \frac{9y}{x}}$$
$$\geq 2\sqrt{\frac{9}{4}}$$
$$\geq 2 \cdot \frac{3}{2}$$
$$\geq 3$$

Thus, the minimum value of $\dfrac{x}{4y} + \dfrac{9y}{x}$ is 3.

93

TJHSST PRACTICE MATH TEST 2
Time — 50 minutes
Number of questions — 28

Directions: Solve each of the following problems using the available space for scratch work. Choose the best answer among the answer choices given and fill in the corresponding circle on the answer sheet.

1. In the equation below, P represents profit, R represents revenue, and E represents expenses. What is the profit when the expenses is \$750 and the revenue is \$1250?

$$P = 2R - 3E$$

(A) 150

(B) 250

(C) 350

(D) 550

(E) 750

2. Let $S(x)$ be the sum of all the positive integers less than or equal to x. For example, $S(5) = 1 + 2 + 3 + 4 + 5 = 15$. What is the value of $S(15) - S(13)$?

(A) 29

(B) 35

(C) 41

(D) 47

(E) 52

3. Let n be the sum of the first five cube numbers. What is the tens digit of n ?

(A) 0

(B) 2

(C) 3

(D) 5

(E) 7

4. Joshua traveled 220 miles at 55 miles per hour. How many minutes longer would the return trip take if he travels at 50 miles per hour?

(A) 60 minutes

(B) 48 minutes

(C) 40 minutes

(D) 24 minutes

(E) 12 minutes

5. Set S has two numbers and the average of set S is x. Set T has three numbers and the average of set T is y. Which of the following expression represents the average of the two sets, S and T ?

(A) $\dfrac{x+y}{2}$

(B) $\dfrac{x+y}{5}$

(C) $\dfrac{xy}{2}$

(D) $\dfrac{2x+3y}{2}$

(E) $\dfrac{2x+3y}{5}$

6. Two numbers are selected at random without replacement from the set $\{1, 2, 3, 4\}$ to form a two-digit number. What is the probability that the two-digit number selected is a prime number?

(A) $\dfrac{5}{12}$

(B) $\dfrac{1}{3}$

(C) $\dfrac{1}{4}$

(D) $\dfrac{1}{6}$

(E) $\dfrac{1}{12}$

$$F, G, H, J, K, F, G, \cdots$$

7. If the pattern above is repeated continuously, what is the 27th letter?

(A) F

(B) G

(C) H

(D) J

(E) K

Popular Sports in Olympics

100M Sprint	36%
Gymnastics	24%
Swimming	17%
Basketball	23%

8. A survey asks people in the US which sport they are going to watch in the upcoming Olympics. The chart above shows the results of the survey. If the US population is 300 million, how many more people, in million, are going to watch the most popular sport compared to the least popular sport in the chart?

(A) 17

(B) 19

(C) 21

(D) 36

(E) 57

9. How many perfect squares are there between 101 and 1025?

   (A) 20

   (B) 21

   (C) 22

   (D) 23

   (E) 24

11. A farmer wants to build a fence around his rectangular field. In addition, he wants to divide it in half with a fence perpendicular to the longer side of the rectangular field so that it becomes two smaller squares. If the total length of the fence is 420 feet, what is the length of the shorter side of the rectangular field?

   (A) 30 feet

   (B) 40 feet

   (C) 50 feet

   (D) 60 feet

   (E) 70 feet

10. You want to burn 468 calories during 36 minutes of exercise. You burn about 12 calories per minute swimming and 15 calories per minute running. How long should you spend running?

   (A) 30 minutes

   (B) 24 minutes

   (C) 18 minutes

   (D) 12 minutes

   (E) 6 minutes

12. A big water bottle on the cooler was full on Monday. Students drank one-fourth the water on Tuesday, one-third of the remaining on Wednesday, one-half of the remaining on Thursday. What fractional part of the water would be remaining in the water bottle?

   (A) $\dfrac{1}{2}$

   (B) $\dfrac{1}{3}$

   (C) $\dfrac{1}{4}$

   (D) $\dfrac{1}{5}$

   (E) $\dfrac{1}{6}$

13. Mr. Rhee, Vivian, Joshua, and Jason are taking a family photo on a long sofa. What is the probability that Mr. Rhee and Vivian sit next to each other?

(A) $\dfrac{1}{6}$

(B) $\dfrac{1}{5}$

(C) $\dfrac{1}{4}$

(D) $\dfrac{1}{3}$

(E) $\dfrac{1}{2}$

14. There are n number of people invited to a party. Each person in the party shakes hands once with other people. If 55 handshakes takes place, what is the value of n ?

(A) 9

(B) 10

(C) 11

(D) 12

(E) 13

15. Both Joshua and Jason rolled a six-sided die and obtained a number. Let m and n be the number that Joshua and Jason obtained, respectively. What is the probability that $m \geq n$?

(A) $\dfrac{1}{3}$

(B) $\dfrac{5}{12}$

(C) $\dfrac{1}{2}$

(D) $\dfrac{7}{12}$

(E) $\dfrac{25}{36}$

$B, E, H, K, N, \underline{\hphantom{XXX}}$

16. Which of the following letter is the next term in the sequence above?

(A) P

(B) Q

(C) R

(D) S

(E) T

17. In a lake, a wildlife biologist captured 10 fish on the first day. He put a tag on each fish's tail fin and released all fish back to the lake. On the second day, the biologist returned and recaptured 100 fish. Of these, 2 fish had tags. How many fish are there in the lake?

    (A) 500

    (B) 1000

    (C) 1500

    (D) 2500

    (E) 5000

18. Joshua can paint a house in 8 days, while Jason takes 12 days to do it. After Joshua works alone for 2 days, Joshua and Jason worked together to finish the job. How many days did Joshua and Jason work together?

    (A) 5.2 days

    (B) 4.8 days

    (C) 4.4 days

    (D) 4.0 days

    (E) 3.6 days

19. Two men at the same position on a circular 4-mile race track start running. If they run in opposite directions, they meet in 12 minutes. However, it takes one hour for the faster runner to gain a lap if they run in the same direction. How fast, in miles per hour, does the faster runner run?

    (A) 5 mph

    (B) 6 mph

    (C) 8 mph

    (D) 10 mph

    (E) 12 mph

20. A book has 256 pages. How many digits are used to number the pages of the book consecutively from page 1?

    (A) 645

    (B) 650

    (C) 655

    (D) 660

    (E) 665

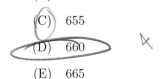

1—9

9 digits

10—99

178 digits → 180

100—256

468 digits → 471

471
180
9
650

21. In a set of five distinct positive integers, the average of the two smallest integers is 2, the average of the three smallest integers is 3, the average of the four smallest is 4, and the average of all five integers is 5. What is the largest integer in the set?

   (A)   9

   (B)   10

   (C)   11

   (D)   12

   (E)   13

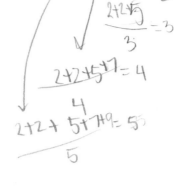

$$\frac{2+2}{2}=2$$

$$\frac{2+2+5}{3}=3$$

$$\frac{2+2+5+7}{4}=4$$

$$\frac{2+2+5+7+9}{5}=5$$

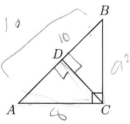

22. In $\triangle ABC$ shown above, $\overline{CD}$ is drawn to $\overline{AB}$ so that $\overline{CD}\perp\overline{AB}$. If $AB = 10$ and $AC = 8$, what is the length of $\overline{CD}$?

   (A)   2

   (B)   2.4

   (C)   4

   (D)   4.8

   (E)   6

   $a^2 + 8^2 = 100$

   $a^2 = 36$

23. n factorial, denoted by $n!$, is the product of an integer n and all the integers below it. For instance, $3! = 3 \times 2 \times 1$. How many positive integers divide $6!$?

   (A)   26

   (B)   30

   (C)   36

   (D)   42

   (E)   48

24. If the sum of two numbers is 3 and their product is 1, what is the sum of their cubes?

   (A)   12

   (B)   15

   (C)   18

   (D)   21

   (E)   24

$$\frac{3}{2}+\frac{3}{2}$$

$$\frac{3}{2}\cdot\frac{3}{2}=\frac{9}{4}$$

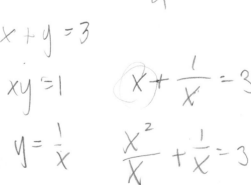

$x+y=3$

$xy=1$

$y=\frac{1}{x}$

$x+\frac{1}{x}=3$

$\frac{x^2}{x}+\frac{1}{x}=3$

$\frac{x^2+1}{x}=3$

$x^2+1=3x$

$x^2-3x+1=0$

100

25. Square $ABCD$ has a length of 1. Point E is selected inside the square. Segment EA represents the distance between point E and the vertex of the square A, and segment EC represents the distance between point E and the vertex of the square C. What is the probability that $EA > EC$?

(A) $\dfrac{1}{4}$

(B) $\dfrac{1}{3}$

(C) $\dfrac{1}{2}$

(D) $\dfrac{3}{5}$

(E) $\dfrac{2}{3}$

27. If the 6-digit number $383A59$ is divisible by 11, what is the value of A ?

(A) 2

(B) 3

(C) 5

(D) 7

(E) 8

26. How many ways can you pay \$79 exactly using only \$5 bills and \$2 bills ?

(A) 11

(B) 10

(C) 9

(D) 8

(E) 7

$$\sqrt{12 + \sqrt{12 + \sqrt{12 + \cdots}}}$$

28. What is the value of the expression above?

(A) 3.5

(B) 4

(C) 4.5

(D) 5

(E) 5.5

Answers and Solutions
TJHSST Math Practice Test 2

Answers

1. B	11. D	21. A
2. A	12. C	22. D
3. B	13. E	23. B
4. D	14. C	24. C
5. E	15. D	25. C
6. A	16. B	26. D
7. B	17. A	27. C
8. E	18. E	28. B
9. C	19. E	
10. D	20. D	

Solutions

1. (B)

   To find P(profit), plug in the given values of R(revenue) and E(expenses) into the equation $P = 2R - 3E$. Since $R = \$1250$ and $E = \$750$,

   $$P = 2R - 3E = 2(1250) - 3(750) = 250$$

   Therefore, when the expenses is \$750 and the revenue is \$1250, the profit of the company is \$250.

2. (A)

   $S(x)$ is the sum of all positive integers less than or equal to x. Thus,

   $$S(15) = 1 + 2 + \cdots + 12 + 13 + 14 + 15$$
   $$\underline{S(13) = 1 + 2 + \cdots + 12 + 13} \qquad \text{Subtract } S(13) \text{ from } S(15)$$
   $$S(15) - S(13) = 14 + 15 = 29$$

   Therefore, the value of $S(15) - S(13)$ is 29.

3. (B)

   $n = 1^3 + 2^3 + 3^3 + 4^3 + 5^3 = 225$. Therefore, 2 is the tens digit of n.

4. (D)

> **Tips**   Use the time formula: time $= \frac{\text{distance}}{\text{speed}}$

Since $\frac{220\,\text{miles}}{55\,\text{miles per hour}} = 4$ hours, it took Joshua 4 hours to travel 220 miles. On the return trip, if he travels at 50 miles per hour, it will take him $\frac{220\,\text{miles}}{50\,\text{miles per hour}} = 4.4$ hours. This means that it will take him 0.4 hour longer on the return trip. Since 0.4 hour is equal to 0.4×60 minutes $= 24$ minutes, it will take Joshua 24 minutes longer on the return trip.

5. (E)

> **Tips**   Sum of elements in a set = average of elements × number of elements

Set S has two numbers and the average of the set is x. Thus, the sum of the two numbers in set S is $2x$. Additionally, Set T has three numbers and the average of the set is y. Thus, the sum of the three numbers in set T is $3y$. The total sum of the numbers in sets S and T is $2x + 3y$. There are five numbers in total in sets S and T. To find the average of sets S and T, divide the total sum of numbers in sets S and T by 5.

$$\text{Average of sets } S \text{ and } T = \frac{\text{Total sum}}{5} = \frac{2x + 3y}{5}$$

Therefore, the average of the two sets, S and T, is $\dfrac{2x + 3y}{5}$.

6. (A)

> **Tips**   The fundamental counting principle: If one event can occur in m ways and another event can occur n ways, then the number of ways both events can occur is $m \times n$.

Two numbers are selected at random without replacement from the set $\{1, 2, 3, 4\}$ to form a two-digit number. To find the total number of two-digit numbers, use the fundamental counting principle. Define event 1 and event 2 as selecting a digit for the tens' place, and ones' place, respectively. Event 1 has 4 ways to select a digit out of 4 digits. After one digit is taken, event 2 has 3 ways to select a digit out of the three remaining digits. Thus, there are $4 \times 3 = 12$ possible two-digit numbers using 1, 2, 3, and 4, which are shown below.

12 possible two-digit numbers: 12, 13, 14, 21, 23, 24, 31, 32, 34, 41, 42, and 43

Out of 12 possible two-digit numbers, there are 5 prime numbers: 13, 23, 31, 41, and 43. Therefore, the probability that the two-digit number selected is a prime number is $\frac{5}{12}$.

7. (B)

The pattern consists of F, G, H, J, and K. It is repeated continuously. Since every 5th is k, the 20th letter and 25th letter is also K. Therefore, the 26th letter is F and 27th letter is G.

8. (E)

According to the survey, the most popular sport is the 100 meter sprint and the least popular sport is swimming.

$$100 \text{ meter sprint} = 300 \times 0.36 = 108$$
$$\text{Swimming} = 300 \times 0.19 = 51$$

Therefore, $108 - 51 = 57$ million more people are going to watch the 100 meter sprint compared to swimming.

9. (C)

The first perfect square greater than 100 is $11^2 = 121$.

$$11^2 = 121$$
$$12^2 = 144$$
$$\vdots$$
$$31^2 = 961$$
$$32^2 = 1024$$

Therefore, there are $32 - 11 + 1 = 22$ the perfect squares between 101 and 1025.

10. (D)

Let's define x as the number of minutes that you spend on swimming, and y as the number of minutes that you spend on running.

$$x + y = 36 \quad \xrightarrow{\text{Multiply by 12}} \quad 12x + 12y = 432$$
$$12x + 15y = 468$$

Use the linear combinations method.

$$12x + 12y = 432$$
$$\underline{12x + 15y = 468} \qquad \text{Subtract two equations}$$
$$-3y = -36$$
$$y = 12$$

Therefore, the number of minutes that you spend on running, y, is 12.

11. (D)

In the figure below, let x be the length of the shorter side of the rectangle. The rectangle is divided into two congruent smaller squares. Thus, the length of each square is x.

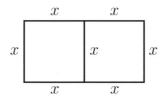

The total length of the fence can be expressed as $7x$ as shown above. Since the total length of the fence is 420 feet, $7x = 420 \implies x = 60$. Therefore, the length of the shorter side of the rectangular field is 60.

12. (C)

On Tuesday, students drank $\frac{1}{4}$ of the water. Thus, $\frac{3}{4}$ of the water would be remaining on Tuesday. Students drank $\frac{1}{3}$ of the remaining water on Wednesday. Thus, $\frac{2}{3}$ of the remaining water would be remaining on Wednesday. This means that $\frac{2}{3} \times \frac{3}{4} = \frac{1}{2}$ of the water would be remaining on Wednesday. Students drank $\frac{1}{2}$ of the remaining water on Thursday. Thus, $\frac{1}{2}$ of the remaining water would be remaining. Therefore, $\frac{1}{2} \times \frac{1}{2} = \frac{1}{4}$ of the water would be remaining on Thursday.

13. (E)

Mr. Rhee, Vivian, Joshua, and Jason are taking a family photo. To count the total possible seating arrangements for Mr. Rhee's family, use the fundamental counting principle. Mr. Rhee has 4 ways to choose his seat out of four seats. After his seat is taken, Vivian has 3 ways to choose her seat out of the three remaining seats. Joshua has 2 ways and Jason has 1 way. Thus, there are $4 \times 3 \times 2 \times 1 = 24$ possible seating arrangements for Mr.Rhee's family. Define R, V, A, and B as Mr. Rhee, Vivian, Joshua, and Jason, respectively. To count the number of seating arrangements in which Mr. Rhee and Vivian sit next to each other, let's consider two cases:

Case 1: Mr. Rhee sits left side of Vivian. There are six possible arrangements as shown below.

$$R \quad V \quad A \quad B \qquad A \quad R \quad V \quad B \qquad A \quad B \quad R \quad V$$
$$R \quad V \quad B \quad A \qquad B \quad R \quad V \quad A \qquad B \quad A \quad R \quad V$$

Case 2: Mr. Rhee sits right side of Vivian. There are six possible arrangements.

$$V \quad R \quad A \quad B \qquad A \quad V \quad R \quad B \qquad A \quad B \quad V \quad R$$
$$V \quad R \quad B \quad A \qquad B \quad V \quad R \quad A \qquad B \quad A \quad V \quad R$$

Thus, there are 12 possible seating arrangements in which Mr. Rhee sits next to Vivian. Therefore, the probability that Mr. Rhee and Vivian sit next to each other is $\frac{12}{24} = \frac{1}{2}$.

14. (C)

There are n number of people. In order have a handshake, you need to select two people out of n people. Thus,

$$\binom{n}{2} = 55$$

$$\frac{n!}{(n-2)! \times 2!} = 55, \qquad \text{where } n! = n \times (n-1) \times (n-2)!$$

$$\frac{n \times (n-1) \times (n-2)!}{(n-2)! \times 2!} = 55$$

$$\frac{n(n-1)}{2} = 55$$

$$n(n-1) = 110$$

$$n(n-1) = 11(10)$$

Thus, $n = 11$. Therefore, 11 people are invited to the party.

15. (D)

m and n are the numbers that Joshua and Jason obtained, respectively.

		n					
		1	2	3	4	5	6
m	1	○					
	2	○	○				
	3	○	○	○			
	4	○	○	○	○		
	5	○	○	○	○	○	
	6	○	○	○	○	○	○

There are 21 outcomes for which the $m \geq n$ represented by circles in the table above. Therefore, the probability that $m \geq n$ is $\frac{21}{36}$ or $\frac{7}{12}$.

16. (B)

The sequence B, E, H, K, N, _____ consists of every third letter of the alphabet. Therefore, the next letter in the sequence should be Q.

17. (A)

> The assumption behind tag-recapture method is that the proportion of tagged individuals recaptured in the second sample represent the proportion of tagged individuals in the population as a whole. In other words,
>
> $$\frac{R}{S} = \frac{T}{N}$$
>
> Tips where
>
> - R is the number of fish recaptured on the second day
> - S is the number of sample on the second day
> - T is the number of fish captured and tagged on the first day
> - N is the fish population

In this problem, $R = 2$, $S = 100$, $T = 10$. Set up the proportion and solve for N.

$$\frac{R}{S} = \frac{T}{N}$$
$$\frac{2}{100} = \frac{10}{N}$$
$$N = 500$$

Therefore, the number of fish in the lake is 500.

18. (E)

Joshua can paint a house in 8 days which means that Joshua can paint $\frac{1}{8}$ house per day. Joshua works alone for 2 days. So he finishes $\frac{2}{8} = \frac{1}{4}$ job and $\frac{3}{4}$ job is remaining. Jason takes 12 days to do it which means that Jason can paint $\frac{1}{12}$ house per day. If Joshua and Jason work together, they can paint $\frac{1}{12} + \frac{1}{8}$ or $\frac{5}{24}$ house per day. Let x be the number of days that Joshua and Jason work together to finish the remaining job.

$$\frac{5}{24}x = \frac{3}{4}$$
$$x = \frac{18}{5}$$
$$x = 3.6$$

Therefore, the number of days that Joshua and Jason work together to finish the remaining job is 3.6 days.

19. (E)

Let x and y be the speed of the faster runner and slower runner in miles per hour, respectively. Two runners meet in 12 minutes if they run in opposite directions means that the sum of the distances that they run in 12 minutes or ($\frac{1}{5}$ hr) is 4 miles. This can be written as

$$\frac{x}{5} + \frac{y}{5} = 4 \qquad \Longrightarrow \qquad x + y = 20$$

It takes one hour for the faster runner to gain a lap if both runners run in the same direction which means that the difference of the distances that they run is 4 miles. This can be written as

$$x - y = 4$$

Thus, set up the system of linear equations and solve for x.

$$\begin{array}{rl} x + y = 20 & \\ \underline{x - y = 4} & \qquad \text{Add two equations} \\ 2x = 24 & \\ x = 12 & \end{array}$$

Therefore, the speed of the fast runner is 12 miles per hour.

20. (D)

In order to number the pages of the book consecutively from page 1, the following number of digits are used.

Page number	Number of digits used
$1 \sim 9$	$9(1) = 9$
$10 \sim 99$	$90(2) = 180$
$100 \sim 256$	$157(3) = 471$

Therefore, $9 + 180 + 471 = 660$ digits are used to number the pages of the book from page 1 to page 256.

21. (A)

Distinct means different. There are five different positive integers in the set. It is necessary to solve this problem in terms of the sum: the sum is the average of the elements in the set times the number of the elements in the set. The average of the two smallest integers in the set is 2. This means that the sum of the two smallest integers is 4. Since the five integers in the set are positive and different, the two smallest positive integers in the set must be 1 and 3, neither 2 and 2, nor 0 and 4. Additionally, the averages of the three smallest integers, four smallest integers, and five integers in the set are 3, 4, and 5, respectively. Thus, the sums of the three smallest integers, four smallest integers and five integers in the set are 9, 16, and 25, respectively. Below shows how to obtain the five positive integers in the set.

$$\text{Sum of two smallest integers} = 1 + 3 = 4$$
$$\text{Sum of three smallest integers} = 1 + 3 + 5 = 9$$
$$\text{Sum of four smallest integers} = 1 + 3 + 5 + 7 = 16$$
$$\text{Sum of five integers in the set} = 1 + 3 + 5 + 7 + 9 = 25$$

Thus, there are 1, 3, 5, 7, and 9 in the set. Therefore, the largest integer in the set is 9.

22. (D)

> **Tips** If a triangle is a right triangle, use the Pythagorean theorem: $c^2 = a^2 + b^2$, where c is the hypotenuse, a and b are the legs of the right triangle.

In the figure below, $\triangle ABC$ is a right triangle with $AB = 10$ and $AC = 8$. To find BC, use the Pythagorean theorem: $10^2 = 8^2 + BC^2$. Thus, $BC = 6$.

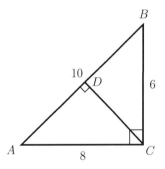

$\overline{AC} \perp \overline{BC}$. Consider $\overline{AC}$ and $\overline{BC}$ as the base and the height of $\triangle ABC$. Thus, the area of $\triangle ABC = \frac{1}{2} \times AC \times BC = \frac{1}{2}(8)(6) = 24$. Additionally, $\overline{CD} \perp \overline{AB}$. If you consider $\overline{AB}$ and $\overline{CD}$ as the base and the height of $\triangle ABC$, the area of $\triangle ABC = \frac{1}{2} \times AB \times CD$.

$$\text{Area of } \triangle ABC = \frac{1}{2} \times AB \times CD = 24 \qquad \text{Substitute 10 for } AB$$
$$\frac{1}{2}(10)\,CD = 24 \qquad\qquad\qquad \text{Solve for } CD$$
$$CD = 4.8$$

23. (B)

Any positive integer that divides 6! is a factor. This question asks you to find the total number of factors of 6!. Since the prime factorization of 6! is $6! = 2^4 \cdot 3^2 \cdot 5$, the total number of factors of 6! is $(4+1) \times (2+1) \times (1+1) = 30$.

24. (C)

Let x and y be the two numbers. The sum of two numbers is 3 can be written as $x + y = 3$, and their product is 1 can be written as $xy = 1$. The sum of their cubes can be calculated by the special patterns shown above.

$$\begin{aligned}
x^3 + y^3 &= (x+y)(x^2 - xy + y^2) \\
&= (x+y)\big((x+y)^2 - 3xy\big) \qquad \text{Substitute } x+y = 3 \text{ and } xy = 1 \\
&= 3(3^2 - 3(1)) \\
&= 18
\end{aligned}$$

Therefore, the sum of their cubes is 18.

25. (C)

If point E is on the segment BD which is a perpendicular bisector of segment AC, $EA = EC$ based on the perpendicular bisector theorem.

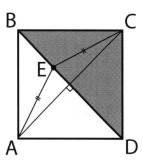

If point E is selected inside the shaded triangular region above, it satisfies $EA > EC$. The area of the square is 1. The area of the shaded triangular region is half the area of the square which is $\frac{1}{2}$. Therefore, the probability that $EA > EC$ is $\frac{1}{2}$.

26. (D)

Let x and y be the number of \$5 bills and \$2 bills, respectively. $5x + 2y = 79$, where x and y are positive integers. $5x + 2y = 79$ gives $y = \frac{79-5x}{2}$.

x	0	1	2	3	5	7	9	11	13	15
$y = \frac{79-5x}{2}$	not integer	37	not integer	32	27	22	17	12	7	2

When x are even, y are not integers. Whereas, x are odd, y are integers as shown above. The values of (x, y) that satisfy $5x + 2y = 79$ are $(1, 37)$, $(3, 32)$, $(5, 27)$, $(7, 22)$, $(9, 17)$, $(11, 12)$, $(13, 7)$, and $(15, 2)$. Therefore, there are 8 ways to pay \$79 exactly using only \$5 bills and \$2 bills.

27. (C)

> **Tips**
>
> Divisibility rule for 11: Take the alternating sum of the digits in the number, read from left to right. If it is 0 or divisible by 11, so is the original number. For instance, 8173 has alternating sum of digits $8 - 1 + 7 - 3 = 11$. Since 11 is divisible by 11, so is 8173.

The alternating sum of the digits, $3 - 8 + 3 - A + 5 - 9 = -6 - A$, must be 0 or divisible by 11. When $A = 5$, the alternating sum, $-6 - A = -11$, is divisible by 11. So is 383559. Therefore, the value of A is 5.

28. (B)

Let $x = \sqrt{12 + \sqrt{12 + \sqrt{12 + \cdots}}}$. So $x > 0$. Square each side of the equation and solve for x.

$$x = \sqrt{12 + \sqrt{12 + \sqrt{12 + \cdots}}}$$

$$x^2 = 12 + \sqrt{12 + \sqrt{12 + \sqrt{12 + \cdots}}}, \qquad \text{Since } x = \sqrt{12 + \sqrt{12 + \sqrt{12 + \cdots}}}$$

$$x^2 = 12 + x$$

$$x^2 - x - 12 = 0$$

$$(x + 3)(x - 4) = 0$$

Solving $x^2 - x - 12 = 0$ gives $x = -3$ or $x = 4$. Since $x > 0$, $x = 4$.

TJHSST PRACTICE MATH TEST 3
Time — 50 minutes
Number of questions — 28

Directions: Solve each of the following problems using the available space for scratch work. Choose the best answer among the answer choices given and fill in the corresponding circle on the answer sheet.

1. The Pythagorean theorem states that in a right triangle, the square of the length of the hypotenuse is equal to the sum of the squares of the lengths of the legs. Which of the following is a set of three positive integers that satisfies the Pythagorean theorem?

    (A) $1, 1, \sqrt{2}$

    (B) $6, 8, 9$

    (C) $5, 12, 15$

    (D) $7, 23, 25$

    (E) $8, 15, 17$

2. Which of the following number has a remainder of 2 if the number is divided by the sum of its digits?

    (A) 12

    (B) 15

    (C) 23

    (D) 26

    (E) 36

3. There are three books on a bookshelf: two math books and a history book. If you arrange these three books, how many different arrangements are possible?

    (A) 27

    (B) 12

    (C) 6

    (D) 3

    (E) 1

4. A clock is malfunctioning. The minute hand of the clock only moves and indicates correct time every 12 minutes. For instance, the clock indicates 12 pm between 12 pm to 12:11 pm and indicates correct time at 12:12 pm. How many times does the clock indicate correct time between 12:10 pm and 5:35 pm?

    (A) 23 times

    (B) 24 times

    (C) 25 times

    (D) 26 times

    (E) 27 times

5. If the sum of two numbers is 3 and their product is 4, what is the sum of their reciprocals?

   (A) $\dfrac{5}{4}$

   (B) $\dfrac{4}{5}$

   (C) $\dfrac{3}{4}$

   (D) $\dfrac{2}{3}$

   (E) $\dfrac{1}{2}$

6. Two standard dice are rolled. What is the probability that the product of the two numbers shown on top of the two dice is odd?

   (A) $\dfrac{3}{4}$

   (B) $\dfrac{2}{3}$

   (C) $\dfrac{1}{2}$

   (D) $\dfrac{1}{3}$

   (E) $\dfrac{1}{4}$

1	x	y	4
		6	9
	11	10	
13			16

7. In the table above, positive integers from 1 to 16 are arranged such that the sum of the numbers in any horizontal, vertical, or main diagonal line is always the same number. If $y > x$, which of the following is the value of x in the table?

   (A) 15

   (B) 14

   (C) 8

   (D) 7

   (E) 3

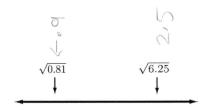

8. On the number line above, a total of nine tick marks will be placed from $\sqrt{0.81}$ to $\sqrt{6.25}$ inclusive. If all the tick marks are evenly spaced, what is the length between any consecutive tick marks?

   (A) 0.16

   (B) 0.18

   (C) 0.20

   (D) 0.22

   (E) 0.24

9. When a fair six-sided die is rolled, you can see numbers on the five faces. What is the probability that the product of these numbers is divisible by 18?

   (A) 1

   (B) $\dfrac{5}{6}$

   (C) $\dfrac{2}{3}$

   (D) $\dfrac{1}{2}$

   (E) $\dfrac{1}{3}$

10. If the ratio of b to a is $3 : 2$, the ratio of b to c is $3 : 4$, and the ratio of d to c is $5 : 4$, what is the ratio of a to d ?

   (A) $2 : 5$

   (B) $3 : 4$

   (C) $4 : 3$

   (D) $5 : 2$

   (E) $15 : 6$

   handwritten:
   b:a
   3:2
   b:c
   3:4
   d:c
   5:4

11. An indoor swimming pool opens at 9 am and children start swimming. Staff at the swimming pool strictly follow a safety rule such that children must take a 10 minute break every 45 minutes. According to the safety rule, children take the first break starting at 9:45 am until 9:55 am. If the swimming pool closes at 5:50 pm, at what time would the last break time begin?

   (A) 4:55 pm

   (B) 5:00 pm

   (C) 5:05 pm

   (D) 5:10 pm

   (E) 5:15 pm

   handwritten:
   10:40 – 10:50
   11:35 – 11:45
   12:30 – 12:40   5:05 – 5:15
   1:25 – 1:35
   2:20 – 2:30
   3:15 – 3:25
   4:10 – 4:20

12. The arithmetic mean of $y - 1, 2y - 2$, and $3y - 4$ is x. The arithmetic mean of $x, 2x - 3$, and $3x - 5$ is y. Which of the following must be the value of $x + y$?

   (A) 10

   (B) 8

   (C) 7

   (D) 6

   (E) 5

   handwritten:
   y - 1 = x
   2x - 3 = y
   y - x = 1
   -y + 2x = 3
   x = 4
   y = 5

13. There are three distinct positive integers. The sums of the two distinct integers are 29, 40, and 41. Which of the following is the largest integer among the three integers?

(A) 27

(B) 26

(C) 23

(D) 19

(E) 18

15. Three fair six-sided dice are rolled. Let x, y, and z be the numbers shown on the 1st die, 2nd die, and third die, respectively. How many outcomes are possible if $x < y < z$?

(A) 72

(B) 60

(C) 36

(D) 20

(E) 12

$$AB, \ FG, \ KL, \ PQ, \ \underline{\hspace{1cm}}$$

14. Which of the following letter is the next term in the sequence above?

(A) UV

(B) NO

(C) WX

(D) MN

(E) XZ

16. What is the sum of the first 100 positive odd integers?

(A) 5050

(B) 7500

(C) 10000

(D) 15500

(E) 20000

17. In the figure above, a target consists of two concentric circles. The ratio of the radius of the smaller circle to that of larger circle is 1 to 2. Assuming a dart only lands either on or inside the target, what is the probability that the dart lands on the shaded area?

(A) $\dfrac{1}{4}$

(B) $\dfrac{3}{8}$

(C) $\dfrac{1}{2}$

(D) $\dfrac{5}{8}$

(E) $\dfrac{2}{3}$

18. What is the number of arrangements of the letters in the word SOLOMON?

(A) 120

(B) 240

(C) 420

(D) 720

(E) 840

123, a, b, c, 207

19. If the numbers above form an arithmetic sequence, which of the following is the value of $a + b - c$?

(A) 89

(B) 123

(C) 258

(D) 495

(E) 537

Column A	Column B
The number of solutions to $x^2 = x$	The number of solutions to $x - 3 = \sqrt{4x}$

20. Which of the following statement is true?

(A) The quantity in Column A is greater.

(B) The quantity in Column B is greater.

(C) The quantity in Column B is greater than or equal to the quantity in Column A.

(D) The two quantities are equal.

(E) Cannot be determined from the information given.

21. In an arithmetic sequence, the sum of the first two terms is 23, and the sum of the next three terms is 72. What is the value of the 6th term?

    (A) 22

    (B) 25

    (C) 29

    (D) 32

    (E) 34

22. How many factors of 864 are perfect squares?

    (A) 6

    (B) 8

    (C) 9

    (D) 10

    (E) 12

23. How many positive two-digit integers are increased by exactly 27 when the digits are reversed?

    (A) 3

    (B) 4

    (C) 5

    (D) 6

    (E) 7

24. When Jason was heading to his office between 7 am and 8 am in the morning, he noticed that the hour hand and the minute hand of a clock formed 90°. When he returned home between 5 pm and 6 pm, he noticed that the hour hand and the minute hand of the clock formed 90° again. Which of the following is closest to the greatest number of hours that he was away from home?

    (A) 8 hours and 20 minutes

    (B) 9 hours

    (C) 9 hours and 40 minutes

    (D) 10 hours and 20 minutes

    (E) 11 hours

25. There are two positive integers: 180 and x. If the greatest common factor of the two numbers is 4, and the least common multiple of the two number is 6840, what is the value of x ?

(A) 92

(B) 122

(C) 152

(D) 182

(E) 212

$$n = 2^2 + 2^3 + \cdots + 2^{98} + 2^{99}$$

27. If the expression n is defined above, what is the units digit of n ?

(A) 1

(B) 2

(C) 3

(D) 4

(E) 5

$$f(a, b, c) = a^2 + b^2 + c^2$$
$$g(a, b, c) = ab + bc + ca$$

26. If $f(x, y, z) = 159$ and $g(x, y, z) = 65$, what is the largest possible value of $x + y + z$?

(A) 18

(B) 17

(C) 16

(D) 15

(E) 14

28. Each side of a cube is painted either blue or red. So you toss a fair coin to determine the color of the 6 faces. What is the probability that no two blue faces are adjacent?

(A) $\dfrac{5}{32}$

(B) $\dfrac{5}{18}$

(C) $\dfrac{1}{3}$

(D) $\dfrac{2}{5}$

(E) $\dfrac{1}{2}$

Answers and Solutions

TJHSST Math Practice Test 3

Answers

1. E	11. C	21. E
2. D	12. E	22. A
3. D	13. B	23. D
4. E	14. A	24. D
5. C	15. D	25. C
6. E	16. C	26. B
7. B	17. B	27. B
8. C	18. E	28. A
9. C	19. B	
10. A	20. A	

Solutions

1. (E)

   Answer choice (A) and (E) satisfy the Pythagorean theorem: $c^2 = a^2 + b^2$. However, $\sqrt{2}$ in answer choice (A) is not a positive integer. Thus, eliminate answer choice (A). Therefore, (E) is the correct answer.

2. (D)

$$(A) \quad 12 \div (1+2) \quad \Longrightarrow \quad \text{remainder of } 0$$
$$(B) \quad 15 \div (1+5) \quad \Longrightarrow \quad \text{remainder of } 3$$
$$(C) \quad 23 \div (2+3) \quad \Longrightarrow \quad \text{remainder of } 3$$
$$(D) \quad 26 \div (2+6) \quad \Longrightarrow \quad \text{remainder of } 2$$
$$(E) \quad 36 \div (3+6) \quad \Longrightarrow \quad \text{remainder of } 0$$

3. (D)

   The list below shows the possible arrangements for the two math books and the history book (M and H are used for the math book and the history book, respectively).

$$
\begin{array}{ccc}
M & M & H \\
M & H & M \\
H & M & M
\end{array}
$$

   Therefore, there are three possible arrangements for the two math books and the history book.

4. (E)

The clock indicates the first correct time at 12:12pm. Afterwards, it indicates correctly at 12:24pm, 12:36pm, 12:48pm and 1:00pm. This means that the clock only indicates 5 correct times every hour. Since there are five hours between 12:10pm to 5:10pm, the clock indicates time correctly $5 \times 5 = 25$ times. There are two additional times that the clock indicates correctly after 5pm: 5:12pm and 5:24pm. Therefore, the clock indicates time correctly 27 times from 12:10pm to 5:35pm.

5. (C)

Let x and y be the two numbers. The sum of two numbers is 3 can be written as $x + y = 3$, and their product is 4 can be written as $xy = 4$. The sum of their reciprocals can be written as $\frac{1}{x} + \frac{1}{y}$ and can be calculated using $x + y = 3$ and $xy = 4$.

$$\frac{1}{x} + \frac{1}{y} = \frac{y}{xy} + \frac{x}{xy}$$
$$= \frac{x + y}{xy}$$
$$= \frac{3}{4}$$

Therefore, the sum of their reciprocals is $\frac{3}{4}$.

6. (E)

> **Tips** The fundamental counting principle: If one event can occur in m ways and another event can occur n ways, then the number of ways both events can occur is $m \times n$.

Use the fundamental counting principle. Define event 1 and event 2 as selecting a number from the first and second die, respectively. There are six outcomes from each event. Thus, the total number of outcomes for event 1 and event 2 is $6 \times 6 = 36$. Define event 3 and event 4 as selecting an odd number from the first and second die, respectively. There are three outcomes from each event: 1, 3, and 5. Thus, the total number of outcomes for event 3 and event 4 is $3 \times 3 = 9$. Thus,

$$\text{Probability that the product is odd} = \frac{9}{36} = \frac{1}{4}$$

Therefore, the probability that the product of the two numbers is odd is $\frac{1}{4}$.

7. (B)

Find the sum of the numbers in any horizontal, vertical, or main diagonal. In table 1, there are four numbers on the diagonal so the sum is $13 + 11 + 6 + 4 = 34$.

Table 1:

1	x	y	4
		6	9
	11	10	
13			16

Table 2:

1	x	y	4
		6	9
	11	10	5
13			16

Table 3:

1	x	y	4
12	7	6	9
8	11	10	5
13			16

Place 5 on the fourth column so that the sum is 34 as shown in table 2. Then, place 8 on the third row, 12 on the first column and 7 on the second row as shown in table 3. There are four numbers remaining: 2, 3, 14, and 15. Either 14 or 15 can not be on the fourth row because the sum exceeds 34. So, 14 and 15 must be on the first row and they are either x or y. Since $y > x$, x is 14.

8. (C)

There are nine tick marks between $\sqrt{0.81} = 0.9$ and $\sqrt{6.25} = 2.5$ inclusive. Let's define interval as the length between any consecutive tick marks. There is one interval between two consecutive tick marks. There are two intervals between three consecutive tick marks, three intervals between four consecutive tick marks, and so on so forth. If the pattern continues, there are eight intervals between nine consecutive tick marks.

$$\text{Length of one interval} = \frac{\text{Distance between 0.9 and 2.5}}{8 \text{ intervals}} = \frac{1.6}{8} = 0.20$$

Therefore, the length between any consecutive tick marks is 0.20.

9. (C)

Number not seen	Product of 5 numbers	Divisible by 18
6	$1 \times 2 \times 3 \times 4 \times 5$	No
5	$1 \times 2 \times 3 \times 4 \times 6$	Yes
4	$1 \times 2 \times 3 \times 5 \times 6$	Yes
3	$1 \times 2 \times 4 \times 5 \times 6$	No
2	$1 \times 3 \times 4 \times 5 \times 6$	Yes
1	$2 \times 3 \times 4 \times 5 \times 6$	Yes

Out of 6 possible products, 4 products are divisible by 18. Therefore, the probability that the product of five numbers is divisible by 18 is $\frac{2}{3}$.

10. (A)

$\frac{a}{b} = \frac{2}{3}$, $\frac{b}{c} = \frac{3}{4}$, and $\frac{c}{d} = \frac{4}{5}$.

$$\frac{a}{d} = \frac{a}{b} \cdot \frac{b}{c} \cdot \frac{c}{d}$$
$$= \frac{2}{3} \cdot \frac{3}{4} \cdot \frac{4}{5}$$
$$= \frac{2}{5}$$

Therefore, the ratio of a to d is $2 : 5$.

11. (C)

Table 1 below shows the first couple of times swimming sessions and when mandatory breaks begin.

9:00am-9:45am	Swim
9:45am-9:55am	Break
9:55am-10:40am	Swim
10:40am-10:50am	Break
10:50am-11:35am	Swim
11:35am-11:45am	Break

Table 1

12:30pm	Break begins
1:25pm	Break begins
2:20pm	Break begins
3:15pm	Break begins
4:10pm	Break begins
5:05pm	Break begins

Table 2

Since this question asks about what time the last break begins, pay close attention to times at which breaks begin in table 1. The first break begins at 9:45am, second break at 10:40am, third break at 11:35am and so forth. These three breaks suggest a pattern such that as the value of hours is increased by one: from 9_{am} to 10_{am} to 11_{am}, the value of minutes is decreased by five: from 45_{min} to 40_{min} to 35_{min}. Thus, the following breaks after 11:35am are 12:30pm, 1:25pm, 2:20 pm, and so on so forth as shown in table 2. Therefore, the last break begins at 5:05pm.

12. (E)

Arithmetic mean: the sum of all elements in a set divided by the number of elements in the set.

$$\frac{x+2x-3+3x-5}{3} = y \implies \frac{6x-8}{3} = y \implies 6x - 3y = 8$$

$$\frac{y-1+2y-2+3y-4}{3} = x \implies \frac{6y-7}{3} = x \implies 3x - 6y = -7$$

To find the value of $x+y$, it is not necessary to solve for x and y directly from the two equations shown above. Instead, subtract the second equation from the first equation. It will give you the value of $x+y$.

$$6x - 3y = 8$$
$$3x - 6y = -7 \qquad \text{Subtract two equations}$$
$$\overline{}$$
$$3x + 3y = 15 \qquad \text{Divide each side by 3}$$
$$x + y = 5$$

Therefore, the value of $x+y$ is 5.

13. (B)

Let x, y, and z be the three distinct positive integers. The sum of the two distinct integers are 29, 40, and 41 can be written as $x+y=29$, $x+z=40$, and $y+z=41$. Add 3 equations to get the sum of the three distinct integers.

$$x + y = 29$$
$$x + z = 40$$
$$y + z = 41 \qquad \text{Add three equations}$$
$$\overline{}$$
$$2x + 2y + 2z = 110 \qquad \text{Divide each side by 2}$$
$$x + y + z = 55$$

$x+y=29$ and $x+y+z=55$ gives $z=26$. $x+z=40$, $y+z=41$ and $x+y+z=55$ gives $y=15$ and $x=14$. Thus, the three distinct positive integers are 14, 15, and 26. Therefore, the largest integer is 26.

14. (A)

The sequence AB, FG, KL, PQ, _____ consists of two consecutive letters in the alphabet. For any two consecutive terms, there are three letters between them. For instance, the three letters between the 4th term and the 5th terms are R, S, and T. Therefore, the 5th term in the sequence should be UV.

15. (D)

Since $x < y < z$, x, y, and z are three distinct positive integers from $\{1,2,3,4,5,6\}$. There are $\binom{6}{3} = 20$ ways to select three distinct integers from $\{1,2,3,4,5,6\}$. Once you select three distinct integers, you can assign these integers to x, y, and z so that it satisfies $x < y < z$. Therefore, 20 outcomes that satisfy $x < y < z$.

16. (C)

$$1 = 1^2$$
$$1 + 3 = 2^2$$
$$1 + 3 + 5 = 3^2$$
$$\vdots$$
$$1 + 3 + 5 \cdots + 197 + 199 = 100^2$$

Using the pattern shown above, the sum of the first 100 positive odd integers is $100^2 = 10000$.

17. (B)

For simplicity, let the radii of the two concentric circles be 1 and 2. Thus, the area of the shaded region is $\frac{1}{2} \times (\pi(2)^2 - \pi(1)^2) = \frac{3}{2}\pi$.

$$\text{Geometric probability} = \frac{\text{Area of the shaded region}}{\text{Area of larger circle}} = \frac{\frac{3}{2}\pi}{4\pi} = \frac{3}{8}$$

Therefore, the probability that the dart lands on the shaded area is $\frac{3}{8}$.

18. (E)

Solomon consists of 7 letters. Out of 7 letters, there are 3 O's.

$$\text{Number of arrangements:} \quad \frac{7!}{3!} = 840$$

Therefore, the number of arrangements of the letters in the word SOLOMON is 840.

19. (B)

Since the numbers $123, a, b, c, 207$ form an arithmetic sequence, b is the arithmetic mean of 123 and 207. Thus,

$$b = \frac{123 + 207}{2} = 165$$

a is the arithmetic mean of 123 and b, and c is the arithmetic mean of b and 207. Thus,

$$a = \frac{123 + 165}{2} = 144, \qquad c = \frac{165 + 207}{2} = 186$$

Therefore, value of $a + b - c$ is $144 + 165 - 186 = 123$.

20. (A)

$x^2 = x$ or $x^2 - x = 0$ can be factored as $x(x-1) = 0$. Thus, the number of solutions to $x^2 = x$ is 2: $x = 0$, or $x = 1$. In order to find the solutions to $x - 3 = \sqrt{4x}$, square each side of the equation.

$$x - 3 = \sqrt{4x}$$
$$(x-3)^2 = 4x$$
$$x^2 - 6x + 9 = 4x$$
$$x^2 - 10x + 9 = 0$$
$$(x-1)(x-9) = 0$$

Thus, the possible solutions to $x - 3 = \sqrt{4x}$ are 1 or 9. However, when $x = 1$, $-2 \neq \sqrt{4}$. So the number of solutions to $x - 3 = \sqrt{4x}$ is 1: $x = 9$. Therefore, the quantity in Column A is greater than the quantity in Column B.

21. (E)

Tips nth term of an arithmetic sequence: $a_n = a_1 + (n-1)d$, where a_1 is the first term, and d is the common difference.

Using the nth term formula $a_n = a_1 + (n-1)d$, write the first 5 terms as follows:

$$a_1 = a$$
$$a_2 = a + d$$
$$a_3 = a + 2d$$
$$a_4 = a + 3d$$
$$a_5 = a + 4d$$

Thus, the sum of the first two terms is 23 can be written as $a + a + d = 2a + d = 23$, and the sum of the next three terms is 72 can be written as $a + 2d + a + 3d + a + 4d = 3a + 9d = 72$.

$$2a + d = 23 \xrightarrow{\text{Multiply by 3}} 6a + 3d = 69$$
$$3a + 9d = 72 \xrightarrow{\text{Multiply by } -2} -6a - 18d = -144$$

Setting up the system of equations and solve for a and d.

$$6a + 3d = 69$$
$$\underline{-6a - 18d = -144} \qquad \text{Add two equations}$$
$$-15d = -75 \qquad \text{Divide each side by } -15$$
$$d = 5$$

$d = 5$ and $2a + d = 23$ gives $a = 9$. Therefore, the value of the 6th terms is $a_6 = a + 5d = 34$.

22. (A)

The prime factorization of $864 = 2^5 \cdot 3^3$. In order for a factor of 864 to be a perfect square, its prime factorization should be of the form $2^a \cdot 3^b$, where a is either 0, 2, or 4 and b is either 0 or 2. Since there are 3 values for a and 2 values for b, $3 \times 2 = 6$ factors of 864 are perfect squares.

126

23. (D)

Let x and y be the tens digit and units digit, respectively. The value of the two-digit integer xy can be written as $10x + y$. When the digits of xy are reversed, the value of yx can be written as $10y + x$. Since the value of yx is 27 greater than the value of xy,

$$10y + x - (10x + y) = 27$$
$$9y - 9x = 27$$
$$y - x = 3$$

we get the relationship between y and x. Below shows the list of (x, y) that satisfies $y - x = 3$.

y	x	yx	xy
4	1	41	14
5	2	52	25
6	3	63	36
7	4	74	47
8	5	85	58
9	6	96	69

Thus, the positive two-digit integers which are increased by exactly 27 when the digits are reversed are 14, 25, 36, 47, 58, and 69. Therefore, the number of positive two-digit integers which are increased by exactly 27 when the digits are reversed is 6.

24. (D)

In the morning, Jason headed to his office at an approximation of either 7:20 am or 7:55 am. Returning home, he looked at the clock at an approximation of either 5:10 pm or 5:40 pm.

$$\text{Greatest Time Away} = 5{:}40 \text{ pm} - 7{:}20 \text{ am}$$
$$= 17{:}40 - 7{:}20$$
$$= 10 \text{ hours and } 20 \text{ minutes}$$

25. (C)

> **Tips**
>
> The product of two numbers ab equals the product of $GCF(a, b)$ and $LCM(a, b)$.
>
> $$ab = GCF \times LCM$$

Two numbers are 180 and x. $GCF = 4$ and $LCM = 6840$.

$$180x = 4 \times 6840$$
$$x = \frac{4 \times 6840}{180}$$
$$x = 152$$

Therefore, the value of x is 152.

26. (B)

> [Tips] $$(x + y + z)^2 = x^2 + y^2 + z^2 + 2(xy + yz + zx)$$

$x^2 + y^2 + z^2 = 159$ and $xy + yz + zx = 65$. Thus,

$$(x + y + z)^2 = x^2 + y^2 + z^2 + 2(xy + yz + zx)$$
$$= 159 + 2(65)$$
$$= 289$$

Since $(x + y + z)^2 = 289 = 17^2$, $x + y + z$ is either 17 or -17. Therefore, the largest possible value of $x + y + z$ is 17.

27. (B)

> [Tips] $$1 + 2 + 2^2 + 2^3 + \cdots + 2^n = 2^{n+1} - 1$$

$$2^2 + 2^3 + \cdots + 2^{99} = 1 + 2 + 2^2 + 2^3 + \cdots + 2^{99} - (1 + 2)$$
$$= (2^{100} - 1) - 3$$
$$= 2^{100} - 4$$

Let's find the units digit of 2^{100} using the pattern below.

Power of 2	2	2^2	2^3	2^4	2^5	2^6	2^7	2^8	2^9	2^{10}	$\cdots$
Units digit	2	4	8	6	2	4	8	6	2	4	$\cdots$

If the power of 2 is multiple of 4, the units digit is 6. Thus, units digit of $2^4, 2^8, \cdots, 2^{100}$ is 6. Since $n = 2^{100} - 4$, the units digit of n is 2.

28. (A)

Each of 6 faces of the cube has 2 choices: painted blue or red. So there are $2^6 = 64$ ways to paint the cube. Let's consider three cases where no two blue faces are adjacent.

- Case 1: Six faces are painted red. There is only 1 way.

- Case 2: One blue face and 5 white faces. There are 6 ways.

- Case 3: Two opposite sides are painted blue and other 4 sides are painted red. There are 3 ways.

Out of 64 ways, there are 10 ways to paint the cube so that no two blue faces are adjacent. Therefore, the probability that no two blue faces are adjacent is $\frac{10}{64}$ or $\frac{5}{32}$.

TJHSST PRACTICE MATH TEST 4

Time — 50 minutes
Number of questions — 28

Directions: Solve each of the following problems using the available space for scratch work. Choose the best answer among the answer choices given and fill in the corresponding circle on the answer sheet.

1. Three points A, B, and C lie on the same number line, not necessarily in that order. Point A and point B are 50 units apart and point C and point A are 17 units apart. What is the maximum distance that point C and point B are apart?

   (A) 17

   (B) 33

   (C) 50

   (D) 67

   (E) 80

2. What is the arithmetic mean of the first ten nonnegative even integers?

   (A) 7

   (B) 8

   (C) 9

   (D) 10

   (E) 11

3. If a car factory produces x cars in y months, how many cars does the car factory produce in z years?

   (A) $\dfrac{xz}{y}$

   (B) $\dfrac{xy}{z}$

   (C) $\dfrac{12yz}{x}$

   (D) $\dfrac{12xz}{y}$

   (E) $\dfrac{12xy}{z}$

4. Two numbers, y and 3, are on the number line. If the midpoint of y and 3 is x, what is the value of y in terms of x ?

   (A) $2x + 3$

   (B) $2x - 3$

   (C) $3 - 2x$

   (D) $6 + x$

   (E) $6 - x$

5. In a circular track whose circumference is 60 m, Joshua and Jason are running in opposite directions from a starting position. Joshua is running 2 m/s and Jason is running 1 m/s. By the time Joshua and Jason meet each other for the first time, how many meters did Joshua run?

(A) 45

(B) 40

(C) 36

(D) 30

(E) 24

$$2, 9, 28, 65, \cdots$$

6. The sequence above is neither an arithmetic sequence nor a geometric sequence. What is the next term in the sequence?

(A) 99

(B) 114

(C) 126

(D) 142

(E) 163

7. Set S consists of 5 positive integers: 6, x, 10, y, and 15. If the mode and the mean of set S are 10 and 11 respectively, what is the product of x and y ?

(A) 150

(B) 140

(C) 130

(D) 120

(E) 110

8. Eight cards, each labeled with a number from 1 through 8, are in a bag. What is the smallest number of cards you need to select so that at least one prime number is guaranteed among the selected cards?

(A) 5

(B) 4

(C) 3

(D) 2

(E) 1

MR. RHEE'S BRILLIANT MATH SERIES

TJHSST MATH TEST 4

9. The length, width, and height of a rectangular box is three, four, and five feet respectively. Each length, width, and height is divided by 3, 4, and 5 so that the rectangular box is divided into smaller cubes with sides of 1 foot. If one can of paint is needed to paint 12 square feet, how many cans of paint are needed to paint the surface area of all smaller cubes?

(A) 22

(B) 24

(C) 26

(D) 28

(E) 30

11. An airplane is flying back and forth from city A to city B. The two cities are d miles apart. If the plane is flying with the wind, it takes 2 hours to travel from city A to city B. However, if the plane is flying against the wind, it takes 3 hours to travel from city B to city A. Assuming that the speed of the airplane and the wind remain the same throughout the trip, which of the following must be the speed of the wind in terms of d ?

(A) $\dfrac{5d}{12}$

(B) $\dfrac{d}{2}$

(C) $\dfrac{d}{5}$

(D) $\dfrac{d}{6}$

(E) $\dfrac{d}{12}$

10. A geometric sequence has 101 terms. If the first term is 6 , and the 101th term is 216, what is the value of the 51st term?

(A) 96

(B) 64

(C) 48

(D) 36

(E) 32

12. How many 4-digit integers greater than 1000 have exactly two pairs of equal digits such as 1122 or 8383?

(A) 81

(B) 90

(C) 486

(D) 540

(E) 900

13. A ball is dropped from a height of 16 yards. Each time it strikes the ground, it bounces up to half its previous height. What is the total distance, in feet, that ball traveled when the ball strikes the ground 4th time?

    (A) 30

    (B) 44

    (C) 90

    (D) 132

    (E) 138

14. In the figure above, all the nine points are equally spaced. how many different lines that connect at least two points can be drawn?

    (A) 8

    (B) 16

    (C) 20

    (D) 22

    (E) 24

15. A cube with the side length 4 cut into exactly 22 smaller cubes with the side length either 1 or 2, and no material is wasted. How many of the 22 smaller cubes have the side length 1?

    (A) 16

    (B) 14

    (C) 12

    (D) 10

    (E) 8

16. s and t are the solutions to $2x^2 + x - 2 = 0$. What is the value of $s^2t + st^2$?

    (A) $-\dfrac{3}{2}$

    (B) -1

    (C) 0

    (D) $\dfrac{1}{2}$

    (E) 3

$$T, T, F, F, S, S, \cdots$$

17. Which of the following letter is the next term in the sequence above?

(A) E

(B) H

(C) M

(D) W

(E) Z

$$k = \frac{1}{1 \cdot 2} + \frac{1}{2 \cdot 3} + \frac{1}{3 \cdot 4} + \cdots + \frac{1}{20 \cdot 21}$$

19. If the expression k above equals a fraction $\frac{m}{n}$, where m and n are positive integers, and the greatest common factor of m and n is 1, what is the value of $m + n$?

(A) 43

(B) 41

(C) 39

(D) 37

(E) 35

18. Let x, y, and z be the nonzero integers. How many ordered triples (x, y, z) satisfy that each integer is the product of other two integers?

(A) 0

(B) 1

(C) 3

(D) 4

(E) 5

20. How many positive integers less than 1000 are divisible by 2 or 3 but not both?

(A) 466

(B) 500

(C) 666

(D) 700

(E) 832

$$\sqrt{28 + 10\sqrt{3}}$$

21. If the expression above equals $a + \sqrt{b}$, where a and b are integers, what is the value of $a^2 + b$?

(A) 20

(B) 22

(C) 24

(D) 26

(E) 28

22. Three numbers are selected from the set $\{1, 2, 3, 4, 5, 6, 7\}$ without replacement. What is the probability that the sum of the three numbers is prime?

(A) $\dfrac{1}{5}$

(B) $\dfrac{2}{7}$

(C) $\dfrac{13}{35}$

(D) $\dfrac{3}{8}$

(E) $\dfrac{1}{2}$

23. If a positive integer n is divided by 7, the remainder is 6. In addition, if it is divided by 6, 5, 4, 3, and 2, the remainders are 5, 4, 3, 2, and 1, respectively. What is the smallest possible value of n ?

(A) 391

(B) 399

(C) 407

(D) 419

(E) 431

24. If the product of all factors of 1000 is 10^n, what is the value of n ?

(A) 24

(B) 26

(C) 28

(D) 30

(E) 32

25. Using the digits 2, 3, 4, 5, 7, 8, and 9 only once, you can make 3 two-digit prime numbers and 1 prime number. What is the sum of the four prime numbers?

    (A) 139

    (B) 142

    (C) 148

    (D) 157

    (E) 164

$$4, 7, 1, 8, 9, 7, \cdots$$

27. For $n > 2$, the nth term, denoted by a_n, of the sequence is the units digit of the sum of the two preceding terms. Let $S_n = a_1 + a_2 + \cdots + a_n$. Which of the following is the value of S_{100} ?

    (A) 400

    (B) 428

    (C) 464

    (D) 500

    (E) 524

26. Jason selects two numbers from the set $\{1, 2, 3, 4\}$ without replacement, and Joshua selects one number from the set $\{1, 2, 3, 4, 5, 6\}$. What is the probability that number selected by Joshua is greater than the sum of two numbers selected by Jason?

    (A) $\dfrac{1}{8}$

    (B) $\dfrac{1}{6}$

    (C) $\dfrac{7}{36}$

    (D) $\dfrac{1}{4}$

    (E) $\dfrac{5}{12}$

28. Square $ABCD$ has the side length 2. If point E is chosen at random from inside the square, the probability that $\triangle ABE$ is an acute triangle is $\frac{m-\pi}{n}$. Which of the following is the value of $m + n$?

    (A) 12

    (B) 14

    (C) 16

    (D) 18

    (E) 20

Answers and Solutions
TJHSST Math Practice Test 4

Answers

1. D	11. E	21. E
2. C	12. C	22. B
3. D	13. D	23. D
4. B	14. C	24. A
5. B	15. A	25. E
6. C	16. D	26. C
7. B	17. A	27. D
8. A	18. D	28. C
9. E	19. B	
10. D	20. B	

Solutions

1. (D)

   Place point A in the middle on the number line as shown in figure 1. Since points A, B, and C lie on the same number line, not necessarily in that order, place point B 50 units left of point A or 50 units right of point A.

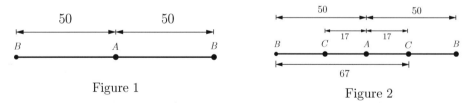

Figure 1   Figure 2

   Point C and point A are 17 units apart. So, place point C 17 units left of point A or 17 units right of point A as shown in figure 2. Therefore, the maximum distance that point C and point B are apart is 67 units.

2. (C)

   The first ten nonnegative even integers are $0, 2, 4, \cdots 18$.

   $$\text{Arithmetic mean} = \frac{0 + 2 + 4 + \cdots + 18}{10} = \frac{90}{10} = 9$$

   Therefore, the arithmetic mean of the first ten nonnegative even integers is 9.

3. (D)

There are 12 months in 1 year. Convert z years to $12z$ months. Define p as the number of cars that the car factory produce in $12z$ months. Set up a proportion in terms of cars and months.

$$x \,_{\text{cars}} : y \,_{\text{months}} = p \,_{\text{cars}} : 12z \,_{\text{months}}$$
$$\frac{x}{y} = \frac{p}{12z} \qquad \text{Use cross product property}$$
$$py = 12xz$$
$$p = \frac{12xz}{y}$$

Therefore, the number of cars that the car factory produce in z years is $\frac{12xz}{y}$.

4. (B)

| Tips | If m is the midpoint of p and q on the number line, $m = \frac{p+q}{2}$ or $2m = p+q$. |

x is the midpoint of y and 3 on the number line. Thus, $x = \frac{y+3}{2}$ or $2x = y+3$, which implies that $y = 2x - 3$. Therefore, y in terms of x is $2x - 3$.

5. (B)

| Tips | Use the distance formula: distance = rate × time. |

Joshua is running 2 m/s and Jason is running 1 m/s. Define t, in seconds, as how long Joshua and Jason have been running until they meet each other for the first time. Then, the distance that Joshua and Jason run for t seconds are $2t$ and t, respectively. When Joshua and Jason meet each other, the sum of the distance that both run equals to the circumference of the circular track, 60 m. Thus,

$$2t + t = 60$$
$$3t = 60$$
$$t = 20$$

This means that Joshua runs for 20 seconds. Therefore, Joshua runs $20 \times 2 = 40$ meters.

6. (C)

The nth term of the sequence can be defined as $a_n = n^3 + 1$ as shown below.

$$2 = 1^3 + 1$$
$$9 = 2^3 + 1$$
$$28 = 3^3 + 1$$
$$65 = 4^3 + 1$$

Therefore, the 5th term of the sequence is $a_5 = 5^3 + 1 = 126$.

7. (B)

Set S consists of 5 positive integers: 6, x, 10, y, and 15. The mean of the five integers in set S is 11, which means that the sum of the five integers is $5 \times 11 = 55$. Set up an equation in terms of the sum and find the value of $x + y$.

$$x + y + 6 + 10 + 15 = 55 \qquad \text{Subtract 31 from each side}$$
$$x + y = 24$$

Thus, $x + y = 24$. Since the mode of set S is 10, either x or y is 10. If $x = 10$, $y = 14$ so that $x + y = 24$. For the same reason, if $y = 10$, $x = 14$. Therefore, the product of xy is $xy = 10(14) = 140$.

8. (A)

There are four non-prime numbers from 1 to 8: 1, 4, 6, and 8. There are four prime numbers: 2, 3, 5, and 7. If all four non-prime numbers are selected, the next number will be a prime number. Therefore, five cards must be selected to guarantee that at least one prime number is selected.

9. (E)

In the figure below, each length, width, and height of the rectangular box is divided by 3, 4, and 5, respectively so that there are $3 \times 4 \times 5 = 60$ smaller cubes with sides of 1 foot.

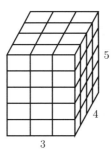

Each smaller cube has six faces. Thus, each has a surface area of 6 square feet. The total surface area of the 60 smaller cubes is $60 \times 6 = 360$ square feet. Since one can of paint is needed to paint 12 square feet, the total number of cans of paint is needed to paint the surface area of the 60 smaller cubes is $\frac{360 \text{ square feet}}{12 \text{ square feet/can}} = 30$ cans.

10. (D)

> Tips   Geometric mean of a and b is $\sqrt{ab}$.

The sequence has 101 terms. Thus, the 51th term is the middle term of the sequence and is the geometric mean of the first term and 101th term. Therefore, the value of 51th term is $\sqrt{6 \cdot 6^3} = 36$.

11. (E)

Define x as the speed of the airplane and y as the speed of the wind. Then, the speed of the airplane with the wind is $x + y$. The speed of the airplane against the wind is $x - y$. Use the Time $= \frac{\text{Distance}}{\text{Speed}}$ formula to set up two equations in terms of time. Let T_{AB} and T_{BA} be the time needed for the airplane to travel from city A to city B and from city B to city A, respectively.

$$\text{With wind:} \quad T_{AB} = \frac{d}{x+y} \implies 2 = \frac{d}{x+y} \implies x+y = \frac{d}{2}$$

$$\text{Against wind:} \quad T_{BA} = \frac{d}{x-y} \implies 3 = \frac{d}{x-y} \implies x-y = \frac{d}{3}$$

Use the linear combinations method to solve for y.

$$
\begin{aligned}
x + y &= \tfrac{d}{2} \\
\underline{x - y} &= \underline{\tfrac{d}{3}} \\
2y &= \tfrac{d}{2} - \tfrac{d}{3} \\
2y &= \tfrac{d}{6} \\
y &= \tfrac{d}{12}
\end{aligned}
$$

Subtract two equations

Therefore, the speed of the wind is $\frac{d}{12}$.

12. (C)

Let A and B be the digits for the first pair and the second pair, respectively. There are 6 arrangements to make 4-digit integers using A and B: $AABB$, $ABAB$, $ABBA$, $BAAB$, $BABA$, and $BBAA$. In each arrangement, there are 9 ways to select A and 9 ways to select B. Therefore, there are $6 \times 9 \times 9 = 486$ 4-digit integers greater than 1000 have exactly two pairs of equal digits.

13. (D)

Each time the tall strikes the ground, it bounces up to half its previous height and fall down to the ground.

	Distance(Up)	Distance(Down)
Before 1st strike	0	16 yd
Between 1st and 2nd strikes	8 yd	8 yd
Between 2nd and 3rd strikes	4 yd	4 yd
Between 3rd and 4th strikes	2 yd	2 yd
Total distance	44 yd	

Therefore, the total distance that ball traveled when the ball strikes the ground 4th time is $3 \times 44 = 132$ feets.

14. (C)

In figure 1 below, there are 8 lines that connect three points. In figure 2, there are 4 lines that connect two points. In figure 3, there are 8 additional lines that connect other two points.

Figure 1

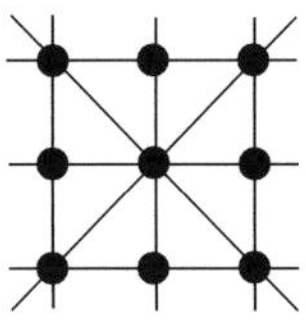

Figure 2

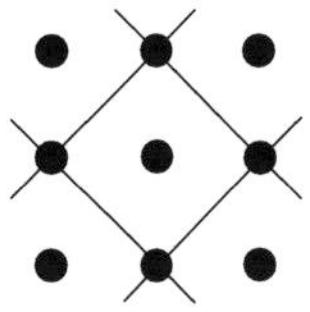

Figure 3

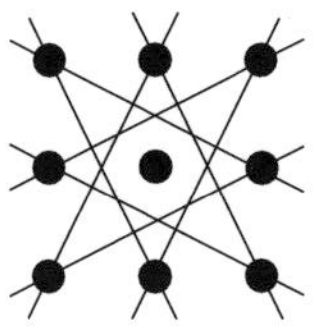

Therefore, there are $8 + 4 + 8 = 20$ different lines that connect at least two points.

15. (A)

Let x be the number of cubes with the side length 1, and y be number of cubes with the side length 2. The volume of a cube with the side length 1 is $1^3 = 1$, the volume of a cube with the side length 2 is $2^3 = 8$, and the volume of a cube with the side length 4 is $4^3 = 64$. Set up the system of equations in terms of the volume and the number of smaller cubes, and solve for x and y.

$$x + 8y = 64$$
$$\underline{x + y = 22} \qquad \text{Subtract two equations}$$
$$7y = 42$$
$$y = 6$$

$y = 6$ and $x + y = 22$ gives $x = 16$. Therefore, there are 16 smaller cubes with the side length 1.

16. (D)

> Tips
>
> Vieta's formulas relate the coefficients of a polynomial to the sum and product of its zeros. Let s and t be the solutions to $ax^2 + bx + c = 0$.
>
> $$s + t = -\frac{b}{a}$$
> $$st = \frac{c}{a}$$

If s and t are the solutions to $2x^2 + x - 2 = 0$, according to the Vieta's formulas,

$$s + t = -\frac{b}{a} = -\frac{1}{2}$$
$$st = \frac{c}{a} = \frac{-2}{2} = -1$$

Thus,

$$s^2t + st^2 = st(s + t) = -1\left(-\frac{1}{2}\right) = \frac{1}{2}$$

the value of $s^2t + st^2$ is $\frac{1}{2}$.

17. (A)

The sequence $T, T, F, F, S, S, \cdots$ consists of the first letter of counting number names starting from two to seven. Since the number after seven is eight, the next term of the sequence is E.

18. (D)

x, y, and z are the nonzero integers. Each integer is the product of other two integers can be written as $x = yz$, $y = xz$, and $z = xy$. Multiplying three equations, you get

$$x = yz$$
$$y = xz$$
$$\underline{z = xy}$$
$$xyz = (xyz)^2 \qquad \text{Multiply three equations}$$

Let $t = xyz$. Then, $xyz = (xyz)^2$ can be written as $t = t^2$ or $t(t-1) = 0$. Since x, y, and z are the nonzero integers, $t = xyz > 0$. Thus, the only solution to $t(t-1) = 0$ is $t = 1$. The table below shows the possible values of x, y, and z so that $t = xyz = 1$.

x	y	z
1	1	1
−1	−1	1
−1	1	−1
1	−1	−1

Therefore, there are 4 ordered triples (x, y, z) that satisfy each integer is the product of other two integers: $(1, 1, 1)$, $(−1, −1, 1)$, $(−1, 1, −1)$, and $(1, −1, −1)$.

19. (B)

Tips

The partial fraction decomposition:

$$\frac{1}{n(n+1)} = \frac{1}{n} - \frac{1}{n+1}$$

For instance, $\frac{1}{2 \cdot 3} = \frac{1}{2} - \frac{1}{3}$.

Adding many fractions with different denominators takes long time to evaluate. Instead, let's use the partial fraction decomposition method shown above.

$$
\begin{aligned}
k &= \frac{1}{1 \cdot 2} + \frac{1}{2 \cdot 3} + \frac{1}{3 \cdot 4} + \cdots + \frac{1}{20 \cdot 21} \\
&= \frac{1}{1} - \frac{1}{2} + \frac{1}{2} - \frac{1}{3} + \frac{1}{3} - \frac{1}{4} + \cdots + \frac{1}{19} - \frac{1}{20} + \frac{1}{20} - \frac{1}{21} \\
&= 1 - \frac{1}{21} \\
&= \frac{20}{21}
\end{aligned}
$$

Thus, $k = \frac{20}{21}$, where $m = 20$ and $n = 21$. Therefore, the value of $m + n = 41$.

20. (B)

A venn diagram is very useful in counting. It helps you count numbers correctly.

A   B

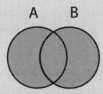

$$A \cup B = A + B - A \cap B$$

Tips

In the figure above, $A \cup B$ represents the combined area of two circles A and B. $A \cap B$ represents the common area where the two circles overlap. The venn diagram suggests that the combined area $(A \cup B)$ equals the sum of areas of circles $(A + B)$ minus the common area $(A \cap B)$.

In counting, each circle A and B represents a set of numbers. $n(A)$ and $n(B)$ represent the number of elements in set A and B, respectively. For instance, $A = \{2, 4, 6, 8, 10\}$ and $n(A) = 5$. Thus, the total number of elements that belong to either set A or set B, $n(A \cup B)$, can be counted as follows:

$$n(A \cup B) = n(A) + n(B) - n(A \cap B)$$

Let's find out how many positive integers less 1000 are divisible by 2 or 3 or both. Define A as the set of numbers divisible by 2 and B as the set of numbers divisible by 3.

$$A = \{2, 4, 6, \cdots, 998\}, \qquad\qquad n(A) = 499$$
$$B = \{3, 6, 9, \cdots, 999\}, \qquad\qquad n(B) = 333$$
$$A \cap B = \{6, 12, 18, \cdots, 996\}, \qquad\qquad n(A \cap B) = 166$$

The shaded region in the venn diagram below represents the total number of positive integers less than 1000 are divisible by 2 or 3 but not both.

A   B

Shaded region $= A \cup B - A \cap B$

Thus,

$$
\begin{aligned}
n(\text{Shaded region}) &= n(A \cup B) - n(A \cap B) \\
&= n(A) + n(B) - n(A \cap B) - n(A \cap B) \\
&= n(A) + n(B) - 2 \times n(A \cap B) \qquad\qquad = n(A) + n(B) - n(A \cap B) \\
&= 499 + 333 - 2(166) \\
&= 500
\end{aligned}
$$

Therefore, the total number of positive integers less than 1000 are divisible by 2 or 3 but not both is 500.

21. (E)

Let $a + \sqrt{b} = \sqrt{28 + 10\sqrt{3}}$ and square each side of the equation.

$$(a + \sqrt{b})^2 = \left(\sqrt{28 + 10\sqrt{3}}\right)^2$$
$$a^2 + 2a\sqrt{b} + b = 28 + 10\sqrt{3}$$
$$(a^2 + b) + 2a\sqrt{b} = 28 + 10\sqrt{3}$$

Thus, $a^2 + b = 28$ and $2a\sqrt{b} = 10\sqrt{3}$. Therefore, the value of $a^2 + b = 28$.

22. (B)

There are $\binom{7}{3} = 35$ ways to select three numbers from the set $\{1, 2, 3, 4, 5, 6, 7\}$ without replacement. The sum of the three smallest numbers is $1 + 2 + 3 = 6$, and the sum of the three largest numbers is $5 + 6 + 7 = 18$. Thus, there are four prime numbers between 6 and 18: 7, 11, 13, and 17.

- When the sum is 7: $1 + 2 + 4$
- When the sum is 11: $1 + 3 + 7$, $1 + 4 + 6$, $2 + 3 + 6$, and $2 + 4 + 5$
- When the sum is 13: $1 + 5 + 7$, $2 + 4 + 7$, $2 + 5 + 6$, and $3 + 4 + 6$
- When the sum is 17: $4 + 6 + 7$

Therefore, the probability that the sum of the three digits is prime is $\frac{10}{35}$ or $\frac{2}{7}$.

23. (D)

If a positive integer n is divided by 7, 6, 5, 4, 3, and 2, the remainder is 6, 5, 4, 3, 2, and 1, respectively. If n is increased by 1, $n + 1$ is divisible by 2, 3, 4, 5, 6, and 7. In other words, $n + 1$ is a least common multiple of 2, 3, 4, 5, and 7, which is 420. Therefore, the smallest possible value of n is 419.

24. (A)

> **When the prime factorization of a number n is $2^a \cdot 3^b$,**
>
> Tips   Number of factors $= (a + 1) \times (b + 1)$
>
> Product of factors $= n^{\frac{\text{Number of factors}}{2}}$

Since the prime factorization of 1000 is $10^3 = 2^3 \cdot 5^3$, the number of factors of 1000 is $(3 + 1) \times (3 + 1) = 16$. Thus,

$$\text{Product of all factors of } 1000 = 1000^{\frac{16}{2}} = 1000^8 = (10^3)^8 = 10^{24}$$

the product of all factors of 1000 is 10^{24}. Therefore, the value of n is 24.

25. (E)

Using the digits 2, 3, 4, 5, 7, 8, and 9 only once, you can make 3 two-digit prime numbers and 1 prime number. The four prime numbers are 83, 47, 29, and 5. Therefore, the sum of the four prime numbers is 164.

26. (C)

Jason selects two numbers from the set $\{1, 2, 3, 4\}$ without replacement. So the sum of the two number is either $1 + 2 = 3$, $1 + 3 = 4$, $1 + 4 = 5$, $2 + 3 = 5$, $2 + 4 = 6$, or $3 + 4 = 7$.

Let Ja and Jo be the numbers that Jason and Joshua obtained, respectively.

		Jo					
		1	2	3	4	5	6
Ja	3				○	○	○
	4					○	○
	5						○
	5						○
	6						
	7						

There are 7 outcomes for which $Ja \le Jo$ represented by circles in the table above. Therefore, the probability that number selected by Joshua is greater than the sum of two numbers selected by Jason is $\frac{7}{36}$.

27. (D)

List the terms of the sequence until you find the pattern.

$$4, 7, 1, 8, 9, 7, 6, 3, 9, 2, 1, 3, 4, 7, 1, 8, \cdots$$

The pattern is 4, 7, 1, 8, 9, 7, 6, 3, 9, 2, 1, 3. The pattern suggests that

$$a_{12} = a_{24} = a_{36} = \cdots = a_{84} = a_{96} = 3$$

Let's find the sum S_{12}, S_{24}, and S_{96}.

$$S_{12} = a_1 + a_2 + \cdots + a_{12} = 4 + 7 + 1 + 8 + 9 + 7 + 6 + 3 + 9 + 2 + 1 + 3 = 60$$
$$S_{24} = 2 \cdot S_{12} = 2(60) = 120$$
$$\vdots$$
$$S_{96} = 8 \cdot S_{12} = 8(60) = 480$$

From the pattern, $a_{97} = 4$, $a_{98} = 7$, $a_{99} = 1$, and $a_{100} = 8$. Thus,

$$S_{100} = s_{96} + a_{97} + a_{98} + a_{99} + a_{100}$$
$$= 480 + 4 + 7 + 1 + 8$$
$$= 500$$

Therefore, the value of S_{100} is 500.

28. (C)

> (Tips) A triangle that is inscribed inside a semi-circle is a right triangle.

Draw a semi-circle with AB as a diameter as shown below.

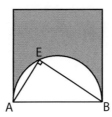

If point E is chosen on the semi-circle, $\triangle ABE$ that is inscribed inside the semi-circle is a right triangle. If point E is chosen on the shaded region inside the square with the side length 2, $\triangle ABE$ is an acute triangle. Thus,

$$\text{Probability that } \triangle ABE \text{ is an acute triangle} = \frac{\text{Area of shaded region}}{\text{Area of square}}$$

$$= \frac{4 - \frac{1}{2}\pi}{4}$$

$$= \frac{8 - \pi}{8}$$

the probability that $\triangle ABE$ is an acute triangle is $\frac{8-\pi}{8}$. Therefore, the value of $m+n = 8+8 = 16$.

TJHSST PRACTICE MATH TEST 5
Time — 50 minutes
Number of questions — 28

Directions: Solve each of the following problems using the available space for scratch work. Choose the best answer among the answer choices given and fill in the corresponding circle on the answer sheet.

1. If February 4th is on Sunday, on what day of the week is February 24th?

   (A) Thursday

   (B) Friday

   (C) Saturday

   (D) Sunday

   (E) Monday

2. If $3^n = 2$, what is the value of 3^{n+1}

   (A) 3

   (B) 4

   (C) 6

   (D) 7

   (E) 9

3. Joshua starts running. For the first second, he is running due east 5 meters from the starting position. For the next second, he is running due west 2 meters. If he continues running in this pattern, how far is Joshua away from the starting position after 13 seconds?

   (A) 19 meters

   (B) 20 meters

   (C) 21 meters

   (D) 22 meters

   (E) 23 meters

$$ny - nx - 6n = 0$$

4. If $n > 0$, what is the value of $y - x$?

   (A) 1

   (B) 2

   (C) 4

   (D) 6

   (E) 12

147

5. There are thirty questions on a math exam worth a total of one hundred points. Each question is worth either three points or five points. How many questions on the math exam are worth five points?

(A) 4

(B) 5

(C) 6

(D) 7

(E) 8

6. For all positive integers k, $k\blacklozenge$ is defined as the product of all positive consecutive even integers less than or equal to k. For instance, $6\blacklozenge = 6 \times 4 \times 2$. Which of the following expression equals $\dfrac{10!}{3 \times 5 \times 7 \times 9}$?

(A) $6\blacklozenge$

(B) $7\blacklozenge$

(C) $8\blacklozenge$

(D) $9\blacklozenge$

(E) $10\blacklozenge$

7. If both n and k are prime numbers, which of the following statement must be true?

(A) nk is an even number.

(B) Greatest common factor of n and k is 1.

(C) $n + k$ is an even number.

(D) $n + k$ is divisible by 2.

(E) $n + k$ is a prime number.

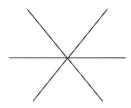

8. In the figure above, three lines intersect at one point to form six angles. If the degree measures of the six angles are integer values and they are not all congruent, what is the smallest possible degree measure of the largest angle?

(A) 59

(B) 60

(C) 61

(D) 177

(E) 178

9. All of the following numbers are prime numbers **except**

   (A) 139

   (B) 157

   (C) 197

   (D) 227

   (E) 253

11. Two standard dice are rolled. What is the probability that the sum of the two numbers on top of each die is either 8 or 10?

   (A) $\dfrac{2}{9}$

   (B) $\dfrac{1}{4}$

   (C) $\dfrac{1}{3}$

   (D) $\dfrac{5}{12}$

   (E) $\dfrac{1}{2}$

10. A print shop has two machines: machine A and machine B. Machine A can print 12 posters in 10 minutes and machine B can print 17 posters in 15 minutes. In the first half hour, only machine A prints posters. In the next hour, machine A and B print together. What is the total number of posters that machine A and machine B print?

   (A) 126

   (B) 128

   (C) 140

   (D) 176

   (E) 208

12. There are forty students in a class. They are taking either math or chemistry or both. The number of students taking math is twice as many as the number of students taking chemistry. If there are five students taking both math and chemistry, what is the number of students taking math?

   (A) 15

   (B) 20

   (C) 25

   (D) 30

   (E) 35

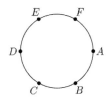

13. In the circular track whose circumference is 120 meters shown above, Joshua and Jason are running in opposite directions from the starting position, A. Joshua is running at 4 meters per second clockwise and Jason is running at 2 meters per second counterclockwise. Which of the following lettered position represents the second time Joshua and Jason meet after they begin running? (Assume that all the lettered positions are equally spaced.)

   (A) B

   (B) C

   (C) D

   (D) E

   (E) F

14. Let x and y be positive integers. How many ordered pairs (x, y) satisfy $3x + 4y \leq 12$?

   (A) 2

   (B) 3

   (C) 4

   (D) 5

   (E) 6

$$\binom{n}{r} = \frac{n!}{(n-r)! \times r!}$$

15. If the combination notation $\binom{n}{r}$ is defined as above, which of the following statement must be true?

   (A) $\binom{10}{0} = \binom{10}{1}$

   (B) $\binom{10}{2} = \binom{10}{9}$

   (C) $\binom{10}{3} = \binom{10}{8}$

   (D) $\binom{10}{4} = \binom{10}{6}$

   (E) $\binom{10}{6} = \binom{10}{5}$

16. The tens digit of a two-digit numbers is 3 more than its units digit. If the original number is 2 more than twice the number obtained by reversing the digits of the original number, what is the sum of the digits of the original number?

   (A) 5

   (B) 6

   (C) 7

   (D) 10

   (E) 12

150

$$25! = 2^a \cdot 3^b \cdot 5^c \cdots$$

17. If the prime factorization of 25! is shown above, what is the value of c ?

    (A) 4

    (B) 5

    (C) 6

    (D) 7

    (E) 8

$$(a_{51} - a_1) + (a_{52} - a_2) + \cdots + (a_{100} - a_{50})$$

19. The nth term of an arithmetic sequence is denoted by a_n. If $a_1 + a_2 + \cdots + a_{50} = 20$, and $a_1 + a_2 + \cdots + a_{100} = 220$, what is the value of the expression above?

    (A) 80

    (B) 100

    (C) 120

    (D) 150

    (E) 180

18. If the sum of three consecutive positive integers is 38 less than the sum of the squares of these integers, what is the sum of cubes?

    (A) 99

    (B) 216

    (C) 405

    (D) 684

    (E) 1584

20. For how many integers n is $\dfrac{30-n}{n}$ the square of an integer?

    (A) 4

    (B) 5

    (C) 6

    (D) 7

    (E) 8

21. If a point (x, y) is randomly chosen inside the square with vertices $(1, 1)$, $(-1, 1)$, $(-1, -1)$, and $(1, -1)$, what is the probability that the point (x, y) chosen satisfies $|x| + |y| \leq 1$?

    (A) $\dfrac{1}{5}$

    (B) $\dfrac{1}{4}$

    (C) $\dfrac{1}{3}$

    (D) $\dfrac{2}{5}$

    (E) $\dfrac{1}{2}$

$$\binom{8}{0} + \binom{8}{1} + \binom{8}{2} + \cdots + \binom{8}{8}$$

23. What is the value of the expression above?

    (A) 96

    (B) 120

    (C) 256

    (D) 782

    (E) 1024

22. In a donut store, only 3 flavors are available: Glazed, Chocolate, and Cinnamon-sugar. If Jason is ordering 4 donuts in the donut store, how many different donut orders are possible?

    (A) 7

    (B) 12

    (C) 15

    (D) 21

    (E) 28

24. A box contains 1 black marble, and 2 white marbles. Each trial, you pull out a marble and replace it with a black marble regardless of the color of the marble. What is the probability that all marbles in the box are black after 3 trials?

    (A) $\dfrac{5}{18}$

    (B) $\dfrac{5}{24}$

    (C) $\dfrac{4}{9}$

    (D) $\dfrac{13}{35}$

    (E) $\dfrac{5}{12}$

Move	Direction	Distance
1st	South	1 foot
2nd	West	2 feet
3rd	North	3 feet
4th	East	4 feet
5th	South	5 feet
6th	West	6 feet
7th	North	7 feet
8th	East	8 feet

25. Mr. Rhee starts walking according to the directions above. For instance, on the first move, he walks 1 foot due south from the starting position. He then walks 2 feet due west on the second move, walks 3 feet due north on the third move, and so on and so forth. When Mr. Rhee finishes the 8th move, how far is he from the starting position?

(A) $4\sqrt{2}$

(B) $5\sqrt{2}$

(C) $6\sqrt{2}$

(D) 5

(E) 10

26. If $4^{16} \cdot 9^8 \cdot 49^4 = m^n$, where m and n are positive integers, what is the smallest possible value of $\dfrac{m}{n}$?

(A) 64

(B) 72

(C) 96

(D) 126

(E) 152

27. The binomial expansion of $(2x - y)^2$ is $4x^2 - 4xy + y^2$. Thus, the sum of all coefficients in the expansion is $4 - 4 + 1 = 1$. What is the sum of all coefficients in the expansion $(2x - y)^8$?

(A) 0

(B) 1

(C) 64

(D) 128

(E) 512

$$\lfloor\sqrt{1}\rfloor + \lfloor\sqrt{2}\rfloor + \lfloor\sqrt{3}\rfloor + \cdots + \lfloor\sqrt{49}\rfloor$$

28. The greatest function of x, denoted by $\lfloor x \rfloor$, produces the greatest integer less than or equal to x. For instance, $\lfloor 3 \rfloor = 3$, and $\lfloor 10 \rfloor = 10$. What is the value of the expression above?

(A) 197

(B) 210

(C) 232

(D) 255

(E) 283

Answers and Solutions

TJHSST Math Practice Test 5

Answers

1. C	11. A	21. E
2. C	12. D	22. C
3. E	13. B	23. C
4. D	14. B	24. C
5. B	15. D	25. A
6. E	16. C	26. D
7. B	17. C	27. B
8. C	18. B	28. B
9. E	19. E	
10. D	20. A	

Solutions

1. (C)

   The days of the week repeat every 7 days. If February 4th falls on a Sunday, the 11th, 18th, and 25th are Sundays. Since February 24th is the day before February 25th, it is a Saturday.

2. (C)

   > Tips   Use the property of exponents: $a^{x+y} = a^x \cdot a^y$

   Based on the property of exponents, $3^{n+1} = 3^n \times 3^1$. Thus,

   $$3^{n+1} = 3^n \times 3^1 \qquad \text{Since } 3^n = 2$$
   $$= 2 \times 3$$
   $$= 6$$

   Therefore, the value of 3^{n+1} is 6.

3. (E)

   Joshua starts running. For the first second, he is running due east 5 meters from the starting position. For the next second, he is running due west 2 meters. This means that Joshua is 3 meters farther away from the starting position every 2 seconds. After 12 seconds, Joshua is $6 \times 3 = 18$ meters away from the starting position. At the 13th second, Joshua is running another 5 meters away from the starting position. Therefore, after 13 seconds, Joshua is $18 + 5 = 23$ meters away from the starting position.

154

4. (D)

Since $n > 0$, divide each side of the equation $ny - nx - 6n = 0$ by n and solve for $y - x$.

$$\frac{ny - nx - 6n}{n} = \frac{0}{n}$$ Divide each side by n

$$\frac{ny}{n} - \frac{nx}{n} - \frac{6n}{n} = 0$$ Simplify

$$y - x - 6 = 0$$ Add 6 to each side

$$y - x = 6$$

Therefore, the value of $y - x$ is 6.

5. (B)

There are two different type of questions on the math exam. One is worth 3 points and another is worth 5 points. Let x be the number of questions worth 5 points. Since there are 30 questions on the math exam, $30 - x$ is the number of questions worth 3 points. Below shows how to obtain the sum of points for each type of questions.

	A question worth 5 points	A question worth 3 points	Total
Number of questions	x	$30 - x$	30
Sum of points	$5x$	$3(30 - x)$	100

Since the math exam is worth a total of 100 points, set up an equation in terms of the sum of points shown on the table above.

$$5x + 3(30 - x) = 100$$ Expand $3(30 - x)$

$$5x - 3x + 90 = 100$$ Subtract 90 from each side

$$2x = 10$$ Divide each side by 2

$$x = 5$$

Therefore, the number of questions that are worth 5 points is 5.

6. (E)

$$\frac{10!}{3 \times 5 \times 7 \times 9} = \frac{1 \times 2 \times \cdots \times 9 \times 10}{3 \times 5 \times 7 \times 9}$$

$$= 2 \times 4 \times 6 \times 8 \times 10$$

$$= 10\blacklozenge$$

Therefore, the expression $10\blacklozenge$ equals $\dfrac{10!}{3 \times 5 \times 7 \times 9}$.

7. (B)

List prime numbers: $2, 3, 5, 7, 11, \cdots$. It is worth noting that 2 is the smallest and the first prime number, and the only even prime number. Other than 2, all the prime numbers are odd numbers. If $n = 3$ and $k = 5$, $n + k = 8$ and $nk = 15$. Thus, eliminate answer choices (A) and (E). If $n = 2$ and $k = 3$, $n + k = 5$, which is not an even number and is not divisible by 2. Thus, eliminate answer choices (C) and (D). Since n and k are prime numbers, the greatest common factor of n and k is 1. Therefore, (B) is the correct answer.

8. (C)

The degree measure of the arc in a circle is $360°$. If all six angles in the figure below were congruent, the measure of each angle would be $\frac{360}{6} = 60°$.

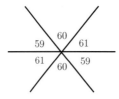

However, the measures of the six angles are integer values and not all congruent. Thus, the measure of some of the six angles are not $60°$. To determine the smallest possible degree measure of the largest angle, add the smallest positive integer value of the measure of an angle, $1°$, to $60°$. Therefore, the smallest possible degree measure of the largest angle is $61°$.

9. (E)

The number 253 in answer choice (E) is not divisible by 2, 3, 5, and 7. $\sqrt{256} = 16$ and $\sqrt{253} < \sqrt{256}$. Thus, the prime numbers less than $\sqrt{253}$ are 2, 3, 5, 7, 11, and 13. Since 253 is divisible by 11, 253 is not a prime number. Therefore, (E) is the correct answer.

10. (D)

Machine A can print 12 posters in 10 minutes or $12 \times 6 = 72$ posters in 60 minutes. Machine B can print 17 posters in 15 minutes or $17 \times 4 = 68$ posters in 60 minutes. In the first half hour, only machine A prints the posters. Thus, it prints $72 \times \frac{1}{2} = 36$ posters alone. In the next hour, both machine A and B print together. Thus, they print $72 + 68 = 140$ posters together. Therefore, the total number of posters that machine A and machine B print is $36 + 140 = 176$.

11. (A)

The first and the second die have 6 possible outcomes each: 1, 2, 3, 4, 5, and 6, which are shown in the second row and the second column of the table below. There are total number of $6 \times 6 = 36$ possible outcomes. Each of the 36 outcomes represents the sum of the two numbers on the top of the first and the second die. For instance, when 2 is on the first die and 6 is on the second die, expressed as $(2, 6)$, the sum of the two numbers is 8.

		1ˢᵗ die					
		1	2	3	4	5	6
2ⁿᵈ die	1						
	2						8
	3					8	
	4				8		10
	5			8		10	
	6		8		10		

There are 8 outcomes for which the sum of the two numbers is either 8 or 10: $(2, 6)$, $(3, 5)$, $(4, 4)$, $(5, 3)$, $(6, 2)$, and $(4, 6)$, $(5, 5)$, and $(6, 4)$. Therefore, the probability that the sum of the two numbers on the top of each die is either 8 or 10 is $\frac{8}{36}$ or $\frac{2}{9}$.

12. (D)

In the venn diagram below, define M, C, $M \cup C$, and $M \cap C$ as the number of students who are taking math, chemistry, either math or chemistry, and both math and chemistry, respectively.

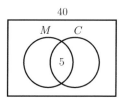

There are 40 students who are taking either math or chemistry and 5 students who are taking both math and chemistry. Thus, $M \cup C = 40$ and $M \cap C = 5$. Since the number of students taking math is twice as many as the number of students taking chemistry, $M = 2C$.

$$M \cup C = M + C - M \cap C \qquad \text{Substitute } 2C \text{ for } M$$
$$40 = 2C + C - 5$$
$$3C = 45$$
$$C = 15$$

Since $M = 2C$, $M = 2 \times 15 = 30$. Therefore, the number of students taking math is 30.

13. (B)

A circular track whose circumference is 120 meters has 6 different labeled positions: $A, B, C, D, E,$ and F. There are $\frac{120}{6} = 20$ meters in between each different labeled position. Joshua and Jason run in opposite directions from position A at a rate of 4 meters per second clockwise and 2 meters per second counterclockwise, respectively. Let t be the time when Joshua and Jason meet for the first time. Then, the distances that Joshua and Jason run for time t are $4t$ and $2t$, respectively. When Joshua and Jason meet for the first time, the sum of the distances they run is equal to the circumference of the circular track, 120 meters. Set up an equation in terms of the sum of distances and solve for t.

$$4t + 2t = 120 \qquad \Longrightarrow \qquad t = 20$$

$t = 20$ implies that Joshua and Jason meet each other every 20 seconds. Joshua and Jason meet for the first time at $t = 20$ and second time at $t = 40$. At $t = 40$, Joshua runs $4 \times 40 = 160$ meters and Jason runs $2 \times 40 = 80$ meters. Therefore, Joshua and Jason meet each other for the second time at position C.

14. (B)

x and y are positive integers. The ordered pairs (x, y) that satisfy $3x + 4y \leq 12$ are $(1, 1)$, $(1, 2)$, and $(2, 1)$. Therefore, the number of ordered pairs that satisfy $3x + 4y \leq 12$ is 3.

15. (D)

$$\binom{10}{4} = \frac{10!}{6! \times 4!}, \qquad \binom{10}{6} = \frac{10!}{4! \times 6!}$$

Since both $\binom{10}{4}$ and $\binom{10}{6}$ have the same numerator and denominator, $\binom{10}{4} = \binom{10}{6}$.

16. (C)

Let x and y be the tens digit and units digit of the original number, respectively. The tens digit of a two-digit numbers is 3 more than its units digit can be written as $x - y = 3$ or $x = y + 3$. The value of the original number, xy, can be written as $10x + y$. The value of the number obtained by reversing the digits of the original number, yx, can be written as $10y + x$. Thus, the original number is 2 more than twice the number obtained by reversing the digits of the original number can be written as $10x + y = 2(10y + x) + 2$, which simplifies to $8x - 19y = 2$. Substitute $x = y + 3$ into $8x - 19y = 2$ to solve for y.

$$8x - 19y = 2$$
$$8(y + 3) - 19y = 2$$
$$-11y + 24 = 2$$
$$-11y = -22$$
$$y = 2$$

Since $y = 2$, $x = y + 3 = 5$. Thus, the original number xy is 52. Therefore, the sum of tens and units digit of 52 is 7.

17. (C)

Let's consider what numbers from 1 to 25 contribute the power of 5. If a number is a multiple of 5, it contributes the power of 5. There are four numbers(5, 10, 15, and 20) that contribute one 5 each, and one number(25) that contributes two 5's. Thus, the power of 5 is $4 + 2 = 6$. Therefore, the value of c is 6.

18. (B)

Let $x-1$, x, and $x+1$ be three consecutive positive integers. Thus, the sum of the three consecutive positive integers is $3x$,

$$(x-1)^2 = x^2 - 2x + 1$$
$$(x)^2 = x^2$$
$$(x+1)^2 = x^2 + 2x + 1$$

and the sum of squares is $3x^2 + 2$. Write the sum of the three consecutive positive integers is 38 less than the sum of the squares as $3x = (3x^2 + 2) - 38$ or $3x^2 - 3x - 36 = 0$ and solve for x.

$$3x^2 - 3x - 36 = 0$$
$$x^2 - x - 12 = 0$$
$$(x+3)(x-4) = 0$$

The solutions to $3x^2 - 3x - 36 = 0$ are $x = -3$ and $x = 4$. However, $x > 0$, $x = 4$. Thus, the three consecutive positive integers are 3, 4, and 5. Therefore, the sum of cubes is $3^3 + 4^3 + 5^3 = 216$.

19. (E)

$a_1 + a_2 + \cdots + a_{50} = 20$, and $a_1 + a_2 + \cdots + a_{100} = 220$ implies that $a_{51} + a_{52} + \cdots + a_{100} = 220 - 20 = 200$.

$$(a_{51} - a_1) + (a_{52} - a_2) + \cdots + (a_{100} - a_{50}) = (a_{51} + a_{52} + \cdots + a_{100}) - (a_1 + a_2 + \cdots + a_{100})$$
$$= 200 - 20$$
$$= 180$$

Therefore, the value of the expression $(a_{51} - a_1) + (a_{52} - a_2) + \cdots + (a_{100} - a_{50})$ is 180.

20. (A)

Let $\dfrac{30-n}{n} = k^2$, where k is an integer.

$$\frac{30-n}{n} = k^2$$
$$nk^2 = 30 - n$$
$$nk^2 + n = 30$$
$$n(k^2 + 1) = 30$$
$$n = \frac{30}{k^2 + 1}$$

Since n is an integer, $k^2 + 1$ must be factors of 30.

Factors of 30	1	2	3	5	6	10	15	30
$k^2 + 1$	$k = 0$	$k = 1$	NA	$k = 2$	NA	$k = 3$	NA	NA

Thus,

	$k = 0$	$k = 1$	$k = 2$	$k = 3$
$n = \frac{30}{k^2+1}$	$n = 30$	$n = 15$	$n = 6$	$n = 3$

Therefore, there are four possible integer values of n for which $\dfrac{30-n}{n}$ is the square of an integer.

21. (E)

The graph of $|x| + |y| \leq 1$ is the shaded region inside the square as shown below.

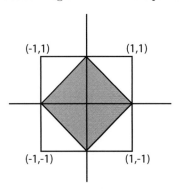

The area of the square is 4. The area of the shaded region, half the area of the square, is 2. Therefore,

$$\text{Probability} = \frac{\text{Area of the shaded region}}{\text{Area of the square}} = \frac{2}{4} = \frac{1}{2}$$

the probability that the point (x, y) chosen satisfies $|x| + |y| \leq 1$ is $\frac{1}{2}$.

22. (C)

Since there are 3 flavors, we need $3 - 1 = 2$ dividers. In the figure below, 2 lines represent 2 dividers, and 4 circles represent 4 donuts.

One of the possible arrangements of 4 donuts and 2 dividers is shown below.

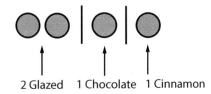

2 Glazed   1 Chocolate   1 Cinnamon

2 circles to the left of the first divider represent 2 glazed donuts, 1 circle between the first divider and the second divider represents 1 chocolate donut, and 1 circle to the right of the second divider represents 1 cinnamon-sugar. Simply, the number of different donut orders is the same as the number of arrangements of 4 circles and 2 lines. Out of 6 blanks, we choose 2 blanks for the 2 dividers. Therefore, there are $\binom{6}{2} = 15$ different donut orders are possible.

23. (C)

Tips

The sum of the entries in the nth row of Pascal's triangle is 2^n.

$$\binom{n}{0} + \binom{n}{1} + \binom{n}{2} + \cdots + \binom{n}{n} = 2^n$$

The expression below represents the sum of the entries in the 8th row of Pascal's triangle.

$$\binom{8}{0} + \binom{8}{1} + \binom{8}{2} + \cdots + \binom{8}{8} = 2^8 = 256$$

Therefore, the value of the expression is 256.

24. (C)

In order to have all marbles in the box are black after 3 trials, consider following three cases.

- WWB(The first marble is white, the second marble is white, and the third marble is black) are pulled out. The probability is

$$\frac{2}{3} \cdot \frac{1}{3} \cdot 1 = \frac{2}{9}$$

- WBW are pulled out. The probability is

$$\frac{2}{3} \cdot \frac{2}{3} \cdot \frac{1}{3} = \frac{4}{27}$$

- BWW are pulled out. The probability is

$$\frac{1}{3} \cdot \frac{2}{3} \cdot \frac{1}{3} = \frac{2}{27}$$

Therefore, the probability that all marbles in the box are black after 3 trials is $\frac{2}{9} + \frac{4}{27} + \frac{2}{27} = \frac{4}{9}$.

25. (A)

It will take too much time to calculate the distance between Mr. Rhee and the starting position in each move as shown below. Instead, calculate the overall distances for the north and south direction, and the east and west direction. It is easier and faster to calculate the distance between Mr. Rhee and the starting position after the 8th move.

To calculate the overall distances for the north and south direction, assign + to the north direction and − to the south direction. For instance, walk 3 feet due north can be written as +3 and walk 1 foot due south as −1. Thus,

Overall distances for north and south $= -1 + 3 - 5 + 7 = +4$

+4 indicates that Mr. Rhee has moved 4 feet north overall. Next, calculate the overall distances for the east and west direction. Assign + to the east direction and − to the west direction.

Overall distances for east and west $= -2 + 4 - 6 + 8 = +4$

+4 indicates that Mr. Rhee has moved 4 feet east overall. Thus, Mr. Rhee has moved 4 feet north and 4 feet east after the 8th move. In the figure below, O represent the starting position and P represents where Mr. Rhee is after the 8th move.

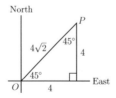

To find the distance between Mr. Rhee and the starting postion, OP, use the 45°-45°-90° special right triangle ratio: $1 : 1 : \sqrt{2}$, or use the Pythagorean theorem: $OP^2 = 4^2 + 4^2$. Thus, $OP = 4\sqrt{2}$. Therefore, Mr. Rhee is $4\sqrt{2}$ feet away from the staring position after the 8th move.

26. (D)

Use the following exponent properties:

- $(a^m)^n = a^{mn}$

- $a^n \cdot b^n = (a \cdot b)^n$

$4^{16} \cdot 9^8 \cdot 49^4 = m^n$, where m and n are positive integers. In order to have the smallest possible value of $\dfrac{m}{n}$, n should have the largest possible value.

$$4^{16} \cdot 9^8 \cdot 49^4 = 2^{32} \cdot 3^{16} \cdot 7^8$$
$$= (2^4)^8 \cdot (3^2)^8 \cdot 7^8$$
$$= (2^4 \cdot 3^2 \cdot 7)^8$$

Thus, $m = 2^4 \cdot 3^2 \cdot 7$ and $n = 8$. Therefore, the smallest possible value of $\frac{m}{n}$ is $\dfrac{16 \cdot 9 \cdot 7}{8} = 126$.

27. (B)

To find the sum of all coefficients in the expansion, substitute $x = 1$, and $y = 1$. For instance,

$$(2x - y)^2 = 4x^2 - 4xy + y^2, \qquad \text{Substitute } x = 1 \text{ and } y = 1$$
$$(2(1) - 1)^2 = 4(1)^2 - 4(1)(1) + (1)^2 = 1$$

Substituting $x = 1$, and $y = 1$ into $(2x - y)^8$ gives $(2(1) - 1)^8 = 1$. Therefore, the sum of all coefficients in the expansion $(2x - y)^8$ is 1.

28. (B)

The value of the first $3(2^2 - 1^2)$ terms is 1, the value of the next $5(3^2 - 2^2)$ terms is 2, the value of the next $7(4^2 - 3^2)$ terms is 3, the value of the next $9(5^2 - 4^2)$ terms is 4, the value of the next $11(6^2 - 5^2)$ terms is 5, the value of the next $13(7^2 - 6^2)$ terms is 6, and the value of the last term is 7. Therefore, the value of the expression is $3(1) + 5(2) + 7(3) + 9(4) + 11(5) + 13(6) + 7 = 210$.

TJHSST PRACTICE MATH TEST 6
Time — 50 minutes
Number of questions — 28

Directions: Solve each of the following problems using the available space for scratch work. Choose the best answer among the answer choices given and fill in the corresponding circle on the answer sheet.

1. A penny, a nickel, a dime, and a quarter are in a bag. If you select two coins at random, how many different total values are possible?

   (A) 5

   (B) 6

   (C) 7

   (D) 8

   (E) 9

Yellow, Green, Blue, Red, Black, $\cdots$

2. In a clothing store, all the T-shirts are arranged in the pattern shown above. What is the color of the 37th T-shirt?

   (A) Yellow

   (B) Green

   (C) Blue

   (D) Red

   (E) Black

Time	Average Speed
9 am to 10:30 am	40 miles per hour
10:30 am to 11:30 am	50 miles per hour
11:30 am to 12:30pm	Break
12:30 pm to 3:00 pm	60 miles per hour

3. According to the chart above, what is the total distance that Mr. Rhee traveled between 9 am to 3 pm?

   (A) 220 miles

   (B) 230 miles

   (C) 240 miles

   (D) 250 miles

   (E) 260 miles

4. There are three red marbles and a certain number of black and white marbles in a bag. If the probability of selecting a red marble is $\frac{1}{5}$, how many non-red marbles are in the bag?

   (A) 13

   (B) 12

   (C) 11

   (D) 10

   (E) 9

165

5. Jason has $10. If Joshua gives one-fourth of the amount of his money to Jason, both have the same amount of money. What is the amount of money that Joshua has in the beginning?

(A) 36

(B) 32

(C) 28

(D) 24

(E) 20

Year	$\cdots$	3	5	7	$\cdots$
Amount	$\cdots$	$1950	$2450	$2950	$\cdots$

7. The table above shows the amount of money that Sue has in her savings account over time. If the amount of money increases at a constant rate throughout the years, how much money did Sue deposit in her savings account in the beginning?

(A) 1150

(B) 1200

(C) 1250

(D) 1300

(E) 1350

6. A ferris wheel with a diameter of 60 feet takes 40 seconds to make a rotation. If Jason rides the ferris wheel for 1 minute and 40 seconds, through what angle, in degrees, does he rotate?

(A) 360°

(B) 684°

(C) 720°

(D) 810°

(E) 900°

8. The length, width, and height of a rectangular box is three, four, and five feet respectively. Each length, width, and height is divided by 3, 4, and 5 so that the rectangular box is divided into smaller cubes with sides of 1 foot. If 20 cans of paint are needed to paint the surface area of all smaller cubes, how many square feet can be painted with one can of paint?

(A) 10 square feet

(B) 12 square feet

(C) 14 square feet

(D) 16 square feet

(E) 18 square feet

$E(n)$ = Sum of the first n positive even integers

$O(n)$ = Sum of the first n positive odd integers

9. If $E(n)$ and $O(n)$ are defined above, what is the value of $E(501) - O(500)$?

(A) 250

(B) 500

(C) 1002

(D) 1502

(E) 2002

10. What is the probability that a randomly selected positive factor of 180 is odd?

(A) $\dfrac{1}{6}$

(B) $\dfrac{1}{5}$

(C) $\dfrac{1}{4}$

(D) $\dfrac{1}{3}$

(E) $\dfrac{2}{5}$

11. Let x and y be integers such that $2 \leq x \leq 7$, and $8 \leq y \leq 13$. What is the smallest possible value of $\dfrac{xy}{y - x}$?

(A) $\dfrac{10}{7}$

(B) $\dfrac{8}{3}$

(C) $\dfrac{26}{11}$

(D) $\dfrac{41}{15}$

(E) $\dfrac{71}{20}$

12. At a homecoming party, a group of boys and girls exchange dances. Each boy at the party dances with exactly five girls at the party, and each girl at the party dances with exactly six boys at the party. If there are sixty boys at the party, how many girls are at the party?

(A) 45

(B) 50

(C) 55

(D) 60

(E) 65

$$J, F, M, A, M, J, \cdots$$

13. Which of the following letter is the next term in the sequence above?

(A) J

(B) L

(C) P

(D) R

(E) X

14. If the length of the diagonal of a rectangle is 8, and the area of the rectangle is 18, what is the perimeter of the rectangle?

(A) 18

(B) 20

(C) 22

(D) 24

(E) 26

15. Joshua has 19 coins that consist of only quarters and dimes. If his quarters were dimes and his dimes were quarters, he would have 45 cents less. How much, in cents, are his coins worth?

(A) 325

(B) 340

(C) 355

(D) 370

(E) 385

16. Jason is about to make a sandwich. He has three types of breads: wheat, rye, and sourdough. He has four types of deli meats: ham, chicken, turkey, and pastrami. If Jason chooses one type of bread and any collection of deli meats(no meat is possible), how many different sandwiches can Jason make?

(A) 12

(B) 24

(C) 36

(D) 48

(E) 64

17. Mr. Rhee has three squares with different side lengths. The smallest square can be inscribed in the second largest square, and the second largest square can be inscribed in the largest square. What is the ratio of the area of the largest square to the area of the smallest square?

(A) 3:1

(B) $2\sqrt{2} : 1$

(C) 4:1

(D) $3\sqrt{2} : 1$

(E) 5 : 1

19. Two six-sided fair dice are rolled. What is the probability that the sum of the two numbers on the dice is greater than the product of the two numbers on the dice?

(A) $\dfrac{1}{6}$

(B) $\dfrac{5}{36}$

(C) $\dfrac{1}{4}$

(D) $\dfrac{11}{36}$

(E) $\dfrac{1}{3}$

18. Each point in the grid above has the same probability of being selected. If three distinct points are randomly selected, what is the probability that the three points are on the same line?

(A) $\dfrac{2}{21}$

(B) $\dfrac{5}{42}$

(C) $\dfrac{1}{6}$

(D) $\dfrac{1}{5}$

(E) $\dfrac{1}{4}$

20. The first term, denoted by a_1, of a sequence is 50. Each succeeding term is the sum of squares of the digits of the preceding term. Which of the following is the first term in the sequence less than 10? (a_n is the nth term of the sequence)

(A) a_8

(B) a_9

(C) a_{10}

(D) a_{11}

(E) a_{12}

21. Joshua has a biased coin such that the probabilities of getting a head, and a tail are not the same. If Joshua tosses the coin three times, the probabilities of getting two heads is $\frac{2}{9}$, and that of getting two tails is $\frac{4}{9}$. What would be the probability of getting a head when Joshua tosses the coin once?

(A) $\dfrac{1}{6}$

(B) $\dfrac{1}{5}$

(C) $\dfrac{1}{4}$

(D) $\dfrac{1}{3}$

(E) $\dfrac{2}{5}$

22. Mr. Rhee, Joshua, and Jason paint a house at different rates. When Mr. Rhee and Joshua paint together, they finish the house in $\frac{4}{3}$ days. When Mr. Rhee and Jason paint together, they finish the house in $\frac{3}{2}$ days. When Joshua and Jason paint together, they finish the house in $\frac{12}{5}$ days. If all three paint together, what fractional part of the house would they finish for one day?

(A) $\dfrac{5}{6}$

(B) $\dfrac{11}{12}$

(C) 1

(D) $\dfrac{13}{12}$

(E) $\dfrac{7}{6}$

23. A licence plate in a certain state consists of three digits and three letters, not necessarily distinct. If three digits must appear next to each other, how many different license plates are possible?

(A) 9×26^3

(B) 26×10^3

(C) $10^3 \times 26^3$

(D) $4 \times 10^3 \times 26^3$

(E) $6 \times 10^3 \times 26^3$

$$a_n = \{997, 994, 991, \cdots\}$$
$$b_n = \{10, 14, 18, \cdots\}$$

24. Two sequences a_n and b_n above are arithmetic sequences. The first terms of the sequences are $a_1 = 997$, and $b_1 = 10$. The second terms of the sequences are $a_2 = 994$, and $b_2 = 14$. What is the first term of sequence b_n such that $b_n > a_n$?

(A) b_{139}

(B) b_{140}

(C) b_{141}

(D) b_{142}

(E) b_{143}

$$\nabla(a,b,c) = \frac{a}{\frac{1}{b} + \frac{1}{c}}$$

25. For real numbers a, b, and c, the operator $\nabla(a,b,c)$ is defined above. What is the value of the expression shown below?

$$\nabla(\nabla(6,4,2), \nabla(5,2,2), \nabla(4,3,1))$$

(A) 9

(B) 12

(C) 15

(D) 18

(E) 21

26. A wooden cube with a side length of 4 is painted red on all six faces and then cut into smaller cubes with side length 1. If one smaller cube is randomly selected, what is the probability that the selected smaller cube has at least 1 face painted red?

(A) $\dfrac{2}{3}$

(B) $\dfrac{11}{16}$

(C) $\dfrac{3}{4}$

(D) $\dfrac{13}{16}$

(E) $\dfrac{7}{8}$

27. Let S be the sum of all 4-digit numbers that can be formed by using each of the digits 1, 3, 5, and 7 exactly once. What is the value of $\dfrac{S}{96}$?

(A) 1111

(B) 2222

(C) 3333

(D) 4444

(E) 5555

$$\cfrac{1}{2 + \cfrac{1}{2 + \cfrac{1}{2 + \cdots}}}$$

28. If the expression above simplifies to $a + \sqrt{b}$, what is the value of $a + b$?

(A) 0

(B) 1

(C) 2

(D) 3

(E) 4

Answers and Solutions

TJHSST Math Practice Test 6

Answers

1. B	11. C	21. D
2. B	12. B	22. B
3. E	13. A	23. D
4. B	14. B	24. E
5. E	15. C	25. C
6. E	16. D	26. E
7. B	17. C	27. A
8. E	18. A	28. B
9. D	19. D	
10. D	20. B	

Solutions

1. (B)

   A penny, a nickel, a dime, and a quarter are in a bag. Two coins are selected at random. The table below shows different possible total values if two coins are selected. Define P, N, D, and Q as a penny, a nickel, a dime, and a quarter, respectively.

$P + N$	6 cents
$P + D$	11 cents
$P + Q$	26 cents
$N + D$	15 cents
$N + Q$	30 cents
$D + Q$	35 cents

   Therefore, there are six different possible total values.

2. (B)

   The pattern consists of five different colors: Yellow, Green, Blue, Red, and Black and it is repeated. This means that every fifth shirt is Black. Thus, the $10^{\text{th}}, 15^{\text{th}}, \cdots, 30^{\text{th}}$, and 35th shirts are Black, the 36th shirt is Yellow, and the 37th shirt is Green.

3. (E)

Tips Use the distance formula: distance = speed × time.

Below shows the distance that Mr. Rhee traveled during the different time intervals.

Time	Average Speed	Distance traveled
9 am to 10:30 am	40 miles per hour	40 mph × 1.5 hour = 60 miles
10:30 am to 11:30 am	50 miles per hour	50 mph × 1 hour = 50 miles
11:30 am to 12:30pm	Break	0 mile
12:30 pm to 3:00 pm	60 miles per hour	60 mph × 2.5 hour = 150 miles

Therefore, the total distance that Mr. Rhee traveled between 9 am to 3 pm is $60 + 50 + 150 = 260$ miles.

4. (B)

Let x be the total number of marbles in the bag. There are three red marbles and the probability of selecting a red marble is $\frac{1}{5}$.

$$\text{Probability of selecting a red marble} = \frac{\text{Number of red marbles}}{\text{Total number of marbles}}$$
$$\frac{1}{5} = \frac{3}{x} \qquad \text{Cross multiply}$$
$$x = 15$$

Thus, the total number of marbles in the bag is 15. Therefore, there are $15 - 3 = 12$ non-red marbles in the bag.

5. (E)

Let x be the amount of money that Joshua has in the beginning. If Joshua gives one-fourth of the amount of his money to Jason, Jason has $\frac{x}{4} + 10$ and Joshua has $x - \frac{x}{4} = \frac{3x}{4}$. Since Joshua and Jason have the same amount of money,

$$\frac{3x}{4} = \frac{x}{4} + 10 \qquad \text{Multiply each side by 4}$$
$$3x = x + 40 \qquad \text{Subtract } x \text{ from each side}$$
$$2x = 40 \qquad \text{Divide each side by 2}$$
$$x = 20$$

Therefore, the amount of money that Joshua has in the beginning is $20.

173

6. (E)

There are 60 seconds in one minute. Convert 1 minute and 40 seconds to 100 seconds. Let x be the angle, in degrees, that the ferris wheel rotates for 100 seconds. Since the ferris wheel rotates $360°$ every 40 seconds, set up a proportion in terms of degrees ($°$) and seconds.

$$40_{\text{seconds}} : 360_{\text{degrees}} = 100_{\text{seconds}} : x_{\text{degrees}}$$

$$\frac{40}{360} = \frac{100}{x} \qquad \text{Use cross product property}$$

$$40x = 100(360) \qquad \text{Solve for } x$$

$$x = 900$$

Thus, the ferris wheel rotates $900°$ in one minute and 40 seconds, so does Jason. Therefore, Jason rotates $900°$ in one minute and 40 seconds.

7. (B)

The amount of money in Sue's savings account increases at a constant rate throughout the years. This suggests that a linear function best describes the information in the table. Create two ordered pairs, $(3, 1950)$ and $(5, 2450)$ from the table and find the slope of the linear function, which determines the rate at which the amount of money increases per year.

$$\text{Slope} = \frac{y_2 - y_1}{x_2 - x_1} = \frac{2450 - 1950}{5 - 3} = 250$$

Thus, the linear function can be written as $y = 250x + b$, where x represents the number of years, b represents the initial amount of money that Sue deposited in the beginning, and y represents the total amount of money in the savings account in x years. To find b, substitute 3 for x and 1950 for y.

$$y = 250x + b \qquad \text{Substitute 3 for } x \text{ and 1950 for } y.$$

$$1950 = 250(3) + b \qquad \text{Solve for } b$$

$$b = 1200$$

Therefore, Sue deposited \$1200 in her savings account in the beginning.

8. (E)

In the figure below, each length, width, and height of the rectangular box is divided by 3, 4, and 5, respectively so that there are $3 \times 4 \times 5 = 60$ smaller cubes with sides of 1 foot.

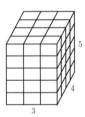

Each smaller cube has six faces. Thus, each has a surface area of 6 square feet. The total surface area of the 60 smaller cubes is $60 \times 6 = 360$ square feet. Since 20 cans of paint is needed to paint 360 square feet, the number of square feet can be painted with one can of paint is $\frac{360}{20} = 18$. Therefore, (E) is the correct answer.

9. (D)

$$E(501) = 2 + 4 + 6 + \cdot + 1000 + 1002$$
$$- O(500) = 1 + 3 + 5 + \cdot + 999$$
$$= 1 + 1 + 1 + \cdots + 1 + 1002$$
$$= 500(1) + 1002$$
$$= 1502$$

Therefore, the value of $E(501) - O(500)$ is 1502.

10. (D)

| Tips | If a prime factorization of a number, n, is $n = 2^a \times 3^b \times 5^c$, the total number of factors of n is $(a+1) \times (b+1) \times (c+1)$. |

The prime factorization of 180 is $2^2 \cdot 3^2 \cdot 5$. Thus, the number of factors of 180 is $3 \cdot 3 \cdot 2 = 18$. Out of 18 factors, there are 6 odd factors: 1, 3, 5, 9, 15, and 45. Therefore, the probability that a randomly selected positive factor of 180 is odd is $\frac{6}{18} = \frac{1}{3}$.

11. (C)

		x	
		2	7
y	8	$\frac{16}{6}$	$\frac{56}{1}$
	13	$\frac{26}{11}$	$\frac{91}{6}$

Therefore, the smallest possible value of $\dfrac{xy}{y-x}$ is $\dfrac{26}{11}$.

12. (B)

There are 60 boys at the party and each boy dances with exactly 5 girls. Thus, the total number of dances at the party is $60 \times 5 = 300$. Since each girl at the party dances with exactly 6 boys,

$$\text{Number of girls at the party} = \frac{\text{Total number of dances}}{6} = \frac{300}{6} = 50$$

the number of girls at the party is 50.

13. (A)

The sequence $J, F, M, A, M, J, \cdots$ consists of the first letter of the names of the months. Since the month after June is July, the next term of the sequence is J.

14. (B)

Tips
$$(x+y)^2 = x^2 + 2xy + y^2$$

Let x and y be the length, the width of the rectangle respectively.

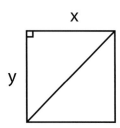

Then, the length of the diagonal of the rectangle is 8 can be written as $\sqrt{x^2 + y^2} = 8$ or $x^2 + y^2 = 64$, and area of the rectangle is 18 can be written as $xy = 18$.

$$\begin{aligned}
(x+y)^2 &= x^2 + 2xy + y^2 \\
&= x^2 + y^2 + 2xy \\
&= 64 + 2(18) \\
&= 100
\end{aligned}$$

Thus, $x + y = 10$ or $x + y = -10$. The perimeter of the rectangle P can be written as $P = 2(x+y)$. Since $P > 0$, $P = 2(x+y) = 2(10) = 20$. Therefore, the perimeter of the rectangle is 20.

15. (C)

Let x and y be the numbers of quarters and dimes, respectively. Joshua has 19 coins can be written as $x + y = 19$, and his coins worth can be written as $25x + 10y$. If his quarters were dimes and his dimes were quarters, his coins worth can be written as $25y + 10x$. Thus, If his quarters were dimes and his dimes were quarters, he would have 45 cents less can be written as $25x + 10y = 25y + 10x + 45$, which simplifies to $x - y = 3$. Set up the system of linear equations and solve for x.

$$\begin{aligned}
x + y &= 19 \\
\underline{x - y = 3} \quad & \qquad \text{Add two equations} \\
2x &= 22 \\
x &= 11
\end{aligned}$$

Thus, $x = 11$ and $y = 8$. Therefore, Joshua's coins are worth $11 \times 25 + 8 \times 10 = 355$ cents.

16. (D)

- The fundamental counting principle: If one event can occur in m ways and another event can occur in n ways, then the number of ways both events can occur is $m \times n$.

- The sum of the entries in the nth row of Pascal's triangle is 2^n.

$$\binom{n}{0} + \binom{n}{1} + \binom{n}{2} + \cdots + \binom{n}{n} = 2^n$$

Let event 1 be selecting the type of bread, and event 2 be selecting any collection of deli meats. For event 1, there are $\binom{3}{1} =$ ways to select the type of bread. For event 2, Jason can select either 0, 1, 2, 3, or 4 deli meats. This can be calculated as follows:

$$\binom{4}{0} + \binom{4}{1} + \binom{4}{2} + \binom{4}{3} + \binom{4}{4} = 2^4 = 16$$

Thus, event 1 has 3 outcomes and event 2 has 16 outcomes. According to the fundamental counting principle, Jason can make $3 \times 16 = 48$ different sandwiches.

17. (C)

If a smaller square is inscribed inside a larger square, the area of the smaller square is half the area of the larger square.

For simplicity, let the area of the largest square be 100. Then, the area of the second largest square which is inscribed inside the largest square is 50, and the area of the smallest square which is inscribed inside the second largest square is 25. Therefore, the ratio of the area of the largest square to the area of the smallest square is $100 : 25$ or $4 : 1$.

18. (A)

Out of 9 points, the 3 points are randomly selected. So there are $\binom{9}{3} = 84$ ways of selecting the three points.

There are 8 ways to draw a line that contains the three points as shown above. Therefore, the probability that the three points are on the same line is $\frac{8}{84} = \frac{2}{21}$.

19. (D)

		\multicolumn{6}{c}{2nd die}

		1	2	3	4	5	6
1st die	1	○	○	○	○	○	○
	2	○					
	3	○					
	4	○					
	5	○					
	6	○					

There are 11 outcomes for which the sum of the two numbers is greater than the product of the two numbers. They are represented by circles in the table above. Therefore, the probability that the sum of the two numbers on the dice is greater than the product of the two numbers on the dice is $\frac{11}{36}$.

20. (B)

Each succeeding term is the sum of squares of the digits of the preceding term. The second term, a_2, and the third terms, a_3, are as follows:

$$a_2 = 5^2 + 0^2 = 25$$
$$a_3 = 2^2 + 5^2 = 29$$

Thus,

a_n	a_1	a_2	a_3	a_4	a_5	a_6	a_7	a_8	a_9
Value	50	25	29	85	89	145	42	20	4

Therefore, the 9th term, a_9, is less than 10.

21. (D)

Let n be the probability of getting a head when Joshua tosses a biased coin once. Thus, $1 - n$ becomes the probability of getting a tail when Joshua tosses a biased coin once. The probabilities of getting two heads is $\frac{2}{9}$, and that of getting two tails is $\frac{4}{9}$ when Joshua tosses the coin three times can be written as follows:

$$P(2T) = \binom{3}{2}(1 - n)^2 \cdot n = \frac{4}{9} \tag{1}$$

$$P(2H) = \binom{3}{2}n^2 \cdot (1 - n) = \frac{2}{9} \tag{2}$$

Dividing equation (1) by equation (2) gives

$$\frac{\binom{3}{2}(1 - n)^2 \cdot n}{\binom{3}{2}n^2 \cdot (1 - n)} = \frac{\frac{4}{9}}{\frac{2}{9}}$$

$$\frac{1 - n}{n} = 2$$

$$1 - n = 2n$$

$$3n = 1$$

$$n = \frac{1}{3}$$

Therefore, the probability of getting a head when Joshua tosses the coin once is $\frac{1}{3}$.

22. (B)

Mr. Rhee, Joshua, and Jason paint a house at different rates. When Mr. Rhee and Joshua paint together for one day, they finish $\frac{3}{4}$ of the house. When Mr. Rhee and Jason paint together for one day, they finish $\frac{2}{3}$ of the house. When Joshua and Jason paint together for one day, they finish $\frac{5}{12}$ of the house. Let x, y, z be the fractions of the house that Mr. Rhee, Joshua, and Jason can finish in one day, respectively. Thus,

$$x + y = \frac{3}{4}$$
$$x + z = \frac{2}{3}$$
$$y + z = \frac{5}{12}$$

Adding three equations gives $2(x + y + z) = \frac{22}{12}$ or $x + y + z = \frac{11}{12}$. Therefore, if all three paint together, they finish $\frac{11}{12}$ of house for one day.

23. (D)

There are 10^3 ways to choose three digits and 26^3 ways to choose three letters. Since the three digits must appear next to each other, there are 4 possible locations for the three digits out of 6 blanks. Therefore, the number of different possible license plates is $4 \times 10^3 \times 26^3$.

179

24. (E)

> **Tips** The nth term of the arithmetic sequence is $a_n = a_1 + (n-1)d$, where a_1 is the first term and d is the common difference.

The nth terms of the sequences a_n and b_n are as follows:

$$a_n = 997 + (n-1)(-3) = -3n + 1000$$
$$b_n = 10 + (n-1)4 = 4n + 6$$

Let's find out which terms of the sequences have the same values.

$$4n + 6 = -3n + 1000$$
$$7n = 994$$
$$n = 142$$

Thus, the 142th terms of the sequences are the same. In order words, $b_{142} = a_{142}$. Therefore, the first term of sequence b_n such that $b_n > a_n$ is the 143th term.

25. (C)

Let's simplify $\nabla(a, b, c)$.

$$\nabla(a, b, c) = \frac{a}{\frac{1}{b} + \frac{1}{c}} = \frac{a}{\frac{b+c}{bc}} = \frac{abc}{b+c}$$

Thus,

$$\nabla(6, 4, 2) = \frac{6 \cdot 4 \cdot 2}{4 + 2} = 8, \qquad \nabla(5, 2, 2) = \frac{5 \cdot 2 \cdot 2}{2 + 2} = 5, \qquad \nabla(4, 3, 1) = \frac{4 \cdot 3 \cdot 1}{3 + 1} = 3$$

Therefore,

$$\nabla(\nabla(6, 4, 2), \nabla(5, 2, 2), \nabla(4, 3, 1)) = \nabla(8, 5, 3) = \frac{8 \cdot 5 \cdot 3}{5 + 3} = 15$$

26. (E)

> **Tips** $\text{Prob(At least 1 red face)} = 1 - \text{Prob(Unpainted)}$

A wooden cube with side length 4 is painted red on all six faces and then cut into $4^3 = 64$ smaller cubes with side length 1. The number of unpainted smaller cubes is $2^3 = 8$. Thus,

$$\text{Prob(At least 1 red face)} = 1 - \text{Prob(Unpainted)}$$
$$= 1 - \frac{8}{64}$$
$$= \frac{7}{8}$$

Therefore, the probability that the selected smaller cube has at least 1 face painted red is $\frac{7}{8}$.

27. (A)

There are $4! = 24$ 4-digits numbers if you use each of the digits 1, 3, 5, and 7 exactly once. Let's find out the sum of the digits in one's place of the 24 numbers. Each of the digits 1, 3, 5, and 7 are used exactly 6 times. Thus, the sum of the digits in one's place of the 24 numbers is $6(1+3+5+7) = 96$. The table below shows the sum of the values in thousands, hundreds, tens, and one's place of the 24 numbers.

Place	Thousands	Hundreds	tens	One's
Sum	96000	9600	960	96

The sum of the 24 number is $S = 96(1000 + 100 + 10 + 1)$ or $S = 96(1111)$. Therefore, the value of $\frac{S}{96}$ is $\frac{96(1111)}{96} = 1111$.

28. (B)

Let x be the expression. Then,

$$x = \cfrac{1}{2 + \cfrac{1}{2 + \cfrac{1}{2 + \cdots}}}$$

$$x = \frac{1}{2 + x}$$

$$x(2 + x) = 1$$

$$x^2 + 2x - 1 = 0$$

Solving $x^2 + 2x - 1$ using the quadratic formula gives $x = -1 \pm \sqrt{2}$. Since $x > 0$, the only solution is $-1 + \sqrt{2}$. Thus, $a = -1$ and $b = 2$. Therefore, the value of $a + b = 1$.

TJHSST PRACTICE MATH TEST 7

Time — 50 minutes

Number of questions — 28

Directions: Solve each of the following problems using the available space for scratch work. Choose the best answer among the answer choices given and fill in the corresponding circle on the answer sheet.

1. If $0.2 < \dfrac{1}{x} < 0.5$, how many positive integer values of x are possible?

   (A) 5

   (B) 4

   (C) 3

   (D) 2

   (E) 1

2. One yard of wire is divided into two pieces. If the length of the shorter piece is $\frac{4}{5}$ of the length of the longer piece, what is the length of the longer piece in inches?

   (A) 16 inches

   (B) 18 inches

   (C) 20 inches

   (D) 22 inches

   (E) 24 inches

3. The price of a pen is \$3.60 in November and is increased by 100% in December. What is the price of the pen in December?

   (A) \$7.20

   (B) \$6.60

   (C) \$6.00

   (D) \$5.40

   (E) \$4.80

4. A ladder of 10 feet is leaning against the wall so that the bottom of the ladder is 6 feet away from the wall. If the top of the ladder starts sliding down the wall 1 foot per second, how far away is the bottom of the ladder from the wall after 2 seconds?

   (A) 8 feet

   (B) 7 feet

   (C) 6 feet

   (D) 5 feet

   (E) 4 feet

$$3, 4, 5, 6, 0, 1, 2, 3, 4, \cdots$$

5. The numbers above show the remainders when consecutive integers are divided by an integer, n. What is the value of n ?

(A) 3

(B) 4

(C) 5

(D) 6

(E) 7

$$\frac{x+4}{3} + \frac{y+5}{3} + \frac{z+6}{3}$$

6. In the expression above, x, y, and z represent the measures of the interior angles of a triangle. What is the value of the expression above?

(A) 65°

(B) 70°

(C) 75°

(D) 80°

(E) 85°

7. Mr. Rhee traveled 90 miles at 60 miles per hour to visit his parents. On the way home, he was caught in heavy traffic so that the average speed for the entire trip was 45 miles per hour. How fast did Mr. Rhee travel on the way home in miles per hour?

(A) 44 miles per hour

(B) 40 miles per hour

(C) 36 miles per hour

(D) 32 miles per hour

(E) 28 miles per hour

8. Joshua buys a package of three oranges for $2 and sells a package of two oranges for $3. If Joshua wants to make a profit of $50, how many oranges does he need to sell?

(A) 40

(B) 50

(C) 60

(D) 70

(E) 80

$$3, 3, 5, 4, 4, \cdots$$

9. Which of the following is the next term in the sequence above?

(A) 2

(B) 3

(C) 4

(D) 5

(E) 6

$$S = 2 - 1 + 4 - 3 + 6 - 5 + \cdots + 500 - 499$$

11. If the pattern shown above continues, what is the value of S ?

(A) 175

(B) 200

(C) 225

(D) 250

(E) 275

10. Sue rented a car for two days. She paid the rental company a fixed daily fee plus an hourly charge for driving time. On the first day, she paid $89. On the second day, she drove the car twice as much as she did on the first day. So, she paid $139 on the second day. What is the fixed daily fee?

(A) $79

(B) $69

(C) $59

(D) $49

(E) $39

12. A wallet contains 3 one-dollar bills and 3 five-dollar bills. If two bills are drawn at random without replacement, what is the probability that their sum is $6 or more?

(A) $\dfrac{3}{7}$

(B) $\dfrac{1}{2}$

(C) $\dfrac{2}{3}$

(D) $\dfrac{3}{4}$

(E) $\dfrac{4}{5}$

13. On a certain exam, 15% of the students received 80 points, 20% received 85 points, 25% received 90 points, and the rest received 75 points. What is the difference between the mean and the mode of the scores on this exam?

    (A) 7.5

    (B) 6.5

    (C) 4.5

    (D) 3.5

    (E) 1.5

15. 51 numbers are selected from the integers between 1 and 100 inclusive. What is the probability that 2 of the selected numbers are consecutive?

    (A) $\dfrac{1}{3}$

    (B) $\dfrac{3}{5}$

    (C) $\dfrac{2}{3}$

    (D) $\dfrac{5}{7}$

    (E) 1

$$T = \{ D, \quad B, \quad R, \quad G\}$$

14. Set T has four elements. Which of the following is the most similar to the elements in set T ?

    (A) E

    (B) O

    (C) P

    (D) V

    (E) Z

16. The quadratic equation $8x^2 - 2x - 1 = 0$ has roots that are the reciprocals of the roots of $x^2 + ax - b = 0$. Which of the following is the value of $a + b$?

    (A) 7

    (B) 8

    (C) 9

    (D) 10

    (E) 11

17. How many sets of two or more consecutive positive integers have a sum of 21?

   (A) 2

   (B) 3

   (C) 4

   (D) 5

   (E) 6

$$2f(x) - 3f(-x) = 13$$
$$2f(-x) - 3f(x) = -17$$

18. For real numbers $f(x)$ and $f(-x)$, two equations are defined above. What is the value of $f(x) + f(-x)$?

   (A) 4

   (B) 8

   (C) 12

   (D) 16

   (E) 20

19. A train m meters long, traveling at a constant speed, passes two tunnels. The train takes 10 seconds to pass the first tunnel which is 200 meters long from the moment the front enters the tunnel to the moment the rear leaves it. In addition, the train takes 15 seconds to pass the second tunnel which is 350 meters long. What is the length of the train in meters?

   (A) 75 meters

   (B) 100 meters

   (C) 125 meters

   (D) 150 meters

   (E) 200 meters

20. The first term of a geometric sequence is 3. The product of the first three terms of the sequence is N, and the product of the next three terms of the sequence is $512N$. What is the second term of the sequence?

   (A) 3

   (B) 6

   (C) 9

   (D) 12

   (E) 15

21. Let m and n be two-digit numbers such that n is obtained by reversing the digits of m, and $m > n$. Which of the following integer must divide $m^2 - n^2$?

    (A)   81

    (B)   88

    (C)   92

    (D)   99

    (E)   108

22. For real numbers x, y, and z, the product of x and y is 6, the product of y and z is 10. If $x + z = 4$, what is the product of x, y, and z ?

    (A)   10

    (B)   12

    (C)   15

    (D)   24

    (E)   30

23. A book has a certain number of pages. If 1203 digits are used to number the pages of the book consecutively from page 1, how many pages does the book have?

    (A)   355 pages

    (B)   377 pages

    (C)   399 pages

    (D)   415 pages

    (E)   437 pages

24. In a certain high school, a student ID number consists of two letters followed by three distinct digits. The three digits are distinct and in increasing order. None of the three digits is either 0, 1, 2 or, 3. How many different student ID numbers are possible?

    (A) $26^2 + 20$

    (B) $26^2 + 35$

    (C) $26^2 \cdot 20$

    (D) $26^2 \cdot 35$

    (E) $26^2 \cdot 120$

$$\frac{2(n-1)!}{n+1} = k, \quad \text{where } k \text{ is an integer}$$

25. For a positive integer n less than or equal to 13, how many possible values of n satisfy the equation above?

    (A) 5

    (B) 6

    (C) 8

    (D) 10

    (E) 11

26. Joshua and Jason each have a bag that contains 1 black marble, 1 red marble, 1 green marble, and 1 blue marble. They want to exchange one marble from their bags. First, Joshua randomly selects one marble from his bag and puts it into Jason's bag. Next, Jason randomly selects one marble from his bag and puts it into Joshua's bag. What is the probability that the two bags have the same contents after Joshua and Jason exchange one marble?

    (A) $\frac{1}{4}$

    (B) $\frac{2}{5}$

    (C) $\frac{1}{3}$

    (D) $\frac{3}{7}$

    (E) $\frac{1}{2}$

27. How many three-digit positive integers greater than or equal to 100 have at least one digit that is a multiple of 3?

    (A) 452

    (B) 552

    (C) 557

    (D) 606

    (E) 706

28. A palindrome is a number that reads the same backward as forward. For instance, the number 747 is a 3-digit palindrome. What is the sum of all 3-digit palindromes?

    (A) 48500

    (B) 49500

    (C) 50500

    (D) 51500

    (E) 52500

Answers and Solutions
TJHSST Math Practice Test 7

Answers

1. D	11. D	21. D
2. C	12. E	22. C
3. A	13. B	23. E
4. A	14. C	24. C
5. E	15. E	25. C
6. A	16. D	26. B
7. C	17. B	27. D
8. C	18. A	28. B
9. B	19. B	
10. E	20. B	

Solutions

1. (D)

> **Tips** The inequality symbol is reversed when taking the reciprocal of each side of the inequality.

$$0.2 < \frac{1}{x} < 0.5 \qquad \text{Take the reciprocal of each side}$$

$$\frac{1}{0.2} > x > \frac{1}{0.5} \qquad \text{Inequality symbol is reversed}$$

$$2 < x < 5$$

Since x is a positive integer, the possible values of x for which $2 < x < 5$ is 3 and 4. Therefore, there are two possible integer values of x.

2. (C)

There are 12 inches in one foot and 3 feet in one yard. Thus, there are 36 inches in one yard. Let $5x$ be the length of the longer piece. Since the length of the shorter piece is $\frac{4}{5}$ of the longer piece, the length of the shorter piece can be expressed as $\frac{4}{5} \times 5x = 4x$.

$$4x + 5x = 36 \qquad \text{Simplify}$$

$$9x = 36 \qquad \text{Divide each side by 9}$$

$$x = 4$$

Therefore, the length of the longer piece is $5x = 5(4) = 20$.

3. (A)
The price of the pen is increased by 100%, which means that the price of the pen is doubled. Therefore, the price of the pen in December is $2 \times \$3.60 = \$7.20$.

4. (A)
The length of the ladder is 10 feet. Although the top and bottom of the ladder are sliding down and sliding away, the length of the ladder remains the same. When the bottom of the ladder is 6 feet away from the wall, the top of the ladder is 8 feet above the ground as shown in the diagram below. Use the Pythagorean theorem: $10^2 = a^2 + 6^2$, where a is the height of the wall at which the top of the ladder leans against. Thus, $a = 8$.

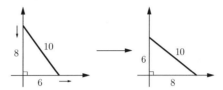

The top of the ladder is sliding down for 2 seconds at a rate of 1 foot per second so it is $8 - 2 = 6$ feet above the ground. To determine the distance between the bottom of the ladder and the wall, b, use the Pythagorean theorem: $10^2 = 6^2 + b^2$. Thus, $b = 8$. Therefore, the bottom of the ladder is 8 feet away from the wall after 2 seconds.

5. (E)

> **Tips** If a number is divided by an integer n, the possible values of the remainder are $0, 1, 2, \cdots, n-1$.

The possible values of the remainder are 0, 1, 2, 3, 4, 5, and 6. This implies that the consecutive integers are divided by 7.

6. (A)
Since x, y, and z represent the measures of the interior angles of a triangle, the sum of the measures of the interior angles expressed as $x + y + z$ is $180°$. Thus,

$$\frac{x+4}{3} + \frac{y+5}{3} + \frac{z+6}{3} = \frac{x+y+z+15}{3} \qquad \text{Substitute 180 for } x+y+z$$

$$= \frac{180+15}{3}$$

$$= 65$$

Therefore, the value of the expression is $65°$.

7. (C)
Mr. Rhee traveled 90 miles at 60 miles per hour to visit his parents. It took him $\frac{90\,\text{miles}}{60\text{mph}}$ or 1.5 hours to drive to his parents's house. The total distance for the entire trip is 2×90 miles or 180 miles. Since the average speed for the entire trip is 45 miles per hour, the total time for the entire trip is $\frac{180\,\text{miles}}{45\text{mph}}$ or 4 hours. This implies that it took Mr. Rhee $4 - 1.5 = 2.5$ hours to drive back to his home. Therefore, the rate at which Mr. Rhee traveled on the way home is $\frac{90\,\text{miles}}{2.5\,\text{hours}}$ or 36 miles per hour.

8. (C)

It's easier to calculate the profit if the number of oranges that Joshua buys and sells is the same. Since Joshua buys a package of 3 oranges and sells a package of 2 oranges, the least common multiple (LCM) of 3 and 2 is 6. This means that if Joshua buys 6 oranges for $2 \times \$2 = \$4$ and sells 6 oranges for $3 \times \$3 = \$9$, he makes $\$9 - \$4 = \$5$ profit for every 6 oranges that he sells. Therefore, the number of oranges that Joshua needs to sell to make a profit of $50 is 10×6 or 60.

9. (B)

1 is spelled as one which has 3 letters. 2 is spelled as two which has 3 letters. 3 is spelled as three which has 5 letters. 4 is spelled as four which has 4 letters. 5 is spelled as five which has 4 letters. The next term in the sequence is 6 which is spelled as six and has 3 letters.

10. (E)

Let x be the fixed daily fee and y be the total hourly charge on the first day. Sue paid $89 which includes the fixed daily fee and the total hourly charge on the first day. This can be expressed as $x + y = 89$. On the second day, she drove the car twice as much as she did on the first day and paid $139, which can be expressed as $x + 2y = 139$. Use the linear combinations method to solve for y.

$$x + 2y = 139$$
$$\underline{x + y = 89} \qquad \text{Subtract two equations}$$
$$y = 50$$

Since $y = 50$ and $x + y = 89$, $x = 39$. Therefore, the fixed daily fee, x, is $39.

11. (D)

Group 2 numbers to make a pair as shown below.

$$S = 2 - 1 + 4 - 3 + 6 - 5 + \cdots + 500 - 490$$
$$= (2 - 1) + (4 - 3) + (6 - 5) + \cdots + (500 - 490)$$
$$= 1 + 1 + 1 + \cdots + 1$$
$$= 250$$

The sum of each pair is 1. Since there are 250 pairs, the sum of the 250 pairs is 250. Therefore, the value of S is 250.

12. (E)

There are 36 possible outcomes which are shown in the table below.

	1	1	1	5	5	5
1	X			O	O	O
1		X		O	O	O
1			X	O	O	O
5	O	O	O	X	O	O
5	O	O	O	O	X	O
5	O	O	O	O	O	X

Since two bills are drawn at random without replacement, eliminate 6 outcomes which are represented by X. Thus, the total number of outcomes is $36 - 6 = 30$. Out of 30 outcomes, 24 outcomes, represented by $\bigcirc$, show that their sum is \$6 or more. Therefore, the probability that their sum is \$6 or more is $\frac{24}{30}$ or $\frac{4}{5}$.

13. (B)

> **Tips** Mode is the number that is shown most frequently.

Assume that 100 students took the exam. Then the distribution of the scores is as follows:

Points received	75	80	85	90
Number of students	40	15	20	25

$$\text{Mean} = \frac{40(75) + 15(80) + 20(85) + 25(90)}{100} = \frac{8150}{100} = 81.5$$

Since 40 students received 75 points, the mode of the scores is 75. Therefore, the difference between the mean and the mode of the scores on this exam is $81.5 - 75 = 6.5$.

14. (C)

Set T consists of the four alphabet letters with straight line segment(s) and curve(s). Since the letter P consists of a straight line segment and a curve, P is the most similar to the elements in set T.

15. (E)

Assume that you selected 50 odd integers from the integers between 1 and 100 inclusive. At this moment, none of the selected numbers were consecutive yet. However, if you select the 51th integer, the number will be an even integer and will pair up with one of the 50 selected odd integers. Therefore, the probability that 2 of the selected numbers are consecutive is 100% or 1.

16. (D)

$8x^2 - 2x - 1 = 0$ or $(2x-1)(4x+1) = 0$ has two roots: $\frac{1}{2}$ and $-\frac{1}{4}$. Thus, the reciprocals of the roots are 2 and -4. The quadratic equation that has roots 2 and -4 can be written as $(x-2)(x+4) = 0$ or $x^2 + 2x - 8 = 0$. Thus, $a = 2$ and $b = 8$. Therefore, the value of $a + b = 10$.

17. (B)

Number of consecutive positive integers	Sum
2	$10 + 11 = 21$
3	$6 + 7 + 8 = 21$
4	$4 + 5 + 6 + 7 = 22$
5	$2 + 3 + 4 + 5 + 6 = 20$
6	$1 + 2 + 3 + 4 + 5 + 6 = 21$

Therefore, there are 3 sets of two or more consecutive positive integers which have a sum of 21.

18. (A)

First, let's arrange $f(x)$ and $f(-x)$ in the equations.

$$2f(x) - 3f(-x) = 13$$
$$-3f(x) + 2f(-x) = -17$$

Let p and q be $f(x)$ and $f(-x)$, respectively, and rewrite the equations in terms of p and q.

$$2p - 3q = 13 \xrightarrow{\text{Multiply by 3}} 6p - 9q = 39$$
$$-3p + 2q = -17 \xrightarrow{\text{Multiply by 2}} -6p + 4q = -34$$

Use the linear combinations method.

$$6p - 9q = 39$$
$$\underline{-6p + 4q = -34} \qquad \text{Add two equations}$$
$$-5q = 5$$
$$q = -1$$

$q = -1$ and $6p - 9q = 39$ gives $p = 5$. Thus, $p = f(x) = 5$, and $q = f(-x) = -1$. Therefore, the value of $f(x) + f(-x) = 4$.

194

19. (B)

The train takes 10 seconds to pass the first tunnel which is 200 meters long, and 15 seconds to pass the second tunnel which is 350 meters long. The train takes 5 additional seconds to travel $350 - 200 = 150$ meters more. It means that the speed of the train is $\frac{150}{5} = 30$ m/s. The train takes 10 seconds to pass the first tunnel 200 meters long from the moment the front enters the tunnel to the moment the rear leaves it, which means that the distance that the train travel for 10 seconds is $m + 200$ meters.

$$\text{Time} = \frac{\text{Distance}}{\text{Speed}}$$
$$10 = \frac{m + 200}{30}$$
$$m + 200 = 300$$
$$m = 100$$

Therefore, the length of the train is 100 meters.

20. (B)

> **Tips**   The nth term of a geometric sequence is $a_n = a_1 \cdot r^{n-1}$, where a_1 is the first term, and r is the common ratio.

Let a be the first term, and r be the common ratio of the geometric sequence.

a_n	a_1	a_2	a_3	a_4	a_5	a_6
Value	a	ar	ar^2	ar^3	ar^4	ar^5

Thus,

$$\text{Product of the first three terms} = a \cdot ar \cdot ar^2 = a^3 r^3 = N \qquad (3)$$
$$\text{Product of the next three terms} = ar^3 \cdot ar^4 \cdot ar^5 = a^3 r^{12} = 512N \qquad (4)$$

Dividing equation (2) by equation (1) gives

$$\frac{a^3 r^{12}}{a^3 r^3} = \frac{512N}{N}$$
$$r^9 = 512$$
$$r^9 = 2^9$$
$$r = 2$$

the common ratio of the sequence r, which is $r = 2$. Therefore, the second term of the sequence, ar, is $ar = 3 \cdot 2 = 6$.

21. (D)

> **Tips** $\qquad\qquad x^2 - y^2 = (x+y)(x-y)$

Let $m = pq$, where p is the tens digit, and q is the units digit. Thus, the value of m is $10p + q$, and the value of $n = 10q + p$.

$$
\begin{aligned}
m^2 - n^2 &= (m+n)(m-n) \\
&= (10p + q + 10q + p)(10p + q - (10q + p)) \\
&= (11p + 11q)(9p - 9q) \\
&= 11(p+q) \cdot 9(p-q) \\
&= 11 \cdot 9 \cdot (p+q)(p-q) \\
&= 99(p+q)(p-q)
\end{aligned}
$$

$m^2 - n^2$ can be written as $99(p+q)(p-q)$. Therefore, 99 must divide $m^2 - n^2$.

22. (C)

The product of x and y is 6, the product of y and z is 10 can be written as $xy = 6$ and $yz = 10$. Add two terms xy and yz, and then factor y out.

$$
\begin{aligned}
xy + yz &= y(x+z) \\
6 + 10 &= y(4) \\
y &= 4
\end{aligned}
$$

$y = 4$, $xy = 6$, and $x + z = 4$ give $x = \frac{3}{2}$ and $z = \frac{5}{2}$. Therefore, the product of x, y, and z is $\frac{3}{2} \cdot 4 \cdot \frac{5}{2} = 15$.

23. (E)

Let x be the total number of pages of the book. In order to number the pages of the book consecutively from page 1, following number of digits are used.

Page number	Number of digits used
$1 \sim 9$	$9(1) = 9$
$10 \sim 99$	$90(2) = 180$
$100 \sim x$	$(x - 100 + 1)(3)$

Since 1203 digits are used to number the pages of the book consecutively from page 1,

$$
\begin{aligned}
9 + 180 + (x - 100 + 1)(3) &= 1203 \\
(x - 99)(3) &= 1014 \\
x - 99 &= 338 \\
x &= 437
\end{aligned}
$$

Therefore, the total number of pages of the book is 437.

24. (C)

Let event 1 be selecting two letters and event 2 be selecting 3 digits. There are 26×26 or 26^2 ways to select two letters. None of the three digits is either 0, 1, 2 or 3. Thus, 6 digits are possible to select: 4, 5, 6, 7, 8, and 9. Out of 6 possible digits, you select 3 digits and put them in increasing order. Thus, there are $\binom{6}{3} = 20$ ways to select the three digits. According to the fundamental counting principle, event 1 has 26^2 outcomes, and event 2 has 20 outcomes. Therefore, the total number of different possible student ID numbers is $26^2 \cdot 20$.

25. (C)

The table below shows what values of n satisfy the equation $\dfrac{2(n-1)!}{n+1} = k$, where k is an integer.

n	1	2	3	4	5	6	7	8	9	10	11	12	13
$\frac{2(n-1)!}{n+1}$	◯	X	◯	X	◯	X	◯	◯	◯	X	◯	X	◯

◯ means that n satisfies the equation $\dfrac{2(n-1)!}{n+1} = k$, and X means that n does not satisfy the equation. Therefore, there are 8 possible values of n that satisfy the equation $\dfrac{2(n-1)!}{n+1} = k$.

26. (B)

In order for two bags to have the same contents after Joshua and Jason exchange one marble, Joshua and Jason each must select one marble of the same color. Let's consider the following case: Joshua and Jason each select a black marble.

The probability that Joshua selects a black marble is $\frac{1}{4}$. After Joshua puts a black marble into Jason's bag, Jason has 2 black marbles, 1 red marble, 1 green marble, and 1 blue marble. So the probability that Jason selects a black marble is $\frac{2}{5}$. Thus, the probability that Joshua and Jason each select a black marble is $\frac{1}{4} \times \frac{2}{5} = \frac{1}{10}$. Since Joshua and Jason can select either a black marble, a red marble, a green marble, or a blue marble, the probability that the two bags have the same contents after Joshua and Jason exchange one marble is $4 \times \frac{1}{10} = \frac{2}{5}$.

27. (D)

The total number of three-digit positive integers is $9 \times 10 \times 10 = 900$. The Multiple of 3 among the digits 0 through 9 are 3, 6, and 9 . Let's count the number of three-digit positive integers that do **NOT** have at least one digit which is a multiple of 3.

	Hundreds place	Tens place	Units place
Number of possible digits	6 (can't be 0, 3, 6, 9)	7 (can't be 3, 6, 9)	7 (can't be 3, 6, 9)

Thus, the number of three-digit positive integers that do **NOT** have at least one digit which is a multiple of 3 is $6 \times 7 \times 7 = 294$. Therefore, the total number of three-digit positive integers greater than or equal to 100 that have at least one digit which is a multiple of 3 is $900 - 294 = 606$.

28. (B)

Event 1 is selecting a digit for hundreds and units digit, and event 2 is selecting a digit for tens digit. Event 1 has 9 ways$(1, 2, \cdots, 9)$ and event 2 has 10 ways$(0, 1, \cdots, 9)$. According to the fundamental counting principle, there are $9 \times 10 = 90$ 3-digit palindromes.

The sum of 90 3-digit palindromes can be written as

$$\text{Sum of all 3-digit palindromes} = 101 + 111 + 121 + \cdots + 979 + 989 + 999$$

If you pair the 1st and 90th palindromes, the 2nd and 89th palindromes, the 3rd and 87th palindromes, and keep pair the palindromes in this manner, the sum of each pair is 1100 as shown below.

$$
\begin{aligned}
\text{Sum of all 3-digit palindromes} &= 101 + 111 + 121 + \cdots + 979 + 989 + 999 \\
&= (101 + 999) + (111 + 989) + (121 + 979) + \cdots + (545 + 555) \\
&= 1100 + 1100 + \cdots + 1100 \\
&= 1100 \times 45 \\
&= 49500
\end{aligned}
$$

Since there are 45 pairs and the sum of each pair is 1100, the sum of all 90 3-digit palindromes is $45 \times 1100 = 49500$.

TJHSST PRACTICE MATH TEST 8
Time — 50 minutes
Number of questions — 28

Directions: Solve each of the following problems using the available space for scratch work. Choose the best answer among the answer choices given and fill in the corresponding circle on the answer sheet.

1. Mr. Rhee went on a diet. If his weight was 180 pounds in August and 150 pounds in September, what percent of his weight did he lose?

    (A) $16\frac{2}{3}\%$

    (B) $33\frac{1}{3}\%$

    (C) 20%

    (D) 25%

    (E) 30%

2. There are two cubes. If the ratio of the volume of the smaller cube to that of the larger cube is 27 to 64, what is the ratio of the surface area of the smaller cube to that of the larger cube?

    (A) $2:3$

    (B) $3:4$

    (C) $9:16$

    (D) $16:9$

    (E) $27:64$

3. Using only the three digits, 1, 2, and 3, three-digit numbers are formed. If all the digits are used once, what is the probability that the three-digit numbers formed are divisible by 2?

    (A) $\dfrac{1}{2}$

    (B) $\dfrac{1}{3}$

    (C) $\dfrac{1}{4}$

    (D) $\dfrac{1}{5}$

    (E) $\dfrac{1}{6}$

4. If $\left(\dfrac{1}{9}\right)^{x} = 4$, what is the value of 3^{x} ?

    (A) 3

    (B) 2

    (C) $\dfrac{1}{3}$

    (D) $\dfrac{1}{2}$

    (E) $\dfrac{4}{9}$

5. Joshua filled a cup with equal amounts of orange juice, apple juice, and grape juice and mixed it well. He drank half of the cup and then only filled the cup with equal amounts of orange juice and apple juice. What fractional part of the cup was filled with the apple juice?

   (A) $\dfrac{5}{12}$

   (B) $\dfrac{1}{3}$

   (C) $\dfrac{1}{4}$

   (D) $\dfrac{1}{6}$

   (E) $\dfrac{1}{12}$

6. Jason spent one-third of the money in his savings account on books. A few days later, he spent half of the remaining money in his savings account on clothes. If Jason then had $175 left, how much money was in his savings account in the beginning?

   (A) $225

   (B) $375

   (C) $525

   (D) $675

   (E) $825

7. Five different points, A, B, E, C, and D, lie on the same line in that order. The two points B and C trisect the segment $\overline{AD}$ whose length is 36. Point E is the midpoint of the segment $\overline{BC}$. What is the length of the segment $\overline{DE}$?

   (A) 18

   (B) 20

   (C) 22

   (D) 24

   (E) 26

8. Six people who work at the same rate painted half of a house in 4 days. How many additional people are needed to paint the remaining part of the house in 3 days?

   (A) 6

   (B) 5

   (C) 4

   (D) 3

   (E) 2

9. Joshua has m liters of a 10% acid solution, and n liters of a 30% acid solution. If he mixes these solutions up, he will make 100 liters of a 15% acid solution. What is the value of $m - n$?

(A) 5

(B) 20

(C) 35

(D) 50

(E) 65

$$0, 4, 8, 12, \cdots, 992$$

11. In the sequence above, what term of the sequence is 992? (a_n is the nth term of the sequence)

(A) a_{247}

(B) a_{248}

(C) a_{249}

(D) a_{250}

(E) a_{251}

$$S_1 = \frac{1}{2}$$
$$S_2 = \frac{1}{2} + \frac{1}{4}$$
$$\vdots$$
$$S_n = \frac{1}{2} + \frac{1}{4} + \frac{1}{8} + \cdots + \frac{1}{2^n}$$

10. S_n is defined as the sum of n fraction(s) as shown above. If n is very large, what value does S_n approach?

(A) 1

(B) $\frac{3}{2}$

(C) 2

(D) $\frac{5}{2}$

(E) 3

12. How many ways can ten people sit around a circular table?

(A) $2 \times 8!$

(B) $9!$

(C) $2 \times 9!$

(D) $10!$

(E) $2 \times 10!$

13. What is the units digit of $7^{1002} - 2^{1002}$?

(A) 2

(B) 3

(C) 4

(D) 5

(E) 7

$$B, Z, C, Y, D, X, \cdots$$

14. Which of the following letter is the next term in the sequence above?

(A) A

(B) E

(C) H

(D) Q

(E) W

15. If a 9-digit number 100001000 is divided by 9, what is the remainder?

(A) 1

(B) 2

(C) 3

(D) 5

(E) 6

16. If the lines $y = 2x + a$ and $y = -\frac{1}{2}x + b$ intersect at the point $(t, t + 1)$, what is the value of $3a + 2b$?

(A) 1

(B) 2

(C) 3

(D) 4

(E) 5

$a_n = a_{n-1} + a_{n-2}$, for $n \geq 3$, $a_1 = 1$, $a_2 = 2$
$b_n = b_{n-1} + b_{n-2}$, for $n \geq 3$, $b_1 = 1$, $b_2 = 1$

17. If the sequences a_n and b_n are defined above, what is the value of $a_{10} - b_{10}$?

  (A) 15

  (B) 23

  (C) 34

  (D) 46

  (E) 55

18. A half full water tank has a square base with side length 200 cm and a height of 400 cm. If a cube with side length 50 cm is placed inside the water tank, how many meters does the water rise?

  (A) $\dfrac{1}{32}$

  (B) $\dfrac{1}{16}$

  (C) $\dfrac{1}{8}$

  (D) $\dfrac{1}{4}$

  (E) $\dfrac{1}{2}$

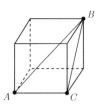

19. A particle can move either inside or on the surface of a cube with side length 10 feet as shown above. The particle moves at a rate of $\frac{1}{2}$ feet per second. The amount of time, in seconds, that the particle can save if it moves from point A to point B directly, rather than to move from point A to point C to point B can be expressed as $a(10 + 10\sqrt{b} - 10\sqrt{c})$. What is the value of abc ?

  (A) 2

  (B) 3

  (C) 8

  (D) 12

  (E) 24

20. For positive integers, m and n, $n^3 = 180m$. Which of the following is the smallest possible value of $m + n$?

  (A) 120

  (B) 135

  (C) 150

  (D) 165

  (E) 180

$$H(1!) + H(2!) + \cdots + H(9!) + H(10!)$$

21. Let $H(n)$ be the hundreds digit of a positive integer n. For instance, $H(321) = 3$. What is the value of the expression above?

    (A) 22

    (B) 23

    (C) 24

    (D) 26

    (E) 27

23. $10! = 10 \times 9 \times \cdots \times 2 \times 1$. If $\sqrt{10!} = n\sqrt{7}$, where n is a positive integer, what is the value of n?

    (A) 362

    (B) 480

    (C) 512

    (D) 624

    (E) 720

22. A drawer contains 10 socks: 2 black, 3 white, and 5 red. If two socks are randomly pulled from the drawer, what is the probability that the two socks have the same color?

    (A) $\dfrac{1}{9}$

    (B) $\dfrac{1}{6}$

    (C) $\dfrac{14}{45}$

    (D) $\dfrac{7}{25}$

    (E) $\dfrac{43}{100}$

24. A set of distinct positive integers are randomly selected between 1 and 1000. What is the minimum number of integers you must select to guarantee that some pair of these integers have a difference that is a multiple of 5?

    (A) 5

    (B) 6

    (C) 7

    (D) 8

    (E) 9

25. On a biased die, some numbers are more likely to be shown than others. If the probability of getting a number n from the biased die is defined by $\frac{n}{21}$, where $n = 1, 2, \cdots, 6$, what is the probability of getting a sum of 7 if you roll the biased die twice?

(A) $\dfrac{8}{63}$

(B) $\dfrac{1}{6}$

(C) $\dfrac{4}{21}$

(D) $\dfrac{1}{4}$

(E) $\dfrac{122}{21^2}$

26. In a rectangular box, the areas of the top face, right face, and front face are 108, 180, and 135, respectively. What is the volume of the rectangular box?

(A) 1240

(B) 1360

(C) 1440

(D) 1560

(E) 1620

27. Suppose Joshua and Jason each select a 1-digit number. What is the probability that the absolute value of the difference of their numbers is less than or equal to 1?

(A) $\dfrac{1}{3}$

(B) $\dfrac{8}{25}$

(C) $\dfrac{1}{4}$

(D) $\dfrac{7}{25}$

(E) $\dfrac{1}{5}$

$$\frac{3x - y}{x - y} = \frac{y - z}{z + y} = \frac{z - x}{-z}$$

28. For real numbers x, y, and z, the equalities are defined above. What is the value of $\dfrac{3x - y}{x - y}$?

(A) $\dfrac{1}{2}$

(B) 1

(C) $\dfrac{3}{2}$

(D) 2

(E) $\dfrac{5}{2}$

Answers and Solutions
TJHSST Math Practice Test 8

Answers

1. A	11. C	21. E
2. C	12. B	22. C
3. B	13. D	23. E
4. D	14. B	24. B
5. A	15. B	25. A
6. C	16. E	26. E
7. A	17. C	27. D
8. E	18. A	28. D
9. D	19. D	
10. A	20. E	

Solutions

1. (A)

> Tips   % decrease $= \dfrac{\text{Final value} - \text{Initial value}}{\text{Initial value}} \times 100\%$

Mr. Rhee's weight was 180 pounds in August and 150 pounds in September. Thus, the final value is 150 and the initial value is 180.

$$\text{\% decrease} = \frac{150 - 180}{180} \times 100\%$$

$$= -\frac{30}{180} \times 100\%$$

$$= -\frac{1}{6} \times 100\%$$

$$= -16\frac{2}{3}\%$$

Therefore, Mr. Rhee lost $16\frac{2}{3}\%$ of his weight.

2. (C)

For simplicity, let the volumes of the smaller cube and the larger cube be 27 and 64, respectively. Thus, the ratio of the volume of the smaller cube to that of the larger cube remains the same: $27 : 64$. The volume of a cube is s^3, where s is the side length of the cube. Thus, the side lengths of the smaller cube and the larger cube are 3 and 4, respectively. Since the surface area of a cube is $6s^2$, the ratio of the surface area of the smaller cube to that of the larger cube is $6(3)^2 : 6(4)^2$ or $9 : 16$.

3. (B)

If the digits, 1, 2, and 3, are used once, there are six three-digit numbers: 123, 132, 213, 231, 312, and 321. Out of six three-digit numbers, only 132 and 312 are divisible by 2. Therefore, the probability that the three-digit numbers formed are divisible by 2 is $\frac{2}{6}$ or $\frac{1}{3}$.

4. (D)

Tips

1. $\dfrac{1}{a} = a^{-1}$

2. $(a^x)^y = a^{xy}$

Since $\frac{1}{9} = \frac{1}{3^2} = 3^{-2}$, $\left(\frac{1}{9}\right)^x = (3^{-2})^x = 3^{-2x}$.

$$\left(\frac{1}{9}\right)^x = 4$$

$$3^{-2x} = 2^2$$

$$\left(3^{-2x}\right)^{-\frac{1}{2}} = (2^2)^{-\frac{1}{2}}$$

$$3^x = 2^{-1}$$

$$3^x = \frac{1}{2}$$

Since $\left(\frac{1}{9}\right)^x = 3^{-2x}$

Raise each side to the power of $-\dfrac{1}{2}$

Therefore, the value of 3^x is $\frac{1}{2}$.

5. (A)

Joshua filled a cup with equal amounts of orange juice, apple juice, and grape juice. Thus, the amount of each fruit juice was equal to $\frac{1}{3}$ of the cup as shown in figure 1.

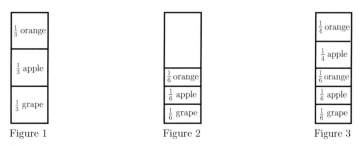

Figure 1   Figure 2   Figure 3

After Joshua drank half of the cup, the remaining fractional part of each fruit juice was $\frac{1}{6}$ of the cup as shown in figure 2. Afterwards, Joshua filled the remaining cup with equal amounts of orange and apple juice. Since only half of the cup was available to fill, Joshua added $\frac{1}{4}$ cup of orange juice and $\frac{1}{4}$ cup of apple juice as shown in figure 3. Therefore, the fractional part of the cup was filled with the apple juice is $\frac{1}{6} + \frac{1}{4} = \frac{5}{12}$.

6. (C)

Let x be the amount of money in Jason's savings account in the beginning. Jason spent one-third of his money, $\frac{x}{3}$, on books. The remaining money in his account is $x - \frac{x}{3}$ or $\frac{2}{3}x$. A few days later, Jason spent half of the remaining money, $\frac{1}{2} \times \frac{2}{3}x$ or $\frac{x}{3}$ on clothes. Thus, the remaining balance in his account after spending money on books and clothes is $x - \frac{x}{3} - \frac{x}{3}$ or $\frac{x}{3}$. The table below summarizes how much money Jason spent on books and clothes and the remaining balance in terms of x.

Initial amount	Books	Clothes	Remaining balance
x	$\frac{x}{3}$	$\frac{1}{2} \times \frac{2}{3}x = \frac{x}{3}$	$\frac{x}{3} = \$175$

Since the remaining balance, $\frac{x}{3}$, is \$175, solve the equation $\frac{x}{3} = 175$. Thus, $x = 525$. Therefore, Jason had \$525 in his savings account in the beginning.

7. (A)

In the figure below, $AB = BC = DC = 12$ and $CE = 6$.

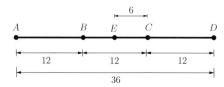

Therefore, $DE = DC + CE = 12 + 6 = 18$.

8. (E)

If it takes 6 people 4 days to paint half a house, 6 people will need 8 days to paint an entire house. In other words, the amount of work required to paint the entire house is equivalent to $6_{\text{people}} \times 8_{\text{days}} = 48_{\text{people}\times\text{days}}$. Since half the house remains unpainted, the amount of work required is $\frac{1}{2} \times 48_{\text{people}\times\text{days}} = 24_{\text{people}\times\text{days}}$. Let x be the total number of people needed to paint half the house in 3 days. Then, the amount of work required in 3 days is $x_{\text{people}} \times 3_{\text{days}} = 3x_{\text{people}\times\text{days}}$. Set up an equation in terms of the amount of work required and solve for x.

$$3x_{\text{people}\times\text{days}} = 24_{\text{people}\times\text{days}}$$
$$x = 8$$

Thus, 8 people are needed to paint half the house in 3 days. Since there are already 6 people working on the house, the number of additional people needed is $8 - 6 = 2$ people.

9. (D)

Joshua has m liters of a 10% acid solution, and n liters of a 30% acid solution. If he mixes these solutions up, he will make 100 liters of a 15% acid solution. Thus, $m + n = 100$ or $n = 100 - m$.

	Liters	Amount of acid
10% solution	m	$0.1m$
30% solution	$100 - m$	$0.3(100 - m)$
15% solution	100	$0.15(100) = 15$

Let's set up an equation in terms of amount of acid and solve for m.

$$0.1m + 0.3(100 - m) = 0.15(100)$$
$$0.1m + 30 - 0.3m = 15$$
$$-0.2m = -15$$
$$m = 75$$

Since $m = 75$, $n = 100 - m = 25$. Therefore, the value of $m - n$ is $75 - 25 = 50$.

10. (A)

> **Tips**
>
> The infinite sum S of a geometric series is
>
> $$S = \frac{a_1}{1 - r}, \qquad \text{if } |r| < 1$$
>
> where a_1 is the first term, and r is the common ratio.

$S = \frac{1}{2} + \frac{1}{4} + \frac{1}{8} + \cdots$ is a geometric series with the first term $a_1 = \frac{1}{2}$, and the common ratio $r = \frac{1}{2}$. Thus,

$$S = \frac{1}{2} + \frac{1}{4} + \frac{1}{8} + \cdots$$
$$= \frac{\frac{1}{2}}{1 - \frac{1}{2}}$$
$$= 1$$

Therefore, $S_n = 1$ when n is very large.

11. (C)

In an arithmetic sequence, add or subtract the same number (common difference) to one term to get the next term. The nth term of the arithmetic sequence is

$$a_n = a_1 + (n-1)d$$

where a_1 is the first term, and d is the common difference.

The sequence $0, 4, 8, 12, \cdots, 992$ is an arithmetic sequence, where the first term, $a_1 = 0$, and the common difference is $d = 4$. Use the nth term formula to find out which term has the value of 992.

$$a_n = a_1 + (n-1)d$$
$$992 = 0 + (n-1)4$$
$$n - 1 = 248$$
$$n = 249$$

Therefore, the 249th term, a_{249}, has the value of 992.

12. (B)

The number of ways n people can sit around a circular table is $(n-1)!$.

In a circular arrangement, you have to fix the position for the first person, which can be performed in only one way since every position is considered same if no one is already sitting on any of the seats. Once you have fixed the position for the first person, you can arrange the remaining 9 people in 9! ways. Therefore, the number of ways 10 people can sit around a circular table is 9!.

13. (D)

The units digits of powers of 7, and powers of 2 are shown below.

$$7^1 = 7, \qquad\qquad 2^1 = 2$$
$$7^2 = 9, \qquad\qquad 2^2 = 4$$
$$7^3 = 3, \qquad\qquad 2^3 = 8$$
$$7^4 = 1, \qquad\qquad 2^4 = 6$$
$$7^5 = 7, \qquad\qquad 2^5 = 2$$
$$\vdots \qquad\qquad\qquad \vdots$$

The units digits of powers of 7 are 7, 9, 3, and 1, and they are repeating. The units digits of powers of 2 are 2, 4, 8, and 6, and they are repeating. Thus,

$$\text{Units digit of } 7^{1002} = \text{units digit of } 7^2 = 9$$
$$\text{Units digit of } 2^{1002} = \text{units digit of } 2^2 = 4$$

Therefore, the units digit of $7^{1002} - 2^{1002}$ is $9 - 4 = 5$.

14. (B)

The odd-numbered terms are letters starting with B (B, C, D, E). The even-numbered terms are letters starting with Z backwards (Z, Y, X). Since the next term of the sequence is the 7th term, letter E is the next term in the sequence.

15. (B)

$100001000 = 99999999 + 1001$. When 99999999 is divided by 9, the remainder is 0. When 1001 is divided by 9, the remainder is 2. Therefore, when 100001000 is divided by 9, the remainder is 2.

16. (E)

The lines $y = 2x + a$ and $y = -\frac{1}{2}x + b$ intersect at the point $(t, t+1)$. It means that the point $(t, t+1)$ is on both lines. Substitute t for x and $t+1$ for y, and then solve for a and b in terms of t.

$$t + 1 = 2t + a \implies a = -t + 1$$
$$t + 1 = -\frac{1}{2}t + b \implies b = \frac{3}{2}t + 1$$

Thus,

$$3a + 2b = 3(-t + 1) + 2\left(\frac{3}{2}t + 1\right)$$
$$= -3t + 3 + 3t + 2$$
$$= 5$$

Therefore, the value of $3a + 2b$ is 5.

17. (C)

The table below shows the sequences a_n and b_n.

n	1	2	3	4	5	6	7	8	9	10
a_n	1	2	3	5	8	13	21	34	55	89
b_n	1	1	2	3	5	8	13	21	34	55

Therefore, the value of $a_{10} - b_{10}$ is $89 - 55 = 34$.

18. (A)

If a cube is placed inside the tank, the water level of the tank will rise by the volume of the cube. Let h be the number of meters that the water level rises. Thus,

$$2 \times 2 \times h = \frac{1}{2} \times \frac{1}{2} \times \frac{1}{2}$$
$$h = \frac{\frac{1}{8}}{4}$$
$$= \frac{1}{32}$$

Therefore, the water level rises $\frac{1}{32}$ meters.

19. (D)

> **Tips**   The longest diagonal of a cube with side length x is $x\sqrt{3}$.

The particle moves at a rate of $\frac{1}{2}$ feet per second, which means that it moves 1 foot in 2 seconds. Since the length of the cube is 10, the length of the path from point A to point B directly or the length of the longest diagonal is $10\sqrt{3}$ feet as shown below. It takes $2 \times 10\sqrt{3}$ seconds for the particle to move from point A to point B directly.

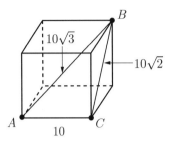

Whereas, the length of a path from point A to point C to point B is $10 + 10\sqrt{2}$ feet. It takes $2 \times (10 + 10\sqrt{2})$ seconds for the particle to move from point A to point C to point B. Thus, the amount of time, in seconds, that the particle can save if it moves from point A to point B directly, rather than to move from point A to point C to point B is $2 \times (10 + 10\sqrt{2}) - 2 \times 10\sqrt{3}$ or $2(10 + 10\sqrt{2} - 10\sqrt{3})$. Since $a = 2$, $b = 3$, and $c = 2$, the value of abc is $2 \times 3 \times 2 = 12$.

20. (E)

The prime factorization of 180 is $2^2 \cdot 3^2 \cdot 5$. If $m = 2 \cdot 3 \times 5^2$, $180m = 2^3 \cdot 3^3 \cdot 5^3 = (2 \cdot 3 \cdot 5)^3$. Thus, $m = 150$ and $n = 30$. Therefore, the smallest possible value of $m + n$ that satisfies $n^3 = 180m$ is 180.

21. (E)

The hundreds digit of $H(1!)$, $H(2!)$, $\cdots$, $H(10!)$ are as follows:

$H(n!)$	$H(1!)$	$H(2!)$	$H(3!)$	$H(4!)$	$H(5!)$	$H(6!)$	$H(7!)$	$H(8!)$	$H(9!)$	$H(10!)$
Hundreds digit	0	0	0	0	1	7	0	3	8	8

Therefore, the value of $H(1!) + H(2!) + \cdots + H(9!) + H(10!)$ is $1 + 7 + 3 + 8 + 8 = 27$.

22. (C)

Let's consider three cases:

(a) Case 1: 2 black socks are pulled. The probability that 2 pulled socks are black is

$$\frac{2}{10} \cdot \frac{1}{9} = \frac{2}{90}$$

(b) Case 2: 2 white socks are pulled. The probability that 2 pulled socks are white is

$$\frac{3}{10} \cdot \frac{2}{9} = \frac{6}{90}$$

(c) Case 3: 2 red socks are pulled. The probability that 2 pulled socks are red is

$$\frac{5}{10} \cdot \frac{4}{9} = \frac{20}{90}$$

Therefore, the probability that the two socks have the same color is $\frac{2}{90} + \frac{6}{90} + \frac{20}{90} = \frac{14}{45}$.

23. (E)

The prime factorization of $10! = 2^8 \cdot 3^4 \cdot 5^2 \cdot 7$. Thus, $\sqrt{10!} = 2^4 \cdot 3^2 \cdot 5 \cdot \sqrt{7} = 720\sqrt{7}$. Therefore, the value of n is 720.

24. (B)

In order for two integers to have a difference that is a multiple of 5, they must have the same remainders when they are divided by 5. For instance, 29 and 14 have the remainder 4 when they are divided by 5, and their difference is a multiple of 5. There are 5 possible values for the remainder when a number is divided by 5: 0, 1, 2, 3, and 4. If you select 5 distinct integers, they might have all different remainders. However, if you select the 6th distinct integer, its remainder must be the same as the remainder of one of 5 selected distinct integers. Therefore, you must select 6 distinct positive integers to guarantee that some pair of these integers have a difference that is a multiple of 5.

25. (A)

The probabilities of getting a number either 1, 2, 3, 4, 5, or 6 are $\frac{1}{21}$, $\frac{2}{21}$, $\frac{3}{21}$, $\frac{4}{21}$, $\frac{5}{21}$, or $\frac{6}{21}$, respectively. Consider the following cases for which the sum of the two numbers is 7.

- Case 1: Two numbers 1 and 6 are selected. Thus, the probability of selecting 1 and 6 is $\frac{1}{21} \cdot \frac{6}{21} = \frac{6}{21^2}$.

- Case 2: Two numbers 2 and 5 are selected. Thus, the probability of selecting 2 and 5 is $\frac{2}{21} \cdot \frac{5}{21} = \frac{10}{21^2}$.

- Case 3: Two numbers 3 and 4 are selected. Thus, the probability of selecting 3 and 4 is $\frac{3}{21} \cdot \frac{4}{21} = \frac{12}{21^2}$.

- Case 4: Two numbers 4 and 3 are selected. Thus, the probability of selecting 4 and 3 is $\frac{4}{21} \cdot \frac{3}{21} = \frac{12}{21^2}$.

- Case 5: Two numbers 5 and 2 are selected. Thus, the probability of selecting 5 and 2 is $\frac{5}{21} \cdot \frac{2}{21} = \frac{10}{21^2}$.

- Case 1: Two numbers 6 and 1 are selected. Thus, the probability of selecting 6 and 1 is $\frac{6}{21} \cdot \frac{1}{21} = \frac{6}{21^2}$.

Therefore, the probability of getting a sum of 7 if you roll the biased die twice is

$$\text{Probability of getting a sum of 7} = \frac{1}{21} + \frac{2}{21} + \frac{3}{21} + \frac{4}{21} + \frac{5}{21} + \frac{6}{21}$$
$$= \frac{56}{21^2}$$
$$= \frac{8}{63}$$

26. (E)

Let x, y, and z be the length, width, and height of the rectangular box as shown below. The volume V of the rectangular box can be expressed as $V = xyz$.

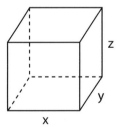

The areas of the top face, right face, and front face can be expressed as xy, yz, and xz, respectively. Thus,

$$xy = 108 = 2^2 \times 3^3$$
$$yz = 180 = 2^2 \times 3^2 \times 5$$
$$xz = 135 = 3^3 \times 5$$

Multiplying three equations above gives $(xyz)^2 = 2^4 \times 3^8 \times 5^2$, or $xyz = 2^2 \times 3^4 \times 5 = 1620$. Therefore, the volume of the rectangular box is $V = xyz = 1620$.

27. (D)

Let x be the 1-digit number that Joshua selected, and y be the 1-digit number that Jason selected. There are $10 \times 10 = 100$ ways to select x and y. The table below the possible values for x and y for which the absolute value of the difference of x and y is less than or equal to 1.

x	Possible values of y	Number of possible values of y
When $x = 0$	$y = 0, 1$	2
When $x = 1$	$y = 0, 1, 2$	3
When $x = 2$	$y = 1, 2, 3$	3
When $x = 3$	$y = 2, 3, 4$	3
When $x = 4$	$y = 3, 4, 5$	3
When $x = 5$	$y = 4, 5, 6$	3
When $x = 6$	$y = 5, 6, 7$	3
When $x = 7$	$y = 6, 7, 8$	3
When $x = 8$	$y = 7, 8, 9$	3
When $x = 9$	$y = 8, 9$	2

Therefore, the probability that the absolute value of the difference of their numbers is less than or equal to 1 is

$$\frac{2 + 3 + 3 + 3 + 3 + 3 + 3 + 3 + 3 + 2}{100} = \frac{28}{100} = \frac{7}{25}$$

28. (D)

> **Tips**
>
> If $\frac{a}{b} = \frac{c}{d} = \frac{e}{f}$, the following equalities are true.
>
> $$\frac{a}{b} = \frac{c}{d} = \frac{e}{f} = \frac{a + c + e}{b + d + f}$$

According to the equalities shown above,

$$\frac{3x - y}{x - y} = \frac{y - z}{z + y} = \frac{z - x}{-z} = \frac{3x - y + y - z + z - x}{x - y + z + y - z} = \frac{2x}{x} = 2$$

215

TJHSST PRACTICE MATH TEST 9
Time — 50 minutes
Number of questions — 28

Directions: Solve each of the following problems using the available space for scratch work. Choose the best answer among the answer choices given and fill in the corresponding circle on the answer sheet.

1. Students walked into the auditorium with rows of two. Jason noticed that his row is the 11th row from the front and the 10th row from the back. How many students went to the auditorium?

   (A) 20

   (B) 21

   (C) 40

   (D) 80

   (E) 82

2. If the radius of a circular garden is $\frac{100}{\pi}$ feet and a post is placed every four feet around the circumference of the garden, how many posts are there?

   (A) 47

   (B) 48

   (C) 49

   (D) 50

   (E) 51

3. What is the probability that a randomly selected positive integer less than 100 will be divisible by 7?

   (A) $\frac{13}{99}$

   (B) $\frac{14}{99}$

   (C) $\frac{15}{99}$

   (D) $\frac{13}{100}$

   (E) $\frac{7}{50}$

4. How many 3-inch square tiles are needed to cover a floor that measures 3 ft by 6 ft ?

   (A) 2

   (B) 36

   (C) 144

   (D) 196

   (E) 288

217

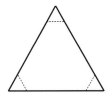

5. In the figure above, each corner of an equilateral triangle, with side length of 25, is cut into a smaller equilateral triangle with side length of 3. What is the perimeter of the remaining figure?

   (A) 66

   (B) 69

   (C) 72

   (D) 75

   (E) 78

$$S = \frac{1 + 3 + 5 + \cdots + 49}{98 + 94 + 90 + \cdots + 2}$$

6. What is the value of the expression S shown above?

   (A) $\dfrac{1}{2}$

   (B) $\dfrac{2}{3}$

   (C) $\dfrac{3}{4}$

   (D) $\dfrac{5}{6}$

   (E) $\dfrac{6}{7}$

7. The coordinates of the three vertices of a right triangle are $(0,0)$, $(5,0)$, and $(5,12)$. What is the value of the length of the longest side of the triangle?

   (A) 13

   (B) 12

   (C) 11

   (D) 10

   (E) 9

8. A track team coach records the lap time after a student finishes his run. The student runs three times and his three lap times are 1 minute and 45 seconds, 1 minute and 55 seconds, and 2 minutes and 26 seconds. What is the average lap time for the three runs?

   (A) 1 minutes and 55 seconds

   (B) 1 minutes and 57 seconds

   (C) 1 minutes and 59 seconds

   (D) 2 minutes and 2 seconds

   (E) 2 minutes and 6 seconds

9. You have a savings account. The amount A you have deposited into your account after t years can be modeled by a linear equation, $A = mt + b$. You have deposited \$1175 into your savings account after three years and deposited \$1850 after 6 years. How much money do you put into your savings account every year?

   (A) \$375

   (B) \$325

   (C) \$275

   (D) \$225

   (E) \$175

11. In the figure above, rectangle $ABCD$ is divided into two smaller rectangles. If the ratio of the area of rectangle $BCFE$ to that of rectangle $AEFD$ is 2 to 5, what is the ratio of BE to AB ?

   (A) $\dfrac{3}{4}$

   (B) $\dfrac{2}{3}$

   (C) $\dfrac{2}{5}$

   (D) $\dfrac{2}{7}$

   (E) $\dfrac{3}{10}$

$$xy = 1$$
$$x + \frac{1}{y} = 3$$

10. If (x, y) is the solution to the system of equations shown above, what is the value of $2x + 3y$?

   (A) 3

   (B) 4

   (C) 5

   (D) 6

   (E) 7

12. When the positive integer k is divided by 5, the remainder is 1. When the positive integer n is divided by 7, the remainder is 2. Which of the following has a remainder of 2 when divided by 6?

   (A) kn

   (B) $kn + 1$

   (C) $kn + 2$

   (D) $kn + 3$

   (E) $kn + 4$

13. How many integers between 100 and 1000 contain only even-numbered digits?

(A) 90

(B) 100

(C) 110

(D) 125

(E) 150

15. In order to determine deer population in a forest, 20 deers were captured, tagged, and released. The next day, 24 deers were captured. Of the 24 deers, 3 are already tagged. What is the size of the deer population in the forest?

(A) 120

(B) 160

(C) 200

(D) 240

(E) 300

$$T = \{ F, \quad H, \quad N \}$$

14. Set T has three elements. Which of the following is the most similar to the elements in set T ?

(A) O

(B) Q

(C) T

(D) V

(E) Y

16. Joshua has five identical bags. Each bag contains at least one nickel and one dime, and has a distinct combination of nickels and dimes, each totaling 55 cents. Joshua randomly selects one bag. What is the probability that the bag contains at least 5 nickels?

(A) $\dfrac{1}{3}$

(B) $\dfrac{1}{2}$

(C) $\dfrac{3}{5}$

(D) $\dfrac{2}{3}$

(E) $\dfrac{3}{4}$

17. What is the tens digit of 11^8 ?

(A) 2

(B) 3

(C) 5

(D) 6

(E) 8

$$f^2(x) = f(f(x))$$
$$f^3(x) = f(f^2(x))$$

18. The functions $f^2(x)$ and $f^3(x)$ are defined above. If $f(x) = mx + n$ and $f^3(x) = 8x + 21$, what is the value of $m + n$?

(A) 4

(B) 5

(C) 6

(D) 7

(E) 8

19. What is the sum of the terms in an arithmetic series $2 + 7 + 12 \cdots + 72$?

(A) 535

(B) 545

(C) 555

(D) 565

(E) 575

20. The digits 2, 3, 5, 7, and 8 are used exactly once to form a 3-digit number and a 2-digit number. If the difference of the two numbers is 247, what is the sum of the two numbers?

(A) 313

(B) 340

(C) 403

(D) 430

(E) 439

21. A set of 25 smaller squares with side length 1 are arranged to make a 5×5 square. How many ways can two smaller squares be selected so that no two squares are in the same row or column?

    (A) 25

    (B) 100

    (C) 200

    (D) 400

    (E) 625

22. If m and n are the solutions to the equation $x^2 - 6x + 1 = 0$, which of the following is the value of $m^3 + n^3$?

    (A) 121

    (B) 148

    (C) 164

    (D) 198

    (E) 212

23. How many ways can you put five distinct marbles into three distinct boxes?

    (A) 10

    (B) 21

    (C) 125

    (D) 180

    (E) 243

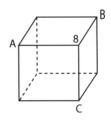

24. The integers from 1 to 8 are placed at the vertices of a cube in a such way that the sums of the four integers on each face of the cube are the same. If the integer 8 is placed on the top face and other integers are placed at A, B and C, what is the value of $A + B + C$?

    (A) 6

    (B) 9

    (C) 12

    (D) 15

    (E) 18

25. For positive integers x and y, how many pairs of x and y satisfy $x^2 - y^2 = 6^3$?

    (A) 1

    (B) 2

    (C) 3

    (D) 4

    (E) 5

$$2x + y + z = 28$$
$$x + 2y + z = 40$$
$$x + y + 2z = 36$$

26. For real numbers x, y, and z, the system of equations are given above. Which of the following is the value of y ?

    (A) 11

    (B) 12

    (C) 13

    (D) 14

    (E) 15

27. If $x^2 + 2$ is divided by $x - 1$, the remainder is 3. If $x^{100} + x^{97} + 2$ is divided by $x + 1$, what is the remainder?

    (A) 1

    (B) 2

    (C) 64

    (D) 128

    (E) 199

28. Jason has 7 coins in his wallet. How many different combinations of pennies, nickels, dimes, and quarters are possible?

    (A) 35

    (B) 66

    (C) 120

    (D) 150

    (E) 180

Answers and Solutions
TJHSST Math Practice Test 9

Answers

1. C	11. D	21. C
2. D	12. C	22. D
3. B	13. B	23. E
4. E	14. E	24. A
5. A	15. B	25. D
6. A	16. C	26. D
7. A	17. E	27. B
8. D	18. B	28. C
9. D	19. C	
10. C	20. C	

Solutions

1. (C)

   Since Jason's row is the 11th row from the front, there are 10 rows in front of Jason. Since Jason's row is the 10th row from the back, there are 9 rows behind Jason. Thus, there are $10 + 1 + 9 = 20$ rows in the auditorium. Since each row is occupied by 2 students, there are $20 \times 2 = 40$ students who went to the auditorium.

2. (D)

   The circumference of a circle with a radius of $\frac{100}{\pi}$ is $2\pi(\frac{100}{\pi}) = 200$. Thus,

   $$\text{Total number of posts on a circle} = \frac{\text{Circumference of a circle}}{\text{Distance between each post}} = \frac{200}{4} = 50$$

   Therefore, the total number of posts around the circular garden is 50.

3. (B)

   There are 99 positive integers less than 100: $1, 2, 3, \cdots, 98, 99$. Out of the 99 integers, there are 14 integers that are divisible by 7: $7, 14, 21, \cdots, 91, 98$. Therefore, the probability that a randomly selected positive integer less than 100 will be divisible by 7 is $\frac{14}{99}$.

4. (E)

One foot equals 12 inches. The dimension of the floor is 3 ft by 6 ft or 36 inches by 72 inches. Thus,

$$\text{Number of 3-in square tiles needed} = \frac{36 \times 72}{3 \times 3}$$
$$= 12 \times 24$$
$$= 288$$

Therefore, the number of 3-in square tiles needed to cover the floor is 288.

5. (A)

In the figure below, each side of the equilateral triangle is cut into a smaller equilateral triangle with side length of 3. So, the remaining figure is a hexagon.

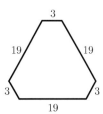

Therefore, the perimeter of the hexagon is $19 \times 3 + 3 \times 3 = 66$.

6. (A)

Factor out 2 from the denominator and simplify the expression.

$$S = \frac{1 + 3 + 5 + \cdots + 49}{98 + 94 + 90 + \cdots + 2} = \frac{1 + 3 + 5 + \cdots + 49}{2 + \cdots + 90 + 94 + 98}$$
$$= \frac{1 + 3 + 5 + \cdots + 49}{2(1 + 3 + 5 + \cdots + 49)} = \frac{1}{2}$$

Therefore, the value of expression S is $\frac{1}{2}$.

7. (A)

In the figure below, the triangle is a 5-12-13 right triangle. Therefore, the length of the longest side, the hypotenuse, is 13.

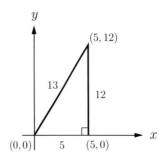

However, the answer can also be derived using the Pythagorean theorem. Define C as the length of the hypotenuse of the right triangle. Since C is the length, $C > 0$.

$$C^2 = 5^2 + 12^2$$
$$C = \sqrt{169}$$
$$C = 13$$

8. (D)

There are 60 seconds in 1 minute. Convert the time from minutes and seconds to just seconds.

$$1 \text{ minute and } 45 \text{ seconds} = 105 \text{ seconds}$$
$$1 \text{ minute and } 55 \text{ seconds} = 115 \text{ seconds}$$
$$2 \text{ minutes and } 26 \text{ seconds} = 146 \text{ seconds}$$

Thus, the total lap time for the three runs is $105 + 115 + 146 = 366$ seconds.

$$\text{Average}_{\text{lap time}} = \frac{366 \text{ seconds}}{3 \text{ laps}}$$
$$= \frac{122 \text{ seconds}}{\text{lap}}$$

Therefore, the average lap time for the three runs is 122 seconds, which is 2 minutes and 2 seconds.

9. (D)

In 3 years, you deposited \$1175 and in 6 years, you deposited \$1850. This can be written as ordered pairs, (x, y), where x represent years and y represents the amount deposited: $(3, 1175)$ and $(6, 1850)$. Find the slope of the line that passes through the points, $(3, 1175)$ and $(6, 1850)$, because it represents the amount of money deposited into the savings account every year.

$$\text{Slope} = \frac{y_2 - y_1}{x_2 - x_1}$$
$$= \frac{1850 - 1175}{6 - 3}$$
$$= \frac{675}{3}$$
$$= 225$$

Therefore, the amount of money deposited into the savings account every year is \$225.

10. (C)

Tips	Use the distributive property: $a(b + c) = ab + ac$.

$$x + \frac{1}{y} = 3 \qquad \text{Multiply each side by } y$$

$$y\left(x + \frac{1}{y}\right) = 3(y) \qquad \text{Use the distributive property}$$

$$xy + 1 = 3y \qquad \text{Since } xy = 1$$

$$1 + 1 = 3y \qquad \text{Divide each side by 3}$$

$$y = \frac{2}{3}$$

Since $y = \frac{2}{3}$ and $xy = 1$, $x = \frac{3}{2}$. Therefore, the value of $2x + 3y$ is $2(\frac{3}{2}) + 3(\frac{2}{3}) = 5$.

11. (D)

Define y as the length of the two smaller rectangles, $BCFE$ and $EFDA$. The areas of the two smaller rectangles $BCFE$ and $AEFD$ are $y \times BE$ and $y \times AE$, respectively. Since the ratio of areas of the two smaller rectangles is $2 : 5$, set up a proportion and find the ratio of BE to AE.

$$\text{Area of BCFE : Area of AEFD} = 2 : 5$$
$$y \times BE : y \times AE = 2 : 5$$
$$\frac{y \times BE}{y \times AE} = \frac{2}{5} \qquad y \text{ cancels each other}$$
$$\frac{BE}{AE} = \frac{2}{5}$$

Thus, the ratio of BE to AE is $2 : 5$. For simplicity, let $BE = 2$ and $AE = 5$. Since $AB = AE + BE = 7$, the ratio of BE to AB is $\frac{2}{7}$.

227

12. (C)

The fastest way to solve this particular problem is to plug in numbers and observe which set of numbers satisfies the requirements in the problem. For instance, $k = 6$ and $n = 9$.

$$(A) \quad kn = 54 \implies \text{remainder of } 0$$
$$(B) \quad kn + 1 = 55 \implies \text{remainder of } 1$$
$$(C) \quad kn + 2 = 56 \implies \text{remainder of } 2$$
$$(D) \quad kn + 3 = 57 \implies \text{remainder of } 3$$
$$(E) \quad kn + 4 = 58 \implies \text{remainder of } 4$$

13. (B)

 Tips The fundamental counting principle: If one event can occur in m ways and another event can occur in n ways, then the number of ways both events can occur is $m \times n$.

Let event 1 be selecting a digit for the hundreds place. There are 4 possible digits: 2, 4, 6 and 8 since integers must be greater than 100. Let event 2 and event 3 be selecting a digit for the tens place and ones place. Event 2 and event 3 each have 5 possible digits: 0, 2, 4, 6, and 8. According to the fundamental counting principle, the number of integers between 100 and 1000 that contain only even-numbered digits is $4 \times 5 \times 5 = 100$.

14. (E)

The letters F, H, N, and Y has three line segments. Therefore, (E) is the correct answer.

15. (B)

Tips The assumption behind tag-recapture method is that the proportion of tagged individuals recaptured in the second sample represent the proportion of tagged individuals in the population as a whole. In other words,

$$\frac{R}{S} = \frac{T}{N}$$

where

- R is the number of deer recaptured on the next day

- S is the number of sample on the next day

- T is the number of deer captured and tagged on the first day

- N is the deer population

In this problem, $R = 3$, $S = 24$, $T = 20$. Set up the proportion and solve for N.

$$\frac{R}{S} = \frac{T}{N}$$
$$\frac{3}{24} = \frac{20}{N}$$
$$N = 160$$

Therefore, the number of deers in the forest is 160.

16. (C)

Let x and y be the number of nickels and dimes, respectively. The 5 possible values for (x, y) such that $5x + 10y = 55$ are $(1, 5)$, $(3, 4)$, $(5, 3)$, $(7, 2)$, $(9, 1)$. Of the 5 possible values, 3 that have at least 5 nickels are $(5, 3)$, $(7, 2)$, and $(9, 1)$. Therefore, the probability that the bag contains at least 5 nickels is $\frac{3}{5}$.

17. (E)

The tens and units digits of the powers of 11 are shown below.

Powers of 11	11^1	11^2	11^3	11^4	11^5	11^6	11^7	11^8
Tens and units digits	11	21	31	41	51	61	71	81

Therefore, the tens digit of 11^8 is 8.

18. (B)

$$f(x) = mx + n$$
$$f^2(x) = f(f(x)) = f(mx + n) = m(mx + n) + n = m^2x + mn + n$$
$$f^3(x) = f(f^2(x)) = f(m^2x + mn + n) = m(m^2x + mn + n) + n = m^3x + m^2n + mn + n$$

Since $f^3(x) = 8x + 21$, $m^3 = 8$ and $m^2n + mn + n = 21$. Solving for m and n gives $m = 2$ and $n = 3$. Therefore, the value of $m + n$ is 5.

229

19. (C)

The sum of the first n terms S_n of an arithmetic series is

$$S_n = \frac{n}{2}(a_1 + a_n)$$

where a_1 is the first term, and $a_n = a_1 + (n-1)d$ is the nth term of the arithmetic sequence.

$2, 7, 12, \cdots, 72$ is the arithmetic sequence with a common difference $d = 5$. Using the nth term formula $a_n = a_1 + (n-1)d$,

$a_n = a_1 + (n-1)d$	Substitute 72 for a_n, 2 for a_1, and 5 for d
$72 = 2 + (n-1)5$	Subtract 2 from each side
$5(n-1) = 70$	Divide each side by 5
$n - 1 = 14$	Add 1 to each side
$n = 15$	

we found that 72 is the 15th term of the arithmetic sequence. Thus, $2 + 7 + 12 + \cdots + 72$ is the sum of the first 15 terms of the arithmetic series.

$S_n = \dfrac{n}{2}(a_1 + a_n)$	Substitute 15 for n
$S_{15} = \dfrac{15}{2}(a_1 + a_{15})$	Substitute 2 for a_1 and 72 for a_{15}
$\quad = \dfrac{15}{2}(2 + 72) = 555$	

Therefore, $2 + 7 + 12 + \cdots + 72 = 555$.

20. (C)

The digits 2, 3, 5, 7, and 8 are used exactly once to form a 3-digit number and a 2-digit number. Since the difference of the two numbers is 247, the 3-digit number is 325, and the 2-digit number is 78. Therefore, the sum of the two numbers is $325 + 78 = 403$.

21. (C)

First, you can select the first square in 25 ways. Once the first square is selected, eliminate 8 squares that are in the same row or same column with the first square. There are 16 remaining smallers squares to select from. So you can select the second square in 16 ways. The number of ways to select the first square and the second square is $25 \times 16 = 400$. However, the order in which you select the squares does not matter. We need to divide the number of ways to select the first square and the second square by 2!. Therefore, the total number of ways that the two smaller squares can be selected so that no two squares are in the same row or column is $\frac{400}{2} = 200$.

22. (D)

- Vieta's formulas relate the coefficients of a polynomial to the sum and product of its zeros. Let s and t be the solutions to $ax^2 + bx + c = 0$.

$$s + t = -\frac{b}{a}$$

$$st = \frac{c}{a}$$

- Special patterns:

$$x^2 + y^2 = (x + y)^2 - 2xy$$
$$x^3 + y^3 = (x + y)(x^2 - xy + y^2)$$

If m and n are the solutions to the equation $x^2 - 6x + 1 = 0$, according to the Vieta's formulas

$$m + n = 6, \qquad mn = 1$$

Since $m^2 + n^2 = (m + n)^2 - 2mn = 6^2 - 2(1) = 34$. Thus,

$$m^3 + n^3 = (m + n)(m^2 - mn + n^2)$$
$$= 6(34 - 1) = 198$$

Therefore, the value of $m^3 + n^3$ is 198.

23. (E)

For each marble, there are 3 ways to put it into 3 distinct boxes. Since there are 5 distinct marbles, there are $3^5 = 243$ way to put 5 distinct marbles into 3 distinct boxes.

24. (A)

If one integer is placed at any vertex of the cube, the integer will be used three times in three different faces. For instance, the integer 8 is placed on the top face as shown below, it will be used on top face, right face, and front face.

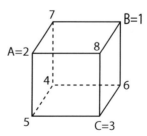

Let's calculate the sum on each face. Since each integer is used three times,

$$\text{Sum of integers on six faces} = 3(1 + 2 + \cdots + 8) = 108$$
$$\text{Sum of integers on each face} = \frac{108}{6} = 18$$

One of the possible arrangements of 8 integers are shown above. Thus, $A = 2$, $B = 1$, and $C = 3$. Therefore, the value of $A + B + C$ is 6.

25. (D)

> **Tips**
> $$x^2 - y^2 = (x+y)(x-y)$$

The prime factorization of $216 = 6^3 = 2^3 \times 3^3$. $x^2 - y^2 = (x+y)(x-y)$. Thus, $(x+y)$ and $(x-y)$ must be factors of 6^3 so that their product equals 6^3. The table below shows the possible values for $(x+y)$ and $(x-y)$, and possible values for integer pairs (x, y) that satisfy $x^2 - y^2 = 6^3$.

$x + y$	$x - y$	(x, y)
216	1	No integer pair
108	2	$(55, 53)$
72	3	No integer pair
54	4	$(29, 25)$
36	6	$(21, 15)$
27	8	No integer pair
24	9	No integer pair
18	12	$(15, 3)$

For instance, when $x + y = 108$, and $x - y = 2$, set the system of equations and solve for x and y.

$$x + y = 108$$
$$\underline{x - y = 2} \qquad \text{Add two equations}$$
$$2x = 110$$
$$x = 55$$

$x = 55$ and $x - y = 2$ gives $y = 53$. Thus, the integer pair (x, y) is $(55, 53)$. The four integer pairs (x, y) that satisfy $x^2 - y^2 = 6^3$ are $(55, 53)$, $(29, 25)$, $(21, 15)$, and $(15, 3)$.

26. (D)

Add three equations as shown below.

$$2x + y + z = 28$$
$$x + 2y + z = 40$$
$$\underline{x + y + 2z = 36} \qquad \text{Add three equations}$$
$$4(x + y + z) = 104$$
$$x + y + z = 26$$

Adding three equations gives $x + y + z = 26$. Comparing $x + y + z = 26$ with $x + 2y + z = 40$ gives $y = 14$. Therefore, the value of y is 14.

27. (B)

> **Tips** The remainder theorem: If a polynomial function $f(x)$ is divided by $x - k$, the remainder is $r = f(k)$, where k is the value of x for which the divisor $x - k$ equals to zero.

If $f(x) = x^2 + 2$ is divided by $x - 1$, the remainder is $r = f(1) = 3$. If $f(x) = x^{100} + x^{97} + 2$ is divided by $x + 1$, the remainder is $r = f(-1) = (-1)^{100} + (-1)^{97} + 2 = 2$.

28. (C)

Since there are 4 different types of coins (Pennies, nickels, dimes, and quarters), we need $4 - 1 = 3$ dividers. In the figure below, 3 lines represent 3 dividers, and 7 circles represent 7 coins.

One of the possible arrangements of 7 coins and 3 dividers is shown below.

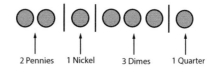

2 Pennies   1 Nickel   3 Dimes   1 Quarter

2 circles to the left of the first divider represent 2 pennies, 1 circle between the first divider and the second divider represents 1 nickel, 3 circles between the second divider and the third divider represents 3 dimes, and 1 circle to the right of the third divider represents 1 quarter. Simply, the number of different combinations of 7 coins is the same as the number of arrangements of 7 circles and 3 lines. Out of 10 blanks, we choose 3 blanks for the 3 dividers. Therefore, there are $\binom{10}{3} = 120$ different combinations of pennies, nickels, dimes, and quarters are possible.

TJHSST PRACTICE MATH TEST 10
Time — 50 minutes
Number of questions — 28

Directions: Solve each of the following problems using the available space for scratch work. Choose the best answer among the answer choices given and fill in the corresponding circle on the answer sheet.

1. Joshua was born in May. May has 31 days. The statements below describe his birthday. When is Joshua's birthday?

   - even number that has 6 factors

   - divisible by 3 but not divisible by 9

   (A) May 30th

   (B) May 24th

   (C) May 18th

   (D) May 12th

   (E) May 6th

$$x + y = 5 - z$$
$$x - z = 7 + y$$

2. In the system of equations above, what is the value of x ?

   (A) 7

   (B) 6

   (C) 5

   (D) 4

   (E) 3

$$0 \le x^2 \le 9$$

3. How many integer values of x satisfy the inequality above?

   (A) 4

   (B) 5

   (C) 6

   (D) 7

   (E) 8

4. The figure above consists of an equilateral triangle and a semicircle. If the diameter of the semicircle is 8, what is the perimeter of the shaded area?

   (A) $8 + 4\pi$

   (B) $12 + 8\pi$

   (C) $16 + 4\pi$

   (D) $16 + 8\pi$

   (E) $24 + 8\pi$

235

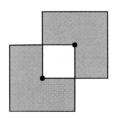

5. In the figure above, two identical squares are overlapped such that one vertex of each square is at the center of the other square. If the length of the square is 8, what is the area of the shaded region?

(A) 60

(B) 72

(C) 84

(D) 90

(E) 96

6. Joshua has taken three tests in math class. The three test scores are 91, 86, and 87. In order for him to get an A in the class, he needs to get an average of at least 90 on the 4 tests. Which of the following score, s, must he receive to get an A ? (Let s be the score on his 4th test.)

(A) $s < 96$

(B) $s \geq 96$

(C) $s \leq 94$

(D) $s > 94$

(E) $s \geq 92$

$$2, 5, 10, 17, \cdots$$

7. In the sequence above, what is the value of the 29th term?

(A) 842

(B) 910

(C) 961

(D) 999

(E) 1024

8. If the pattern shown above continues, which of the following figure is as close as the 997th figure?

(A) Quadrilateral

(B) Rhombus

(C) Octagon

(D) Decagon

(E) Circle

9. Define $a \spadesuit b = a^3 - b$. What is the value of $2 \spadesuit (2 \spadesuit (2 \spadesuit (2 \spadesuit 3)))$?

(A) 3

(B) 5

(C) 7

(D) 8

(E) 10

10. If the volume of a sphere equals its surface area, what is the radius of the sphere?

(A) 1

(B) 2

(C) 3

(D) 4

(E) 5

11. If a rectangle and a triangle intersect, what is the largest number of intersection points if no side of the rectangle coincides with any side of the triangle?

(A) 3

(B) 4

(C) 5

(D) 6

(E) 7

12. Twin primes are pairs of primes which differ by two. The first twin primes are 3 and 5. Which of the following pairs is **NOT** 3-digit twin primes?

(A) 107 and 109

(B) 137 and 139

(C) 141 and 143

(D) 149 and 151

(E) 179 and 181

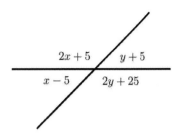

13. Two lines intersect and form two pairs of vertical angles. Which of the following is the value of $x + y$?

(A)   80

(B)   90

(C)   100

(D)   110

(E)   120

14. Points A, B, C, D, and E are arranged on the number line in that order. If $\dfrac{AB}{BC} = \dfrac{1}{2}$, $\dfrac{BC}{CD} = \dfrac{3}{4}$, and $\dfrac{CD}{DE} = \dfrac{5}{6}$, what is the value of $\dfrac{AB}{DE}$?

(A) $\dfrac{1}{4}$

(B) $\dfrac{5}{16}$

(C) $\dfrac{1}{3}$

(D) $\dfrac{3}{8}$

(E) $\dfrac{5}{12}$

15. Suppose N is a positive integer such that $N - 1$ is divisible by 2, $N - 2$ is divisible by 3, $N - 3$ is divisible by 4, and $N - 4$ is divisible by 5. What is the least possible value of N ?

(A)   39

(B)   49

(C)   59

(D)   79

(E)   99

$T, W, T, F, S, S,$ _____

16. Which of the following letter is the next term in the sequence above?

(A)   D

(B)   G

(C)   I

(D)   K

(E)   M

17. The area of a rectangle is 17. If the perimeter of the rectangle is 18, what is the square of the difference of the longer side and shorter side of the rectangle?

   (A) 8

   (B) 13

   (C) 18

   (D) 23

   (E) 28

18. What is the least multiple of 42 that is divisible by 267?

   (A) 2814

   (B) 3192

   (C) 3486

   (D) 3738

   (E) 3948

19. How many squares can be drawn by connecting four dots in the grid above?

   (A) 9

   (B) 14

   (C) 18

   (D) 20

   (E) 22

20. If three vertices of a triangle are given as $(0,0)$, $(50,50)$, and $(51,49)$, what is the area of the triangle?

   (A) 50

   (B) 60

   (C) 75

   (D) 125

   (E) 150

21. Two points A and C are in a plane. Set T contains all points B in the plane for which $\triangle ABC$ is a right triangle, where $m\angle B = 90°$. What best describes T ?

(A) One point

(B) Two points

(C) A line segment

(D) A parabola

(E) A semicircle

22. What is the largest prime factor of 70! ?

(A) 11

(B) 29

(C) 49

(D) 67

(E) 83

23. Since $\frac{1}{4} = 0.25$, the first digit and second digit of the decimal expansion of $\frac{1}{4}$ is 2 and 5, respectively. What is the 60th digit of the decimal expansion of $\frac{1}{7}$?

(A) 4

(B) 5

(C) 7

(D) 8

(E) 9

24. If four vertices of a cube are randomly selected, what is the probability that the four selected points are on the same face of the cube? (Consider 6 faces of the cube: top, bottom, left, right, front, and back)

(A) $\frac{3}{35}$

(B) $\frac{1}{10}$

(C) $\frac{1}{6}$

(D) $\frac{6}{25}$

(E) $\frac{1}{5}$

25. Which of the following is the value of x for which $3^{81^x} = 27^{3^x}$?

    (A) $\dfrac{1}{3}$

    (B) $\dfrac{1}{2}$

    (C) $\dfrac{2}{3}$

    (D) $\dfrac{5}{4}$

    (E) $\dfrac{3}{2}$

27. Joshua and Jason play a game. Each player takes a turn to roll a six-sided die. The first person rolls a two wins the game. If Joshua rolls first, what is the probability that Joshua will win the game?

    (A) $\dfrac{3}{8}$

    (B) $\dfrac{4}{9}$

    (C) $\dfrac{1}{2}$

    (D) $\dfrac{6}{11}$

    (E) $\dfrac{7}{12}$

$$\frac{ab}{a+b} = 1, \qquad \frac{bc}{b+c} = 2, \qquad \frac{ac}{a+c} = 3$$

26. For real numbers a, b, and c, three equalities are defined above. What is the value of $\dfrac{1}{a} + \dfrac{1}{b} + \dfrac{1}{c}$?

    (A) $\dfrac{9}{11}$

    (B) $\dfrac{11}{12}$

    (C) 1

    (D) $\dfrac{13}{12}$

    (E) $\dfrac{12}{11}$

28. x, y, and z are prime numbers such that $xy + z = 79$. Let m be the largest possible value of $x + y + z$, and n be the smallest possible value of $x + y + z$. What is the value of $m + n$?

    (A) 86

    (B) 92

    (C) 98

    (D) 104

    (E) 110

Answers and Solutions
TJHSST Math Practice Test 10

Answers

1. D	11. D	21. E
2. B	12. C	22. D
3. D	13. D	23. C
4. C	14. B	24. A
5. E	15. C	25. A
6. B	16. E	26. B
7. A	17. B	27. D
8. E	18. D	28. C
9. A	19. D	
10. C	20. A	

Solutions

1. (D)

    Use the answer choices to determine which number satisfies all of the given conditions. Eliminate answer choice (C) because 18 is divisible by 9. Eliminate answer choices (A) and (B) because both 30 and 24 have 8 factors. Additionally, eliminate answer choice (E) because 6 has only 4 factors. Therefore, (D) is the correct answer.

2. (B)

    Change the equation $x - z = 7 + y$ to $x - y = 7 + z$, and then add the two equations to eliminate the variables y and z.

    $$x + y = 5 - z$$
    $$\underline{x - y = 7 + z} \qquad \text{Add two equations}$$
    $$2x \quad = 12$$
    $$x = 6$$

    Therefore, the value of x is 6.

3. (D)

    There are 7 integer values of x that satisfy the inequality $0 \leq x^2 \leq 9$: $-3, -2, -1, 0, 1, 2$ and 3.

242

4. (C)

In the figure below, the diameter of the semicircle is 8. This means that the length of the side of the equilateral triangle is 8 and the radius of the semicircle is 4.

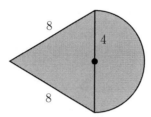

The perimeter is the distance around the figure. Since the diameter of the semicircle is inside the shaded region, it should be excluded from the perimeter of the shaded region. Thus, the perimeter of the shaded region equals the sum of the lengths of two sides of the equilateral triangle and half the circumference of the circle with a radius of 4. Therefore, the perimeter of the shaded region is $8 + 8 + \frac{1}{2}(2\pi(4)) = 16 + 4\pi$.

5. (E)

In the figure below, two identical squares with side length of 8 are overlapped such that one vertex of each square is at the center of the other square. The unshaded region represents the common area where the two squares overlap and is a square with side length of 4. Thus, the area of the unshaded region is 16.

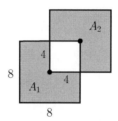

The area of the shaded region is the sum of the areas of A_1 and A_2. The area of each shaded region A_1 and A_2 is equal to the area of the square minus the area of the unshaded region, which is $64 - 16 = 48$. Therefore, the area of the shaded region is $A_1 + A_2 = 48 + 48 = 96$.

6. (B)

Joshua has taken three out of four tests and received the scores: 91, 86, and 87. In order to get an A for the math class, which is an average of 90 or more, the sum of the four tests must be at least $90 \times 4 = 360$. Set up the inequality and solve for s which represents the score needed on the 4th test.

$$91 + 86 + 87 + s \geq 360$$
$$s \geq 96$$

Joshua must obtain a score that is greater than or equal to 96 in order to receive an A for the math class.

7. (A)

nth term of the sequence is defined by $a_n = n^2 + 1$. Therefore, the value of the 29th term is $a_{29} = 29^2 + 1 = 842$.

8. (E)

The pattern shows that the first figure has 4 sides, the second figure has 5 sides, the third figure has 6 sides, and so on. The 997th figure has 1000 sides and looks as close as a circle.

9. (A)

$2 \spadesuit 3 = 2^3 - 3 = 5$ and $2 \spadesuit 5 = 2^3 - 5 = 3$. Thus,

$$2 \spadesuit (2 \spadesuit (2 \spadesuit (2 \spadesuit 3))) = 2 \spadesuit (2 \spadesuit (2 \spadesuit 5))$$
$$= 2 \spadesuit (2 \spadesuit 3)$$
$$= 2 \spadesuit 5$$
$$= 3$$

Therefore, the value of $2 \spadesuit (2 \spadesuit (2 \spadesuit (2 \spadesuit 3)))$ is 3.

10. (C)

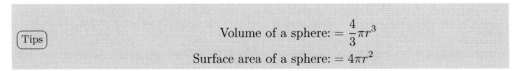

Tips

$$\text{Volume of a sphere:} = \frac{4}{3} \pi r^3$$
$$\text{Surface area of a sphere:} = 4 \pi r^2$$

Let the volume and the surface area of a sphere equal to each other and solve for r.

$$\frac{4}{3} \pi r^3 = 4 \pi r^2 \qquad \text{Divide each side by } 4 \pi r^2$$
$$\frac{r}{3} = 1$$
$$r = 3$$

Therefore, the radius of the sphere is 3 if the volume and the surface area of the sphere are the same.

11. (D)

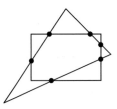

As shown above, if a rectangle and a triangle intersect, and no side of the rectangle coincides with any side of the triangle, the largest number of intersection points is 6.

12. (C)

Tips Divisibility rule for 3: A number is divisible by 3 if the sum of the digits is divisible by 3.

The number 141 is divisible by 3 since the sum of digits, $1 + 4 + 1 = 6$, is divisible by 3. Thus, the number 141 is not a prime number. Therefore, 141 and 143 are **NOT** twin primes.

13. (D)

$2x + 5$ and $x - 5$ are supplementary angles. Thus, the sum of their measures is 180°.

$$2x + 5 + x - 5 = 180$$
$$3x = 180$$
$$x = 60$$

Additionally, $y + 5$ and $2y + 25$ are supplementary angles.

$$y + 5 + 2y + 25 = 180$$
$$3y + 30 = 180$$
$$y = 50$$

Therefore, $x + y = 60 + 50 = 110$.

14. (B)

$$\frac{AB}{DE} = \frac{AB}{BC} \times \frac{BC}{CD} \times \frac{CD}{DE}$$
$$= \frac{1}{2} \times \frac{3}{4} \times \frac{5}{6}$$
$$= \frac{5}{16}$$

Therefore, the value of $\frac{AB}{DE} = \frac{5}{16}$.

15. (C)

N is a positive integer such that $N - 3$ is divisible 4, and $N - 4$ is divisible 5. Thus, the possible values of N are as follows:

$$N = \{19, 39, 59, 79, 99, 119, \cdots\}$$

Since $N - 2$ is divisible by 3, and $N - 1$ is divisible by 2, the possible values of N are as follows:

$$N = \{59, 119, \cdots\}$$

Therefore, the least possible value of N is 59.

16. (E)

The sequence consists of days of a week. Tuesday starts with T, Wednesday starts with W, Thursday starts with T, Friday starts with F, Saturday starts with S, Sunday starts with S, and Monday starts with M. Therefore, the next term in the sequence is M.

17. (B)

$$(x - y)^2 = (x + y)^2 - 4xy$$

Let x and y be the longer side and shorter side of the rectangle, respectively. The area of the rectangle is 17 can be expressed as $xy = 17$. The perimeter of the rectangle is 18 can be expressed as $2(x + y) = 18$ or $x + y = 9$. Thus,

$$(x - y)^2 = (x + y)^2 - 4xy$$
$$= 9^2 - 4(17)$$
$$= 13$$

Therefore, the square of the difference of the longer side and shorter side of the rectangle, $(x - y)^2$, is 13.

18. (D)

The prime factorization of $42 = 2 \times 3 \times 7$. The prime factorization of $267 = 3 \times 89$. In order for the multiples of 42 to be divisible by 267, it must contain 3×89 in its prime factorization. Therefore, the least multiple of 42 that is divisible by 267 is $2 \times 3 \times 7 \times 89 = 3738$.

19. (D)

Below shows the number of squares with different side lengths can be drwan.

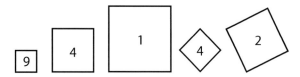

Therefore, there are 20 squares can be drawn by connecting four dots in the grid.

20. (A)

If three vertices of a triangle are $(0,0)$, (a, b), and (c, d), the area A of the triangle is as follows:

$$A = \pm \frac{1}{2}(ad - bc)$$

The three vertices of a triangle are $(0, 0)$, $(50, 50)$, and $(51, 49)$. Therefore,

$$\text{Area of the triangle} = \pm \frac{1}{2}(ad - bc)$$
$$= \pm \frac{1}{2}(50 \times 49 - 50 \times 51)$$
$$= -\frac{1}{2}(-100)$$
$$= 50$$

21. (E)

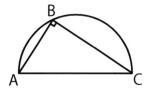

As long as point B is on the semicircle shown above, $\triangle ABC$ is a right triangle.

22. (D)

$70! = 70 \times 69 \times 68 \times \mathbf{67} \times 66 \times \cdots \times 2 \times 1$. Therefore, the largest prime factor of 70! is 67.

23. (C)

$\frac{1}{7} = 0.142857142857\cdots$. The digits 142857 are repeating. Since every 6th digit ends with 7, the 60th digit is 7.

24. (A)

Let's find out the probability of selecting four vertices on the top face. There are 4 vertices on the top face, and 4 vertices on the bottom face. The probability of selecting the first vertex on the top face is $\frac{4}{8} = \frac{1}{2}$. There are 3 vertices remaining on the top face. So the probability of the second vertex on the top face is $\frac{3}{7}$. There are 2 vertices remaining on the top face. So, the probabilities of selecting the third and the fourth vertices are $\frac{2}{6}$ and $\frac{1}{5}$, respectively. Thus, the probability of selecting four vertices on the tops face is

$$\frac{1}{2} \times \frac{3}{7} \times \frac{2}{6} \times \frac{1}{5} = \frac{1}{70}$$

Since we can choose one of the 6 faces of the cube,

$$6 \times \frac{1}{70} = \frac{3}{35}$$

the probability that the four selected points are on the same face of the cube is $\frac{3}{35}$.

25. (A)

$$\bullet \ (3^4)^x = (3^x)^4 = 3^{4x}$$

$$\bullet \ \text{If } a^x = a^y, \text{ then } x = y$$

$$3^{81^x} = 27^{3^x}$$
$$3^{81^x} = (3^3)^{3^x}$$
$$3^{81^x} = 3^{3 \cdot 3^x} \qquad \text{If } 3^x = 3^y, \text{ then } x = y$$
$$81^x = 3 \cdot 3^x$$
$$3^{4x} = 3^{x+1}$$
$$4x = x + 1$$
$$x = \frac{1}{3}$$

26. (B)

$$\frac{ab}{a+b} = 1 \implies \frac{a+b}{ab} = 1 \implies \frac{1}{a} + \frac{1}{b} = 1$$
$$\frac{bc}{b+c} = 2 \implies \frac{b+c}{bc} = \frac{1}{2} \implies \frac{1}{b} + \frac{1}{c} = \frac{1}{2}$$
$$\frac{ac}{a+c} = 3 \implies \frac{a+c}{ac} = \frac{1}{3} \implies \frac{1}{c} + \frac{1}{a} = \frac{1}{3}$$

Adding three equations gives

$$\frac{1}{a} + \frac{1}{b} = 1$$
$$\frac{1}{b} + \frac{1}{c} = \frac{1}{2}$$
$$\frac{1}{c} + \frac{1}{a} = \frac{1}{3} \qquad \text{Add three equations}$$
$$\overline{2\left(\frac{1}{a} + \frac{1}{b} + \frac{1}{c}\right) = \frac{11}{6}}$$
$$\frac{1}{a} + \frac{1}{b} + \frac{1}{c} = \frac{11}{12}$$

Therefore, the value of $\frac{1}{a} + \frac{1}{b} + \frac{1}{c}$ is $\frac{11}{12}$.

27. (D)

The infinite sum S of a geometric series is

$$S = \frac{a_1}{1 - r}, \qquad \text{if } |r| < 1$$

where a_1 is the first term, and r is the common ratio.

Let's consider the following cases.

- Case 1: Joshua wins on the first roll. The probability that he wins on the first roll is $\frac{1}{6}$.

- Case 2: Joshua wins on the 3rd roll. The probability that he wins on the 3rd roll is $\frac{5}{6} \times \frac{5}{6} \times \frac{1}{6}$, or $\frac{1}{6}\left(\frac{5}{6}\right)^2$.

- Case 3: Joshua wins on the 5th roll. The probability that he wins on the 5th roll is $\frac{1}{6}\left(\frac{5}{6}\right)^4$.

- Case 4: Joshua wins on the 7th roll. The probability that he wins on the 7th roll is $\frac{1}{6}\left(\frac{5}{6}\right)^6$.

- Case 5: Joshua wins on the 9th, 11th, 13th roll, and so on.

$$\text{Probability that Joshua will win the game} = \frac{1}{6} + \frac{1}{6}\left(\frac{5}{6}\right)^2 + \frac{1}{6}\left(\frac{5}{6}\right)^4 + \frac{1}{6}\left(\frac{5}{6}\right)^6 + \cdots \qquad (5)$$

The expression in (1) above is the geometric series with the first term $a_1 = \frac{1}{6}$, and the common ratio $r = \left(\frac{5}{6}\right)^2$. Thus,

$$\begin{aligned}
\frac{1}{6} + \frac{1}{6}\left(\frac{5}{6}\right)^2 + \frac{1}{6}\left(\frac{5}{6}\right)^4 + \frac{1}{6}\left(\frac{5}{6}\right)^6 + \cdots &= \frac{a_1}{1 - r} \\
&= \frac{\frac{1}{6}}{1 - \left(\frac{5}{6}\right)^2} \\
&= \frac{6}{11}
\end{aligned}$$

Therefore, the probability that Joshua will win the game is $\frac{6}{11}$.

28. (C)

x, y, and z are prime numbers such that $xy + z = 79$.

$$7 \times 11 + 2 = 79 \qquad \text{(Smallest } x + y + z)$$
$$2 \times 37 + 5 = 79$$
$$\vdots$$
$$2 \times 19 + 41 = 79$$
$$\vdots$$
$$2 \times 3 + 73 = 79 \qquad \text{(Largest } x + y + z)$$

Thus, $m = 2 + 3 + 73 = 78$, and $n = 7 + 11 + 2 = 20$. Therefore, the value of $m + n$ is 98.

Made in the USA
Monee, IL
21 January 2021